DEVISING PERFORMANCE

Theatre and Performance Practices

General Editors: Graham Ley and Jane Milling

Published

Christopher Baugh   *Theatre, Performance and Technology*
Deirdre Heddon and Jane Milling   *Devising Performance*
Helen Nicholson   *Applied Drama*
Michael Wilson   *Storytelling and Theatre*

Forthcoming

Greg Giesekam   *Staging the Screen*
Cathy Turner and Synne K. Behrndt   *Dramaturgy and Performance*
Phillip B. Zarrilli, Jerri Daboo and Rebecca Loukes
   From Stanislavski to Physical Theatre

Devising Performance

A Critical History

DEIRDRE HEDDON AND JANE MILLING

palgrave
macmillan

First published 2006 by
PALGRAVE MACMILLAN
Palgrave Macmillan in the UK is an imprint of Macmillan Publishers Limited, registered in England, company number 785998, of Houndmills, Basingstoke, Hampshire RG21 6XS.

Palgrave Macmillan in the US is a division of St. Martin's Press LLC, 175 Fifth Avenue, New York, NY 10010.

Palgrave Macmillan is the global academic imprint of the above companies and has companies and representatives throughout the world.

Palgrave® and Macmillan® are registered trademarks in the United States, the United Kingdom, Europe and other countries.

ISBN–13: 978 1–4039–0662–5   hardback
ISBN–10: 1–4039–0662–9   hardback
ISBN–13: 978 1–4039–0663–2   paperback
ISBN–10: 1–4039–0663–7   paperback

This book is printed on paper suitable for recycling and made from fully managed and sustained forest sources. Logging, pulping and manufacturing processes are expected to conform to the environmental regulations of the country of origin.

A catalogue record for this book is available from the British Library.

A catalog record for this book is available from the Library of Congress.

10
15   14   13

Contents

General Editors' Preface

This series sets out to explore key performance practices encountered in modern and contemporary theatre. Talking to students and scholars in seminar rooms and studios, and to practitioners in rehearsal, it became clear that there were widely used modes of practice that had received very little critical and analytical attention. In response, we offer these critical, research-based studies that draw on international fieldwork to produce fresh insight into a range of performance processes. Authors who are specialists in their fields have set each mode of practice in its social, political and aesthetic context. The series charts both a history of the development of modes of performance process and an assessment of their significance in contemporary culture.

Each volume is accessibly written and gives a clear and pithy analysis of the historical and cultural development of a mode of practice. As well as offering readers a sense of the breadth of the field, the authors have also given key examples and performance illustrations. In different ways each book in the series asks readers to look again at processes and practices of theatre-making that seem obvious and self-evident, and to examine why and how they have developed as they have, and what their ideological content is. Ultimately the series aims to ask: What are the choices and responsibilities facing performance-makers today?

Graham Ley and Jane Milling

Acknowledgements

We would like to extend our thanks to all the theatre companies and artists who lent their time and insights to our study. The dialogues that this research has opened we hope will continue. Thanks to Graham Ley, Series Editor, for his encouragement, faith and wisdom, and to Kate Wallis at Palgrave Macmillan for her patience. We are also grateful to Gerry Harris for her astute comments. The shortcomings and errors of the work are our own.

Thanks also to the Arts and Humanities Research Council (AHRC). The AHRC funds postgraduate training and research in the arts and humanities, from archaeology and English literature to design and dance. The quality and range of research supported not only provides social and cultural benefits but also contributes to the economic success of the UK. For further information on the AHRC, please see their website: www.ahrc.ac.uk

Our final thanks must be to those whose support is part of our daily collaborative efforts, Rachel Jury and Chris Smith.

1 Introduction

Devising or collaborative creation is a mode of making performance used by many contemporary theatre companies, and widely taught in schools and universities across Europe, America and Australia. Yet little critical attention has been paid to it. In her preface to *Devising Theatre: A Practical and Theoretical Handbook*, Alison Oddey admitted that the main reason for writing the book was that she 'felt there was a lack of information on the subject of devising theatre' (1994, p. xi). Ten years later, and after what turns out to be a surprisingly quick survey of books or articles that specifically concern themselves with this enduring and prevalent practice, it is apparent that very little has changed.[1] Given the widespread use of the mode of practice that we might call 'devising', it is curious that the conversation that Oddey hoped would result from the publication of her book has never really taken place. Perhaps it is precisely because devising *is* so prevalent, so present, that critical enquiry has been so sparse. Devising may appear to be a given, something that simply 'is'. In response to a survey we circulated in 2004 to teachers of degree programmes in Theatre, Drama, Performance and Dance in the UK, one respondent replied, 'Why would you not teach [devising]? It isn't new for goodness sake, or cutting edge, or anything, it's just how people usually make theatre.'[2]

This book sets out to demarcate and explore some of the parameters of devising or collaborative creation and to chart a history of this mode of practice in post-war British, Australian and American culture. Developments in Australian theatre, although less often placed alongside Britain and America in theatre histories, were part of a similar cultural trajectory, influenced by many of the same trends and conditions. Devising practice is taught at universities in all three countries, and exchanges of devising practices and devised performances between Australia and the UK and USA are increasingly significant elements of festivals and collaborative encounters. In studying modes of devising from these three countries we are not aiming to offer a general theory of devising, nor to suggest pragmatic, exemplary or idealised ways of working in collaborative creation. Rather than extrapolate from general principles about devising, we have looked at the companies who used or generated devising processes, and wondered about what they did and why they did it.[3] Our aim here is not to provide a single narrative of origins, but to explore the cultural and political resonances of the emergence of devising processes in the work of British, American and Australian companies which stem largely from the late 1950s and 1960s.[4]

Overall, devising is best understood as a set of strategies that emerged within a variety of theatrical and cultural fields, for example in community arts, performance art/live art, or political theatre. Within these fields, a range of devising processes evolved in relation to specific and continually changing cultural contexts, intimately connected to their moment of production. The purpose of this history is to encourage us to look more carefully at different modes of devising and to consider the implications of our use of these practices today. What are the relationships between today's practice and that of the last century? If the process and form of 'devising' was considered, in the 1950s and 1960s, to be both innovative and experimental, how might we engage with the processes and forms of devising in the twenty-first century? Why, where, when, how, in what way – and arguably, for whom – does devising take place today? How might we critically engage with devising as a practice and interrogate our own practice of it?

What is Devising?

To begin with nomenclature, British and Australian companies tend to use 'devising' to describe their practice, whereas in the USA the synonymous activity is referred to most often as 'collaborative creation'. We shall use the phrases interchangeably in this text, although the terminology itself offers a slight variation in emphasis. While the word 'devising' does not insist on more than one participant, 'collaborative creation' clearly does. A second variation in emphasis takes us to the nub of the issue. When used in non-theatrical settings, 'devising' suggests the craft of making within existing circumstances, planning, plotting, contriving and tangentially inventing.

By contrast, the phrase 'collaborative creation' more clearly empha-sises the origination or bringing into existence, of material *ex nihilo*. Elements of both phrases apply to the practices of companies we study here. At the core of all devising or collaborative creation is a *process* of generating performance, although there is an enormous variety of devising processes used.

The use of the word 'devising' to describe this set of practices for making theatre has led some commentators to suggest that there is no distinction to be made between devised work and other modes of theatre production. One respondent to the questionnaire that we circulated argued that 'devising' could be used to describe the traditional rehearsal and staging of a play-text: 'the terminology [of devising] has a tendency to suggest that script work is not devised, when clearly the performance is devised but with a script as a starting point'. This seems to us unhelpfully broad. In this present study, we examine those theatre companies who use 'devising' or 'collaborative creation' to describe a mode of work in which *no* script – neither written play-text nor performance score – exists prior to the work's creation by the company. Of course, the creation and the use of text or score often occur at different points within the devising pro-cesses, and at different times within a company's *oeuvre*, according to the purposes to which they intend to put their work. However, for the companies studied here, devising is a process for creating performance from scratch, by the group, without a pre-existing script.

Devised performance does not have to involve collaborators. To this extent the scope of devising practices is much larger than can possibly be encompassed here. We have deliberately limited our focus to collaborative creation and therefore place our emphasis on companies, rather than individuals. This decision inevitably produces omissions, particularly in the field of performance art, where the work is undoubtedly devised, though most often by individual artists.[5] Though Chapter 3 explores some crossovers between avant-garde art/performance art and devising practices, our decision to exclude performance art results in the simultaneous exclusion of important radical voices, often of queer and feminist subjects. However, our aim is not to provide a critical history of performance art, nor to give an account of the various ways in which performance artists devise; other books already exist which do that more thoroughly than we could possibly hope to achieve here.[6] This is not to deny that many performance artists, such as Carolee Schneemann, Franko B and Bobby Baker, exert a powerful influence on contemporary devising companies and that such connections remain in need of exploration; but this text must be regarded as only one of many possible engagements with a vast subject.

Also outside the limits of this study is devising which does not result in performance. For many companies, workshop or studio-based discoveries form the bedrock of the performance material; for others, the exploration in a workshop is an end in itself. When the Open Theatre first considered performing in 1963 there was a split in the company between those who wanted to share the studio discoveries and build them into a performance meaningful for an audience, and those for whom the studio sessions were simply actor-training exercises, sufficient in themselves and ultimately about equipping the actor for other kinds of text-based performances. By contrast, for current participants in workshops run by the Living Stage (Washington) discussed in Chapter 5, participation in the processes of devising brings its own reward. Therapeutic uses of play, improvisation, the creation of scenarios and the building of stories offer creative and empowering insight to workshop members, who form their own audience. While one or two examples of devising without performance are included in the chapter concerned with community theatre, to give an indication of the range of work that occurs under this heading, we are centrally concerned with devising as a process of generating *performance*.

For some of the companies we examine here, and for a great deal of the early rhetoric that surrounded devising, the idea of a devised performance being produced collaboratively meant: with all members of the group contributing equally to the creation of the performance or performance script. Moreover, the ideology of 'collaborative' practice equated it with 'freedom'. For Oddey, for example,

there is a freedom of possibilities for all those involved to discover; an emphasis on a way of working that supports intuition, spontaneity, and an accumulation of ideas.   (Oddey, 1994, p. 1)

The rhetoric pertaining to the process of devising is quite transparent here, and it is a rhetoric that is widely shared. In fact, it is possible to construct something of a 'soundbite' of those qualities frequently assumed to be implicit in devising which serve to give it an almost mythical status. Devising is variously: a social expression of non-hierarchical possibilities; a model of cooperative and non-hierarchical collaboration; an ensemble; a collective; a practical expression of political and ideological commitment; a means of taking control of work and operating autonomously; a de-commodification of art; a commitment to total community; a commitment to total art; the negating of the gap between art and life; the erasure of the gap between spectator and performer; a distrust of words; the embodiment of the death of the author; a means to reflect contemporary social reality; a means to incite social change; an escape from theatrical conventions; a challenge for theatre makers; a challenge for spectators; an expressive, creative language; innovative; risky; inventive; spontaneous; experimental; non-literary.[7]

In the twenty-first century, it is more than possible to take to task many of the 'ideals' embodied in the above. For example, is it necessarily the case that devising companies should be non-hierarchical? Were they ever? Judith Malina and Julian Beck, Joseph Chaikin, Richard Schechner, Liz LeCompte, Lin Hixson, Nancy Meckler, John Fox, Naftali Yavin, Hilary Westlake, Tim Etchells, and James Yarker were, or are, leading directors within their ensembles or companies. Does a director, who ultimately has the last word, who accepts final responsibility, complicate the notion of non-hierarchical work or democratic participation? Further, does the fact that many companies now operate as umbrella organisations, often run by one or two key figures, challenge the assumption of ensemble practice? In the pages that follow, it is not our intention definitively to prove or demolish the myths, but instead to ask where these beliefs about devising arise from and whether they are accurate in relation to historical and contemporary practice, and sustainable within contemporary social structures. At the very least, contemporary processes might require us to question what 'collaboration' means.

A shift in the significance of 'collaboration' within contemporary devising practices was articulated by Oddey:

> In the cultural climate of the 1990s, the term 'devising' has less radical implications, placing greater emphasis on skill sharing, specialisation, specific roles, increasing division of responsibilities, such as the role of the director/deviser or the administrator, and more hierarchical company structures. (Oddey, 1994, p. 8)

Two recent books on devising, aimed primarily at the UK market of 17–18-year-olds studying drama or performing arts to examination in 'A' level or GNVQ National Diploma, exemplify the transformation of rhetoric about devising for contemporary companies and audiences. In *Devised and Collaborative Theatre: A Practical Guide* (2002), despite Clive Barker's foreword, which argues that we should see devising 'as attempting to supplant oligarchic, or even dictatorial, control by a more democratic way of working', the content of the volume emphasises the separation of roles and foregrounds that of the director (Bicât and Baldwin, 2002, p. 6).[8] Gill Lamden's *Devising: A Handbook for Drama and Theatre Students* does not offer so radical a reworking of a collaborative 'ideal', in part because she draws on a wider selection of companies at work. Yet the central chapter studies four artistic directors under the heading 'Devising as a profession'. In the 1990s, collaborative creation may have come to mean something rather more akin to traditional theatrical production. The idea of 'devising as a profession' also seems to mark a shift from categorising 'devising' as an innovative, fringe practice, to seeing it within the commercial, mainstream sector. As processes of devising are now so firmly embedded in our training and educational institutions, can we really continue to claim for devising any 'marginal' or 'alternative' status? And why should we wish to do so?

Devising and Script/Text

In the 1990s, Oddey pitted devised theatre as a marginal alternative to the 'dominant literary theatre tradition'. We are in no position to argue, a decade later, that devised performances have become the dominant products of theatrical culture. A brief glance at the theatrical landscape of Britain in 2004 shows that the literary play-text remains central stage. However, any simple binary opposition of devising to script work is not supported by the briefest survey of the actual practice of companies who choose to devise. Many companies see no contradiction between working on pre-existing scripts and devising work, and move seamlessly between the two. For example, Theatre de Complicite produced Dürrenmatt's *The Visit* (1989), Ionesco's *The Chairs* (1997–8) and Shakespeare's *A Winter's Tale* (1992) between and alongside their devised physical theatre work. Judith Malina and Julian Beck of The Living Theatre likewise grew their own devising processes out of work on European Absurdist and American Beat plays. At the height of their period of devising work they also produced a version of Brecht's *Antigone* (1967), and much of The Living Theatre's current work grows from scripts.

While some of the rhetoric that has surrounded devising suggests that it emerges from a distrust of words or a rejection of a literary tradition in theatre, very few devising companies perform without using words. Even groups from a dance or mime tradition have been happy to use text, and the exceptions, such as Trestle Theatre's full-mask shows, or Ralf Ralf's gibberish comedy of political brinkmanship, *The Summit* (1987; revised 2004), still wish to emphasise the story and narrative clarity of their work. Many companies use text as a stimulus for their devising: adapting short stories, poems or novels; using found texts; cutting up existing texts; using historical documents; and quoting, citing or parodying classic play-texts. In some community-theatre contexts devising companies use verbatim performance, reproducing exactly the words of witnesses and interviewees, reassembled and theatricalised in collage.

The role of a writer or writers within a collaboratively created process can be fraught, as the study of the Open Theatre in Chapter 2 illustrates. Most companies we discuss have experimented with crystallising ideas and images into text, or a rehearsal score, at different moments in the devising process, and have explored a variety of relationships between writing and devising modes of work. Some use writers outside the process of devising, some use only the actors driving the devising to generate text, others straddle the difference with a range of involvement for a dramaturg. For a few of the companies here, the collaborative process involves a period of collaborative writing of a script to be performed, as discussed further in Chapter 4. A forthcoming study of the relationship between collaborative creation and writing in recent devised work in the UK will go some way to address this complex area in more detail.[9] The desire, in some early devising companies, to have the actor as a creative contributor to the making of performance, and not an interpreter of text, has perhaps encouraged the idea that devising is anti-literary by nature, but this is by no means accurate. While many companies making work in the 1960s and 1970s were concerned to give voice to the voiceless, and to make new and different points of view heard and seen, this often involved the use of a writer-figure in the rehearsal room. The fuller repercussions of questions of authorship and authority in relation to text within performance are explored in the studies of companies that follow.

Devising and Improvisation

Improvisation has been a key practice in the devising work of many of the companies we look at here. Often, for companies whose working practices involve an initial period of the creative development of ideas in the studio, improvisation of some form *is* that part of the devising process. Frost and Yarrow's study of improvisation briefly charted a range of Western precursors, before they identified three main strands to twentieth-century improvisation:

> (a) the *application* of improvisation to the purposes of the traditional play; (b) the use of *pure* improvisation in the creation of an 'alternative' kind of theatrical experience; and (c) the extension of improvisatory principles *beyond* the theatre itself.   (Frost and Yarrow, 1990, p. 15)

Obviously it is (b), the second strand of work, that primarily concerns us here but, as we discuss more fully in Chapter 2, improvisation developed for actor-training in preparation for work on a text, and creative improvisation for devising, share a heritage, often a form, and are not so clearly demarcated as the distinction between 'applied' and 'pure' above implies.

Moreover, the use of improvisatory techniques in devising re-emerged at a particular moment in social and political culture in America, Australia and Britain. As Daniel Belgrad has argued in his study of *The Culture of Spontaneity* (1998), the appearance of improvisation across art forms in America was indicative of a political moment of resistance to bureaucratisation and established institutions. The uses and styles of improvisation within devising have changed considerably over time as companies' work has been inflected by multiple influences, and by the developing tradition of devising itself. The improvisatory sound-and-movement exercise evolved by Joseph Chaikin and the Open Theatre is no longer so startling that it can be used directly in performance to unsettle the audience, as The Living Theatre did in *Mysteries and Smaller Pieces* (1964).[10] That exercise has become a standard part of drama training in improvisation in all sorts of contexts, enshrined in textbooks. It is important to note that in theatre during the twentieth century, improvisation has been primarily taken to imply an 'acting' exercise, an alien idea to many of the companies and artists discussed in Chapters 3 and 7, below. While these practitioners might improvise in the broadest sense of trying out ideas or experimenting with tasks, this has little to do with the 'acting' focus of many of the textbooks on improvisation or even the more radical manifestations of actor-training.

Some companies have taken the impetus of improvisation further and emphasise the element of spontaneity and its possibility for producing free creative expression. They have evolved performances which are direct displays of improvisation without filtering, as in the TheatreSports work of Keith Johnstone or Second City (Chicago); or within performance structures, as in Keith Johnstone and Improbable Theatre's *Lifegame* (2003), where actors improvised personal stories just recounted by a member of the public interviewed on stage; or in Forced Entertainment's *And on the Thousandth Night ...* (2000), where performers told competing stories for six hours. The metaphor often used about improvisation in performance is that it is 'like jazz'. Cultural critic Henry Gates has emphasised the role of structure, and the limitations of freedom, in jazz improvisation:

> Improvisation, of course, so fundamental to the very idea of jazz, is 'nothing more' than repetition and revision. In this sort of revision, again where meaning is fixed, it is the realignment of the signifier that is the signal trait of expressive genius. The more mundane the fixed text ('April in Paris' by Charlie Parker, 'My Favourite Things' by John Coltrane), the more dramatic is the Signifyin(g) revision. It is this principle of repetition and difference, this practice of intertextuality, which has been so crucial to the black vernacular forms of Signifyin(g), jazz – and even its antecedents, the blues, the spirituals, and ragtime. (Gates, 1988, pp. 63–4)

This idea of repetition and revision is one that holds good in theatrical, improvisational performance. A structured set of givens, rules or games can limit and contain the 'spontaneous' input of the performer. As the performance is prepared and then repeatedly performed, experience of a successful range of interactions between performers and audience inevitably builds. Even in the most apparently chaotic performance or Happening, there is structural order. In the studio or workshop during the making of performance, different devising practices will use improvisation that might involve the repetition and revision of breathing exercises, or physical, dance-based contact between performers, or everyday tasks, or verbal interrogation, or character-based interaction. It is the specific nature of the task, game, rules or structure within which improvisation occurs that conditions the possible outcomes, and contributes to the style of the resultant performance. Of course, improvisation is only part of the process of making work, which might also include editing, designing, structuring, choreographing, writing and rehearsing.

Within the improvisational process used by theatre companies across the various types of devising practice, there is a remarkable repetition of the idea of intuition as a structuring element of that process. Again and again, companies report that they 'just knew' when an image was appropriate, or when they had hit upon an idea, movement, phrase or sequence that 'felt right'. Rather than accept the function of this mechanism as an inexplicable element of the practice, we might remember Foucault's insistence that:

> We believe that feelings are immutable, but every sentiment, particularly the noblest and most disinterested, has a history. We believe in the dull constancy of instinctual life and imagine that it continues to exert its force indiscriminately in the present as it did in the past. But a knowledge of history easily disintegrates this unity.   (Foucault, 1977, p. 153)

Drawing on Foucault's insight here, we should note that intuition functions paradoxically within improvisation in the devising process. An element of material generated by improvisation is recognised by company members as a performance solution, and intuition authenticates that moment as original and a creative revelation. Yet, improvisation is always already conditioned by the mannerisms, physical abilities and training, horizons of expectation and knowledge, patterns of learned behaviour of the performers – their *habitus*, to use Bourdieu's phrase.[11] That moment of intuitive recognition in a group, as a group, is a function of the establishment of a shared set of patterns and experience, and thus is a recognition of what is the 'same', rather than what is original, and is part of what an audience can then recognise as a style of work.

A Moment of Emergence

An improvisational and creative aspect of performance, something akin to devising, has been a part of the folk arts or popular performance across time and across cultures; Tara Arts (London) found inspiration as much from the improvisatory practice of the medieval Gujarati folk drama *Bhavai*, as from Western physical theatre, for example. Many theatre companies who developed devising processes in the 1960s and 1970s looked to earlier popular forms for inspiration in their work. The paradigm they most often cited, although historically it was not by any means always played for popular audiences, was *commedia dell'arte*. Many of the companies we look at in Chapter 2 viewed *commedia* as a form where actors were able to generate material improvisationally within the parameters of a scenario, which might then become the set form of a scene.[12] In continuing the reawakening of interest in *commedia dell'arte* in the twentieth century, some devising companies were influenced by Jacques Copeau, who had set out to 'try to give re-birth to a genre: the New Improvised Comedy, with modern characters and modern subjects' with his company Les Copiaux in Burgundy in 1924 (Frost and Yarrow, 1990, p.25). The company experimented with *commedia*-style masks and improvisations around scenarios for specifically popular audiences, although Copeau was to call a halt to the experiment in 1929, feeling the need for a writer in order to take the experiment further. As Thomas Leabhart charts, Copeau's experiment and writing reinvigorated a French mime tradition and attempted in it to link the political and the popular, an attempt which Jean-Louis Barrault, Jacques Lecoq and Ariane Mnouchkine, amongst others, were to follow (Leabhart, 1989).

The very different trajectory of the European avant-garde also employed elements of chance and improvisation in making performance.[13] While the Futurists, with their production of *sintesi*,[14] had challenged the dominant theatrical convention of realistic verisimilitude introduced to theatre by naturalism, the Dadaists emphasised spontaneity both in their process of working and in their performances, similarly attempting to defy the imposition of conventional 'logic'. Tzara's 'paper-bag' poems were composed by drawing words randomly from a bag, while Hans Arp's 'chance' art allowed scraps of falling paper to form random patterns.[15] Sharing sentiments with the Surrealist movement, Tzara equated spontaneity with creative freedom, arguing 'everything that issues freely from ourselves without the intervention of speculative ideas, represents us' (Melzer, 1980, p.68). The Surrealists further developed the use of 'chance' procedures, such as automatic writing, to try to express the functioning of thought. Automatic writing, like the technique of chance, was intended to allow the artist to escape from the strictures of self-censorship and bypass the individual ego. One writing technique, called *Cadavre exquis*, the exquisite corpse, a phrase taken directly from one of the first results of the writing game, involved collaborators each writing a sentence consecutively, without knowing what the preceding writers had contributed. The visual equivalent of this technique, using drawing or collage, extended the role of chance and collective action, although here the output was imagistic rather than textual. In 1919, André Breton and Philippe Soupault collaborated on what Breton would retrospectively claim as the first surrealist text, *The Magnetic*

Fields, using the technique of 'automatic writing'.[16] The use of 'chance' and various other related processes of generating work – the mistake and the accident, for example – are frequent in contemporary devising.

Another important link between the historical avant-garde and later performance processes is the incorporation of 'found' objects. Bearing some relation to Picasso's paper collage pieces, where real materials were introduced into the representational image, the use of found art also attempts to equate art with life. Kurt Schwitters, who met the Dadaists in 1918, was the most prolific artist to work with 'found' materials, creating 'Merz' collages out of the detritus of everyday life. Schwitters's 1920s concept of the Merz 'composite' stage, in which any and all objects 'are not to be used logically in their objective relationships, but only within the logic of the work of art', pre-empts many of the performance-art developments of the 1950s and 1960s (Kostelanetz, 1980, p. 12).

Although we aim to point to possible continuities with past traditions, this book is centrally concerned with the emergence of a range of devising practices used by companies in the post-World War II period. The companies and the work that we explore were undoubtedly influenced by earlier performance traditions and experiments and we try to chart these where possible in the detailed studies that follow. However, the devised work we look at here is not merely an inevitable evolution of those forms. Its characteristics, diversity, aesthetics and significance signalled a radical disjunction. The emergence of devised work in the 1950s and 1960s was of a different order of magnitude. For example, we might trace an evolution between the revived, twentieth-century *commedia* tradition into actor-centred theatre or dance performance discussed in Chapter 2, but in the latter work, improvisation was used not just within small sections of the performance, but as a structuring mechanism of the whole. Closer connections exist between the 'anti-art', European avant-garde of the early twentieth century and solo European performance artists of the 1950s and 1960s, who evolved devising practices which were pragmatically similar, whilst being politically very different. But in the 1950s and 1960s many *groups* of artists emerged, collaborating to produce performance works. Moreover, as Andreas Huyssen has argued:

neither Dada nor surrealism ever met with much public success in the United States. Precisely this fact made Pop, Happenings, Concept, experimental music, surfiction, and performance art of the 1960s and 1970s look more novel than they really were. The audience's expectation horizon in the United States was fundamentally different from what it was in Europe. Where Europeans might react with a sense of déjà vu, Americans could legitimately sustain a sense of novelty, excitement and breakthrough. (Huyssen, 1986, p. 187)

The other marker of difference in the post-war period was the fact that devising practices were simultaneously emerging across a very wide range of fields in dance, mime, community arts, performance art, storytelling and political theatre, and in some instances also working across performance disciplines.

It seems evident that many of the common conceptions and/or myths of devising that we have inherited arise from the specific political and cultural conditions of the 1950s and 1960s in the West. It is, for example, during the 1950s and 1960s that the process of devising work was considered to be a material expression of political and ideological commitment, and an ideal embodiment of desired aspects of freedom and authenticity.[17] In this respect, devising performance was a practice that echoed other cultural changes of the 1950s and 1960s, when there was a steady 'revolt' evident across art forms, including the work of the Beat writers, and of Pop Artists who framed the material productions of advanced capitalism as art.[18] It was also during the 1950s that Merce Cunningham and John Cage began considering the everyday – movement and sound – as properties of dance and music, alongside 'chance' as a creative property; that Anna Halprin began developing improvisation, gestalt therapy and task-based work to unlock collective creation in dancers; that the action undertaken in action-painting was extended to include space and time; and that the writing of Antonin Artaud, produced originally in the 1940s but not published in English until 1958, was given serious consideration by many performance makers.

Everything came into question: the place of the performer in the theatre; the place of the audience; the function of the playwright and the usefulness of a written script; the structure of the playhouse, and later, the need for any kind of playhouse; and finally, the continued existence of theatre as a relevant force in a changing culture. (Sainer, 1997, p. 12)

The pervasive political mood of the 1950s must itself be understood within the context of the Cold War and the ever-present threat of global nuclear destruction, as the arms race developed between the Soviet Union and the USA and western Europe. Relations between

America and the UK were strained in 1956 when the US did not back Anthony Eden, then Conservative Prime Minister, in the invasion of Egypt he had ordered to maintain control of the Suez Canal, and he was forced to withdraw. The crisis signalled the waning of British imperial prestige and the rise of American imperial ambition. The moment heralded a further process of decolonisation, notably in Africa, commencing in the late 1950s and gathering pace throughout the 1960s, as the struggle for independence and self-government grew. Ghana (formerly the Gold Coast) gained independence in 1957, followed by Nigeria in 1960, the Republic of South Africa in 1961 and Kenya in 1963.

Popular political protest began to become more visible and widespread. The Suez Canal Crisis, set against the backdrop of the enduring Cold War, was a catalyst in the formation of the Campaign for Nuclear Disarmament in the UK, an identifiably New Left organisation. In the USA, the Civil Rights Movement of the 1950s and 1960s provided an important model (and impetus) for collective political protest. In 1954, the National Association for the Advancement of Colored People (NAACP), founded in 1910 to ensure full equality for black Americans, succeeded in getting the Supreme Court to rule that segregation in education was unconstitutional. In 1963, in response to the daily experiences of black Americans, Martin Luther King led 200,000 protesters on a march to Washington, D.C., where he delivered his famous 'I have a dream' speech. Congress finally passed the Civil Rights Act in 1964. In the autumn of that same year, the Free Speech Movement (FSM) of the University of California at Berkeley was founded, in response to the university's restriction of political activity on campus.

Many of the protesters at political rallies and marches during the 1960s were young people and students, part of the affluent post-war generation privileged by university education. The organisation Students for a Democratic Society (SDS), founded in 1959, is a notable example. In the USA, Britain and Australia, the late 1950s was a period of economic prosperity and ideological optimism, set against a background of fascism defeated. The realities of the 1960s, although it was an affluent era, were tested against the utopian promises of the 1950s and found wanting. One major trigger for widespread, international protest was the Vietnam War, which seemed to underline the bankrupt 'democracy' of the West. As Fink reflected, 'The conduct of the war belied the myth of Western innocence and exposed the structural violence of the Western democracies', leading to demonstrations in Washington, Amsterdam, Oslo, Paris, Rome and Tokyo (Fink et al., 1998, p. 26). The international scale of the demonstrations was helped in no small measure by the increasing impact of the mass media, which served not only to report the events of the war internationally, but also to relay the extent of the protest, thereby engendering something of a feeling of a global anti-war movement.

The rhetoric employed within the political movements of the 1960s and 1970s was also applied to ideal (and idealised) models of devising and helps us understand why devising became such a desirable mode of practice during this time. A number of key terms or ideas that belong to the political rhetoric of this period, and which subsequently have an impact on concepts and practices of devising, include 'individual and collective rights', 'self-determination', 'community', 'participation' and 'equality'. For example, Tom Hayden, a member of the Students for a Democratic Society, spoke for thousands of fellow members when he insisted that humans had 'unrealized potential for self-cultivation, self-direction, self-understanding and creativity' (Cavallo, 1999, p. 204). Thus, 'the goal of society should be human independence'. What the students were reacting to, partly, was 'the actual structural separation of people from power' (Marwick, 1998, p. 53).

Embracing its own ideologies through practice, the SDS would arrive at decisions through a consensual process rather than majority rule. The political model desired was that of a popular participatory democracy, which would enable 'ordinary' people to have control over their own lives, 'expressing a new force outside of existing institutions, a society apart from the state' (Cavallo, 1999, p. 209). The 'state' was perceived as being bureaucratic, patriarchal, authoritarian, and repressive, and the individual as alienated. As Robert Daniels summarised the situation,

[the] target of rebellion was power – power over people and power over nations, power exercised on the international plane by great imperial states, by governments within nations, or by people in positions of dominance over the powerless under them, from the industrial bureaucracy to the university classroom. The primary aim of the era was equality.   (Daniels, 1989, p. 5)

The politics of this time, as expressed through the student movement, did not cohere to traditional notions of class politics. Politics, here, referred to every aspect of social life, to the availability of choices, to lifestyle, to working relationships, to personal relationships. Part of this political ideology came from the New Left.

> By invoking early Marx, the insights of psychoanalysis and existentialism, feminism and anticolonialism, the New Left made a broad, sweeping critique of the growing alienation that had developed within the advanced industrial societies. The solution required not only a social, political, and international revolution but also a complete change in the conditions of human existence, from modes of work to forms of private behaviour, from relations between the sexes to the structure of the family.   (Fink et al., 1998, p. 25)

The range of targets identified by the New Left in some senses served to align it with what has been called the 'counter-cultural' movement. Theodore Roszak, who coined that phrase, articulated the connection in an article published in *The Nation* in 1968:

> The counter culture is the embryonic cultural base of New Left politics, the effort to discover new types of community, new family patterns, new personal identities on the far side of power politics, the bourgeois home, and the Protestant work ethic.   (Marwick, 1998, p. 11)

One influential spokesperson for this cross-over of political and cultural life was Herbert Marcuse, author of *One-dimensional Man* (1964). Marcuse argued for a cultural resistance to incorporation by the economic–technical force of established society. His subsequent *An Essay on Liberation* (1969) corresponded with the various international, student-led political demonstrations that had taken place during 1968. What is most notable about *An Essay on Liberation*, and important to locating new theatrical experimentation within a political and cultural context, is Marcuse's insistence on the necessity of a new sensibility. For Marcuse, any economic 'revolution' must involve – in fact be preceded by – a revolution of the senses, which would emerge

> in the struggle against violence and exploitation where this struggle is waged for essentially new ways and forms of life: negation of the entire Establishment, its morality, culture; affirmation of the right to build a society in which the abolition of poverty and toil terminates in a universe where the sensuous, the playful, the calm, and the beautiful become forms of existence and thereby the Form of the society itself.   (Marcuse, 1969, p. 25)

Marcuse read the student movement as symptomatic of the 'Great Refusal' – a rejection of 'the rules of the game that is rigged against them' (ibid., p. 6), and a way of 'methodically disengaging from the Establishment' (Alway, 1999, p. 93). The Great Refusal is the refusal to accept or participate in the given social reality; the Great Refusal is a 'total' politics.

The 1960s also saw the emergence of self-identified marginalised 'groups', a response in part to the fact that the traditional (and indeed sometimes the New) Left did not take full account of the range of oppressions suffered by different people, nor of their various effects. In 1968 the Second Wave feminist movement was founded, followed in 1969 by the Gay Liberation Front. Participants in both movements realised that certain inequalities would or could not be resolved merely by changes in class structure or by a more equitable distribution of wealth. The glut of stereotypical, sexist or homophobic representations of women, gay men and lesbians on stage made the production of alternative representations an urgent necessity. This, combined with the cultural context of the time, suggested collaborative devising – a means of wresting the mode of production from the grip of dominating institutions and dominant ideologies – as an appropriate model of agency for *self*-representation, and a process by which to make visible that which had been previously unseen and unspoken. The collaborative nature of devising also suggested the potential for complex, multiple representations, even if, in practice, this was not always realised.

The upsurge in collectives and collaborative groups during this period, and not just in performance contexts, was remarkable. That there were as many as 2000 to 3000 thousand communes in the USA in the late 1960s (Marwick, 1998, p. 60) is some sort of testimony to the impact of the political rhetoric of participation, collectivity, and democracy. As the ideology of 'participatory democracy' took international root, it was evident that for theatre to play its role in the formation of any new society, the praxis of participatory democracy should also be implemented within the theatre. Set beside the model of hierarchy, specialisation and increased professionalisation in the mainstream theatre industry, devising as a collaborative process offered a politically acceptable alternative. The critique of professionalisation was further evidenced by artists' moving away from, and out of, traditional gallery and theatre spaces.

All over Europe, America ... artists, creative people, stepped aside into a deliberate sell-it-yourself amateurism. This was the beginning of the underground.   (Nuttall, 1968, p. 161)

However, devising practices did not just emerge as part of the alternative, fringe or underground movements; the rhetoric of 'participatory democracy' also led them to emerge within the community, educational and socially-interventionist programmes of mainstream theatres.

This introduction to the context in which devising became an increasingly popular practice has focused on cultural and political shifts and challenges. What has not been addressed here is the longer-term effect of the 1960s: whether these supposed pressures had any lasting impact on culture. What is immediately evident today, of course, is that the 1960s did not usher in a total revolution (nor even a partial one). The contemporary world of the twenty-first century is marked by global capitalism, by continued exploitation, and by the creation (and in some – more privileged – cases, satisfaction) of what Marcuse would refer to as false or 'inauthentic' needs. Arguably, then, in spite of any claims made for the 'revolutionary' zeal of the 1960s, much remains unchanged.

The writers of this book were both born in the 1960s. Our knowledge of the decade is necessarily distanced and second-hand. As 'Thatcher's children', witnesses to the introduction of the sweeping privatisation of previously nationalised industries, the total decimation of other industries (mostly heavy – coal, steel manufacturing, ship-building) with the corollary rise in unemployment, and the erosion of free education for all, we probably also view the 1960s with borrowed nostalgia for both its promises and its failures to deliver. Margaret Thatcher contributed to the 'myth' of the 'sixties' when she declared in March 1982 that 'we are reaping what was sown in the sixties ... fashionable theories and permissive claptrap set the scene for a society in which old values of discipline and restraint were denigrated' (Marwick, 1998, p. 4). This is a theme picked up, somewhat surprisingly, by the Labour Prime Minister Tony Blair in 2004. When announcing new measures on law and order, he regretted a society which had 'spawned a group of young people who were brought up without parental discipline, without proper role models and without any sense of responsibility to or for others. ... Here, now, today, people have had enough of this part of the 1960s consensus.'[19] However, as Richard Cockett has reminded us, though 'the sixties has generally subsided into popular imagination as a collage of revolting students, permissiveness and personal freedom', in reality, for 'most people who lived through the 1960s, the above picture would be scarcely recognisable as an account of their ordinary lives' (Cockett, 1999, p. 85).

While noting the usefulness of the myth of the permissive, failed '1960s' to current political rhetoric, and also admitting that Cockett undoubtedly has a point about the extent of the experience of the 'permissive sixties', it is also important to recognise that throughout the 1950s and 1960s there *were* important international political and cultural events that would have enduring effect and impact (and some of these have already been mentioned – the Cold War, the Suez Canal Crisis, the Vietnam War). The 1960s enacted tangible, long-lasting, material change, alongside the cultural challenges, whose impacts are more difficult to assess. As already noted, in the USA the Civil Rights Act was passed in 1964, followed by the Voting Rights Act of 1965. In Australia, non-European immigration was allowed in 1966, while in 1967 a referendum returned a resounding 'yes' to the question of whether Aboriginals were to be granted citizenship rights including the right to vote, and the Equal Pay Act was introduced in 1969. In the UK, a number of new Acts were passed, including the first Race Relations Act (1965), the Sexual Offences Act (1967) which decriminalised sexual acts in private between consenting males over the age of 21, the Abortion Act (1967), and the Divorce Reform Act (1969). In the UK, of prime importance was the Theatres Act of 1968, which finally removed the Lord Chamberlain's powers of pre-censorship. The legal necessity to submit a written text for approval prior to its performance made devising at worst impossible, and at best hugely restricted.[20] It is in this crucible of change, and amidst the rhetoric of change, that devising as a practice emerged.

Devising and Economics

A key condition that needs to be considered when determining the 'context' for the historic turn to devising is that of economics. In the 1950s and 1960s, many of the companies who began devising were ideologically opposed to – or temperamentally disinclined to comply with – the economic imperatives of the commercial theatrical marketplace, or the post-war development of government subsidy for the arts. It was precisely to escape the restrictions imposed by economic considerations that many artists turned to solo performance work, or street performance events, or set up their own alternative venues. But artists have to live, and as Joan Littlewood's and Julian Beck's memoirs make clear, the life of an unsubsidised or poorly subsidised theatre company, particularly one which places politics and aesthetics over profit, is one of continual, draining struggle.[21] However, not all devising practice happened in the 'alternative' sphere. Those companies who were centrally concerned with educational theatre or community-centred work were usually conceived of and initiated as part of the programme of subsidised regional theatres or local government arts projects, as we explore more fully in Chapter 5.

Direct subsidy has never been, and does not function today as, the only way in which devised performance is funded, particularly devised work in alternative theatre. Sally Banes, writing about American avant-garde performance, has articulated the significance of

> government funding and private funding by individuals, corporations and foundations, but also trust funds from wealthy parents, more modest support by middle-class parents, and even real-estate speculation. ... [I]ntellectual and religious organisations – in particular, colleges, universities, and churches – have played a central role in the development of avant-garde performance, serving as research and development centres, venues, catalysts and patrons.   (Banes, 2000, p.217)

The hidden patronage of the university sector is one that we can also trace in the UK and Australia through the provision of spaces, venues, audiences and technical support, the commissioning of residencies and workshops, and the marketing, discussion and dissemination of many devising companies' performances. The relationship between the emergence of devising companies and training in the university and conservatoire setting is a point that will be picked up in the Conclusion of this book. To evolve a performance through a devising practice usually takes longer than the traditional four-to-five-week rehearsal period of mainstream, text-based theatre in Britain, America and Australia. Without some form of external funding or pre-performance income, such work is, in effect, subsidised by its makers.

In the chapters that follow, where possible we trace the relationship between devising and shifts in the rhetoric and practice of government, business and private funding. For Baz Kershaw, who traced British alternative and community theatre work, the experience became

> ideologically, ... a story of incorporation as companies increasingly became dependent on state agencies, and as those agencies gradually took greater control of the movement's operations in order to dampen its oppositional thrust. Industrially, it is a double-edged success story, as the creation of a

new sector of British theatre with its own infrastructure enabled an increasing number of conservative companies to survive, forcing out more radical
groups in an age of reactionary repressions.   (Kershaw, 1992, p. 252)

No longer a 'fringe' or 'underground' mode of work, devising is
taught at school, university and drama school. Devising companies
have been absorbed into mainstream culture and funded by government subsidy. This trajectory is perhaps most exemplified by Theatre
de Complicite, who were picked up in 1989 by the National
Theatre and offered studio space in which to work, and have been
supported by both mainstream theatre industry and government
subsidy since then. Until 1968 in the UK no company that devised
work received funding; in that year, grants or guarantees were offered
to the Brighton Combination and Inter-Action Trust.[22] Today, the
Arts Council of England revenue-funds 30 companies who devise
work, either as the sole working practice or as part of their activity.[23]

The Question of Process

It was during the 1950s and 1960s that a concern with the creative
'process' itself became so widespread. With the emergence of interest
in improvisation, experimental theatre practice and devising practices,
the language of rehearsal was replaced by references to 'labs', 'workshops' and 'sessions', drawn from the discourses of science, craft
and the music industry.[24] In an attempt to resist the commodification
of performance, to enable connections between life and art, artists
across cultural fields entertained the possibility of presenting work
that was 'unfinished', expecting and ready to integrate or reflect
audience response. While this move was for some a demystification of
creativity, an attempt to blur the divisions between amateur and
professional, ironically, for others it led to an increased professionalisation of the artist, championing and scrutinising the aesthetics of
the *labour* of the creative artist, rather than simply the product. Hence
this is also the period when performances became 'work-in-progress',
which hoped to summon a new kind of viewing from the audience.
The extent to which the open-ended nature of devised performance
continues to conflict with the traditional production expectations of
the theatrical industry is explored by Karen Fricker's study of Robert
Lepage and Ex Machina's work (2003), notably *The Seven Streams of
the River Ota*. Fricker unpacks the uneasy status of performances

which operate as 'work-in-progress', evolving through performance before audiences into a final form, yet sold and marketed as a finished product on the international festival touring circuit.

The Anxiety of Influence

This volume examines the nature and the purposes of devising in a range of theatre fields including political theatre, community arts, physical theatre and postmodern performance. Given the apparent fragmentation of devising practice, is it possible to suggest that a tradition of devising has emerged in British, American or Australian culture? There are two forces at work in this volume: the desire to trace chronology, to follow time forward, to write a history that 'leads' us to think about the work we might make in the present; and the need to move backwards, retracing, in order to find the 'same' thing, the shared, the copy, the tradition. The paradox is captured by Jean-François Lyotard's opposition of tradition with history, which he articulated in a discussion about John Cage's work and about the power of so-called repetitive musics:

> [this power] lies in the fact that [repetitive musics] cause the forgetting of what is being repeated and they make for a nonforgetting of time as a beat in place. Tradition is that which concerns time, not content. Whereas what the West wants from autonomy, invention, novelty, self-determination, is the opposite – to forget time and to preserve, acquire and accumulate contents. To turn them into what we call history, and to think that it progresses because it accumulates. On the contrary, in the case of popular traditions ... nothing is accumulated, that is, the narratives must be repeated all the time because they are forgotten all the time. But what does not get forgotten is the temporal beat that does not stop sending the narratives to oblivion.   (Lyotard, 1985, p. 34)

From our look at devising work we have found the idea of both a tradition and a history. The tradition we explore finds links and coherence in modes of devising work. The devising practitioners examined here saw each other's work, heard about performances or processes they were not part of, participated in workshops, learnt about work in formal educational contexts, influenced each other. The history we explore finds differences in devising across the diverse fields in which it occurs, and also examines what it is that links devising process and performance to the chronology of the cultural, political or social moment.

What is impossible to 'recover' is both the live performance and a definitive history of the making of a piece of devised or collaborative work. Although video documentation now gives some experience of a performance, the different medium renders it a different version from the live event. Further, much of the history of this work predates video-recording technology. Mike Pearson, writing of performances that were staged in Wales throughout the 1970s, captured the problem well:

> these performances, variously described as 'experimental', 'devised', 'physical', 'site-specific', rarely became part of a published record. They have their document in the endlessly elaborated (and increasingly fictionalised) reminiscences and anecdotes of its practitioners, in a discourse akin to an oral culture. Unfortunately, memory fades.   (Pearson, 1997, p. 85)[25]

Memories of process are also unreliable: Who made which suggestion, or initiated a movement that became a moment of performance? Even with video recordings or notation in the studio or workshop, the narrative does not accumulate to an explanation of how work was made, since the process is continually forgotten. A rare example of a remembering of a devised *performance* was offered by Stan's Cafe, who presented or represented Impact Theatre Cooperative's devised performance, *The Carrier Frequency*.[26] Impact's 'original' work had premiered in 1984, and had been a collaboration with writer Russell Hoban, better known for his dystopian novels such as *Ridley Walker*. With its pounding soundtrack, and exhausting, repetitive task-based action, *The Carrier Frequency* had been hailed as a foundational artwork and post-nuclear fantasy. In 1999, Stan's Cafe set out to copy, piece together and re-present the performance from a video of one version of the work.[27] This remembering was in part developed with the intervention of the academy. Stan's Cafe's performance was prefaced by a day conference on 'Archaeology, Repertory and Theatre Inheritance'. Nikki Cooper, one of the performers with Impact, remembered:

> I wasn't in Impact with my brain. It was purely emotional. We would have laughed that what we were doing would ever be discussed, like this, academically.   (Babbage, 2000, p. 98)

Both more and less than repetition and revision, this second performance represented what is always at stake with devised performance, not only the forgetting of its performance, but the forgetting of its making. The second performance was pieced together by quite different means from the first, from a visual and verbal score *without* devising. In this example, then, process had become distinctly divorced from product.

The tradition of devising continually betrays its influences as it repeats, appropriates, copies, and forgets its borrowings, the 'constant folding and faulting of influence and inspiration that is practice and production and document' (Pearson, n.p., 2004). Images and motifs reappear in productions – not only from devised performance, but from the broader social and cultural environment. For Simon McBurney of Theatre de Complicite, 'the pleasure of theatre is impurity, it's the magpie quality of people stealing from everybody else' (McBurney, 1994, p. 24). Gerry Harris has warned against the mis-recognition of style as process, and the production of performances that can only recycle cliché. She bewailed the endless round of productions in the late 1980s and early 1990s which used eastern European folk songs or laments as shorthand for dislocation and isolation, or battered suitcases as symbols for journey, after the success of Grotowski's company and Theatre de Complicite's European adaptations (Harris, 1999a, pp. 6–21). However, for some companies, such as The Wooster Group or Forced Entertainment, a reiteration of their own performance images and previous processes functions as part of the accumulation of layers, often a starting point within a new devising process. Complex images are also borrowed knowingly as quotation, as, for example, the balloon dance in Forced Entertainment's *First Night* (2001). Cathy Turner described actress Claire Marshall in a bathing suit with balloons pinned to it:

> My memory of it (which may not be accurate) is that Claire did a sort of slow, vague dance on a chair (a cross-reference to her dance in *Pleasure* (1997)?). She was smoking and she used the cigarette to burst the balloons one by one, as if utterly bored of being a showgirl – but that boredom was also a tease.[28]

This echoed Pina Bausch's *Masurca Fogo* (1998) where, to draw attention to her possible role as 'object', dancer Julie Shanahan wore a bikini adorned with red balloons and popped them one by one with exaggerated enthusiasm. Chapter 7 discusses in more detail the ideology of knowing quotation as a mechanism of postmodern, devised performance.

Other motifs occur and recur across the tradition of devised performance that are not just performance images, but reflexive functions of devised performance itself. Take, for example, staring wordlessly at the audience. The broader field of experimental performance championed the power of the performer and audience member consciously reflecting on their shared time and space in performance, a recognition of the 'encounter' textually realised in the work of Peter Handke in the 1970s. One of the simplest markers of this encounter is a moment when an actor (not as a character, but as a performer) stands before an audience and looks back at them, observing them, in silence, for an extended period of time. This desire to draw attention to the 'watching' and the contract of watching that the audience and performers have embarked upon, recurs again and again in devised work. At the beginning of The Living Theatre's *Mysteries and Smaller Pieces* (1964), performed first in Paris, a single actor stood in the centre of the stage, looking at the audience, 'defiantly silent' (Aronson, 2000, p. 75), 'at attention ... expecting that some audience response would begin the play' (Tytell, 1995, p. 200). Initially this encounter was designed to run for six minutes; by the time Margaret Croyden saw the performance she described the time period as half an hour (Croyden, 1974, p. 105). Open Theatre's *Mutation Show* (1971) ended with the actors in silence, looking out at the audience, breathless but at rest. Australian performance group The Sydney Front's *Don Juan* (1992) began with the actors in a bank of seating in the studio space, behind an iron barrier, as the audience were ushered in. The actors watched them, eventually beginning to whisper to each other, and finally pushed aside the bar to join them. Forced Entertainment's *Dirty Work* (1998) opened with two actors looking at the audience for what felt an uncomfortably long time, as seduction, as apology or in pity, before they consoled us for what the performance was not, with descriptions of impossible spectacles and improbable theatrical encounters. As part of the marking of tradition, deliberate borrowing or copying, as well as the unconscious work of influence, can be read across the *performances* generated by devised process, and in the chapters that follow we trace some of the ways in which devising *processes* and strategies also cross-fertilise and repeat.

The Plan of the Book

Our intention is to map out an overview, one possible landscape, of the evolution of the mode of devising as a practice. Oddey's *Devising Theatre* (1994) offered pioneering guidance on 'how to' devise, and other workbooks and practice-based books have been produced since.[29]Although we do explore the devising practices and processes of companies here, it is not in order to offer exemplary models to be followed. Rather, by examining the development of different devising processes in their differing moments in history, this study aims to raise questions about the choices and responsibilities that face student and professional practitioners in using devising strategies today.

Recently a number of histories have begun to appear which chart the post-war rise and evolution of alternative theatre companies, political theatre companies, or dance and community groups, although there remains much work to be done here.[30] These histories have provided valuable background and advice for us, but we are not attempting to chart a history of every devising company here, or even to trace the complete histories and influences of the groups at which we do look. Reading the back-run of theatre journals such as *Performance*, *Plays and Players*, or *Theatre Australia* reveals a wealth of devising companies whose work is forgotten or performances which are lost to us. A thorough chronology of devising companies and devised performances in even one of the countries considered here would be an enormous undertaking. Readers will perhaps inevitably identify their own lacunae and begin to construct their own landscapes and histories of the theatre companies we neglect. Such responses will be valuable elements in weaving a history of post-war theatre. Rather than attempting a history of all theatre companies who have devised, or even identifying all devising companies, we are attempting here to trace the evolution of the *mode of devising* itself.

In order to do this, in each chapter we have chosen to study companies that exemplify key elements of devising practices and processes. The sheer scale of this landscape makes choices, inclusions and exclusions, inevitable. We are not implying that the detailed studies that follow are necessarily of the only, or on occasion even the most, important devising companies. However, the companies we have chosen to talk about in detail offer clear examples of the distinctions and complexities of different devising modes. Readers might choose to substitute one company for another depending on their own areas of influence, knowledge, or matters of concern. The danger of any book of this sort is that, through the inclusion of particular examples, those companies become, by default, canonical. Several of the companies discussed here have been thoroughly studied already, and we include them precisely because they are already recognised as pioneers in their particular field of theatre practice.

They have inspired, through performances, occasionally through workshops, and often because they have been well-documented, a range of other companies to replicate their style of work. Of course, the citing of work results in further citing of work. This is an unavoidable effect of the materiality and 'economics' of writing, as distinct from the ephemerality of live performance, an effect that we do not pretend to escape here. We hope that this book might prompt other writers to make different choices and thereby to write over our constructed landscape.

Devising did not suddenly emerge as a practice without relation to existing theatrical fields such as mainstream narrative theatre, community arts or political theatre, for example, and this history attempts to place devising in that theatrical, political and social context. In each case we look not only at the historical context to the emergence of devising as a mode itself, but also at the particularity of specific types of devising. What becomes evident from this history is that devising is a multifarious mode of work. To help give coherence to the picture, we have grouped devising companies together in the chapters that follow because the central concerns of their work, and the devising practices they use or used, are linked. Broadly speaking we have identified three strands of devising practice: theatre predominantly concerned with the actor, acting and story, in Chapters 2 and 6; theatre closely linked to art practices, which dramaturgically places the image as equal to the spoken text and which therefore pays close attention to the visual potentials inherent in the stage 'picture', in Chapters 3 and 7; and theatre predominantly concerned with its impact in a political and/or social context, in Chapters 4 and 5.

It would be disingenuous (not to mention harmful) to suggest that there are clear-cut lines separating any of the types of practices and companies discussed in this book, for the practices, companies, aims, forms, and even personnel blur, and many companies deliberately take an interdisciplinary approach. To take just one example that reveals the extent to which the areas of work discussed below are fluid, we might try to place the company Brith Gof. Founded in 1981, Brith Gof would initially have fitted comfortably into the actor-centred practices explored in Chapter 2, given that their 'group ethos' at this time matched that of the 'encapsulated work group' practised by the Polish Theatre Laboratory (Savill, 1997, p. 100). However, from the outset, the work of this Welsh-based company was culturally political, desiring to create a 'new kind of theatre in Wales' (ibid.). Though this concept of 'new' did refer to 'new forms', their aims also extended beyond formal experimentation. As Charmian Savill recorded, 'their work was inspired by their need to reinscribe Welsh social, mythic, literary, political and historical representation' (ibid., p. 105). Taking seriously this political commitment, we might wish to locate Brith Gof in Chapter 4. However, Brith Gof's productions also typically involved various communities in their devising, inviting contributions from 'students, dancers, musicians, local communities, special needs groups or theatre companies' (ibid., p. 103). In this respect, the company could quite easily sit within the parameters of Chapter 5. From the mid-1980s, both the composition of the group, and its formal style and concept of the 'political', shifted. Temporary members were now invited to work with the company, and the formal codes adopted by the company, intended to interrogate and challenge 'metanarratives', produced effects that bear resemblance to the work explored in Chapter 7, which we have located within a frame of postmodernism. The placing of companies into separate, defined modes of practice presumes neat categories when in fact categories are often deliberately challenged. Moreover, the various cultural, social, political and theatrical influences inevitably work across the different devising modes we have identified. We encourage readers to similarly read across and through the modes/chapters.

There has been a great deal of cross-fertilisation between Australia, America and the UK through the touring of devised performances, workshops by leading companies, and through the teaching of devising at school and university level. We hope that what follows is a contribution to that debate and exchange. We have begun by attempting to resist already knowing what devising 'is', and have tried to proceed by examining the rhetoric used about devising against the practices and processes actually employed by practitioners. The questions that underpin this investigation have significance for our use of devising practices today. Why did devising emerge as a mode of work? What conditioned the evolution of different devising practices? What are the ideological implications of the decision to devise, and of the choice of different devising processes?

2 Devising and Acting

In this chapter we will examine a range of companies who pioneered modes of devising generated by, and drawn from, a concern with acting and the performer. Often cited as companies at the cutting edge of the American theatrical avant-garde, groups like the San Francisco Dancers' Workshop, the San Francisco Mime Troupe, Open Theatre, The Living Theatre and The Performance Group, as well as groups within the European tradition under the leadership of directors such as Joan Littlewood, Jerzy Grotowski and Ariane Mnouchkine began their explorations into devised work through an interest in the possibilities of acting, actor training, and the performer's relationship with the audience. The context and background of the development of games and improvisation in actor training was central to the evolution of this kind of devising. Emerging alongside mainstream theatrical traditions, such devising drew on conventional ideas of character and storytelling, and often used popular forms such as clowning, vaudeville or *commedia dell'arte* to structure work. Ultimately, the devising explored in this chapter was centrally concerned with the rituals of performance itself and the value of the relationship between audience and performer.

Games and Improvisations

Since the turn of the twentieth century, the idea of imaginative and physical 'training' in order to hone the pre-rehearsal capabilities of the performer had been developed by practitioners as diverse as Stanislavski, Meyerhold, Copeau and Piscator. The influence of Japanese, Balinese and South Indian performance traditions, which had been repeatedly 're-discovered' by European practitioners, reinforced the productive possibilities of systematic training. Stanislavski's influence on mainstream actor training offered an emphasis on improvisation, and had been transformed in America into the 'Method' at the Actors' Studio, where it was at its height by the 1950s. The ideology that underpinned improvisation was linked to the emergence of devising, for the groups studied here, in two key ways. First, the use of improvisation presupposed that a performer had an inner creativity that had been repressed, socialised, censored or hidden. Hence, the rhetoric of many groups contained a nostalgic yearning for a childlike attitude and, more questionably, for ritual or 'simpler' forms of theatricality. Improvisation was the means by which this 'return' to the prelapsarian innocence of creativity could be achieved. Secondly, the actor was 'released' from the constraints of the text into creative 'self-expression' by improvisation. Such self-expression is paradoxical, since at the same moment as the performance is made more authentic or truthful by seeming to arise directly from the actor's 'self', it is simultaneously a display of their technical virtuosity and artistry, facilitated by training and exercises. Given the sense of continuum with traditional actor training, it is perhaps not so surprising that the companies who developed this mode of devising felt no ideological exclusivity about devised performance. Whilst most of the groups discussed here positioned themselves as alternative or non-mainstream, those at work in the 1950s and 1960s tended to claim their work as radical or innovative on political grounds rather than because it was devised. They frequently combined devised performance with text-based work in their repertoire, or moved easily from text-based work into devised work generating text, and back, over time.

An early English group to make broader use of improvisation in actor preparation and in the development of performances was Joan Littlewood's aptly named company Theatre Workshop, based at the Theatre Royal, Stratford East, London, from 1953. Littlewood had been working before the Second World War with a company, Theatre of Action, which was a continuation of the political tradition of the 1930s' Workers' Theatre Movement. At the outbreak of war, Littlewood and collaborators began to imagine a new company, Theatre Workshop, which would both stage performance, and train actors

> to handle their bodies with the same degree of skill and control that was generally regarded as the special domain of ballet-dancers and professional athletes. ... As for acting proper, we would combine Stanislavski's method of living the role with the improvisational techniques of the Italian

comedy. And for a repertoire – we would create a tailor-made one for ourselves. (Goorney and MacColl, 1986, p. xlix)

The daily routine of the company involved physical training, using Dalcroze exercises and Laban Movement, and improvisation, as well as the pragmatic tasks of running and maintaining the theatre: painting, cleaning, preparing costumes and scenery, and finally performing. This created a strong feeling of ensemble, although the activity was initially as much a result of the parlously under-funded state of the theatre as it was an ideological decision. The poverty of the Workshop also meant that until the West End transfers of plays from the late-1950s, all of the actors were paid at the same rate.

Work at the Theatre Workshop under the direction of Joan Littlewood was centred on scripts and the development of scripts: Ewan MacColl wrote several of the early plays alongside the development of other new dramatists. However, unlike the newly established English Stage Company, the playwright was not king. Littlewood reflected on their work in a radio interview in 1959:

I believe very much in a theatre of actor-artists ... the playwrights have got to be in the theatre ... then perhaps out of our type of play, which has a great deal of improvisation in them, we shall get better plays. (Goorney, 1981, p. 114)

One of the most significant writers who worked with the company was the Irish dramatist Brendan Behan, whose *The Quare Fellow* arrived in embryonic form with Littlewood in 1956. Goorney described how actors, working on the material about a day in the life of a condemned prisoner, used improvisation first:

The day-to-day routines were improvised, cleaning out cells, the quick smoke, the furtive conversation, trading tobacco, and the boredom and meanness of prison life were explored. The improvisations had, of course, been selected by Joan with the script in mind, and when it was finally introduced, the situation and the relationships had been well explored. (Goorney, 1981, p. 105)

Behan acknowledged the work of the company on the opening night, 'Miss Littlewood's company has performed a better play than I wrote.' This way of working, drawn from Stanislavskian techniques, was more about preparation for performance of a script; nevertheless, improvisation as a means of *generating* a script, and as a mode of live performance, increasingly played a role in the company's work. So much so that the Lord Chamberlain was to rebuke them for performances of *You Won't Always Be On Top* (1956), as:

> the exchanges that arise naturally between men working on a building site lent themselves readily to improvisation and as the cast became more familiar with the situation and their relationship developed, the language became less restrained. (Goorney, 1981, p.106)

The company began to workshop material more extensively in their work on plays in 1958, including both Shelagh Delaney's *A Taste of Honey* and Behan's second play for the company, *The Hostage*, and this mode of work led into the only fully devised production that the group evolved, and probably the one for which they are most remembered, *Oh, What a Lovely War!*

With Shelagh Delaney's play *A Taste of Honey*, Avis Bunnage, who played the mother Helen, explained the working process:

> we did a lot of improvisation. When we came to bits that didn't seem to work we ad-libbed round the ideas, made it up as we went along. We used things that were around, an aspidistra that someone had left on stage became incorporated into the production. I said some of my lines to it. (Goorney, 1981, p.109)

The action of the play had characters directly addressing the audience and absorbing them within the apparently realistic world of a Manchester bedsit. Behan's *The Hostage* had evolved from a much looser interaction between actor and playwright than other plays that the company had worked on. Behan had regaled the actors with anecdotes, they improvised characters, dialogue and scenes and out of this emerged 'material which could be incorporated into the script. . . . Miss Gilchrist, the social worker in the play, emerged during a pub session' (Goorney, 1981, p.110).[1] By the time they were working on *Oh, What a Lovely War!* in March 1963, the actors were more fully involved in generating material:

> each member was given an aspect of the [First World] war to research. After reading and studying the use of gas, the battle of Ypres, the Somme or the visit of the King they would report back and be questioned. It was these discussion groups which gave birth to the play. (Coren, 1984, p.45)[2]

Littlewood described the unusual working process:

> what you see is not a piece of direction by a producer. There were no
> rehearsals as they are known. There was a collection of individuals, more of
> an anti-group than a group, working on ideas, on songs, on settings, on
> facts. (Goorney, 1981, p. 127)

The facts that the actors were discovering were only recently available
in the public realm, as the fifty-year gagging of official papers had just
been lifted. The performance was interlaced with songs and direct
address to the audience in the style of an end-of-pier pierrot show.

This production, and several others from the Theatre Workshop,
transferred into the West End, eliding the apparent boundaries
between the fringe and mainstream venues. The products of this
script-orientated mode of work, where actors were for the most part
'in character' in narrative-driven scenarios, were perhaps felt to be
familiar and were more readily accessible to non-fringe audiences.
Certainly Ewan MacColl and those who had championed the more
overtly political and street-based work of the early Theatre Workshop
group were disappointed by the ease with which such productions
could cross over. Yet the Arts Council remained suspicious and never
provided adequate subsidy, offering only a fraction of the English
Stage Company's grants at the Royal Court, for example (Rebellato,
1999, p. 67). What the Theatre Workshop had demonstrated was
how easily Stanislavskian improvisation could lead to the development of devised performance. Although far less formally intrepid than
Oh, What a Lovely War!, some of the tradition of Theatre Workshop
and the use of character-driven improvisation, closely controlled by a
director, was continued in the heightened naturalism of Mike Leigh's
work, or Hull Truck under Mike Bradwell's direction, in the 1970s.[3]

However, for many young companies of the 1950s, Stanislavskian
technique felt too character-centred, and thus unsuited to equip actors
to play in the strange, characterless texts of the absurdist playwrights
of the 1940s and 1950s, or the poetic dramas of the Beat generation.[4]
Other kinds of actor training were beginning to be looked for.[5] One
of the responses to this need for other kinds of acting exercise was the
increased interest in the game, and it was not just in the performance
arena that games had become significant. Essentially beginning in the
world of mathematics in the 1930s and 1940s, Game Theory as a field
of study developed into economics and social science with J. von

Neumann and O. Morgenstern's influential *Theory of Games and Economic Behaviour* (1944). This interest was in part produced by the search for structures of work or creativity in the rapidly shifting world, and Game Theory seemed to offer some explanatory or guiding models for social change and social organisation. Two important sociological and anthropological studies of games and culture were produced, Johan Huizinga's *Homo Ludens: A Study of the Play Element in Culture* (1955) and Roger Caillois's *Man, Play and Games* (1961). These studies argued for the importance of play and games in the development of the individual, in the growth of a child into maturity, and more broadly as a key to successful interaction and the formation of societies. This interest in childhood, games and the influence of developmental psychology was reflected in the content of many of the devised performances of the 1960s and 1970s, such as the Open Theatre's *Mutation Show* (1971, US) or The Freehold's *Alternatives* (1969, UK).

An early pioneer of the therapeutic use of all kinds of games was Neva Boyd, who worked in the 1930s, through the Works Progress Administration, to evolve a series of exercises and children's games to assist the social development and integration of communities, both immigrant and those shattered by the Depression. Her work was predicated on theories of the beneficial effects of play and of group interaction. In the late 1950s two innovative actor trainers, Nola Chilton and Viola Spolin, had independently developed Boyd's games into a series of connected exercises designed to prepare the actor to work on non-naturalistic play-texts. Spolin acknowledged her debt to Boyd in her collection of games and exercises, *Improvisation in the Theater* (1963), which became one of the most influential post-war actor-training texts. It was a short step to move from exercises or games as a preparation for the performance of an existing text, to using these games as a building block of performance structure or story itself.

Ideas of games and improvisation were picked up by two US dance companies working in the 1950s, Anna Halprin's San Francisco Dancers' Workshop (founded 1955) and the Judson Church Dance Theatre. Halprin was working on the West Coast while Judson Church Dance Theatre, which had evolved from classes taught by a collaborator of John Cage's, Robert Dunn, at the Cunningham Studio in 1960, was experimenting in New York. Anna Halprin worked with dancers to improvise dance from anatomical structure, searching for a 'natural', organic movement beyond the stereotyped range of modern dance. Inspired by the Bauhaus style of cross-art-form collaboration, where architects, musicians, painters and dancers evolved work together, the work processes and the performances shared much with performance artists explored in Chapter 3. The process linked task-based work, games with collaborators, and games in relation to the performance environment in order to reveal new physical possibilities and to create a sensory impact on the audience, as in pieces like *Five-Legged Stool* (1962) and the spectacular opera *Exposizione* (1963).[6] The dancers used breath, voice, dialogue, and their material was often drawn from their personal lives and relationships. While not improvised in performance, dances were made up of units or sections that had been discovered through improvisation, not choreography. *Parades and Changes* (1965–7) exemplified the work-process in its outcome, with its continually shifting patterns of ordinary and extraordinary actions: bathing oneself and another; undressing and redressing; making noises with huge sheets of paper; leaping from a high platform into the arms of others; embracing. In the mid-1960s Halprin's work evolved through a focus on gestalt therapy to become more obviously communal and community-based, involving the audience actively wherever possible as in *Citydance* (1976–7). Halprin crystallised her work on improvisation and her method for collaborative creation into a structure that she called the RSVP cycles – Resources, Scores, Valuaction, Performance.[7] Halprin's work influenced Schechner's Performance Group and Judson Church Dance Theatre, and dancers Kate and Peter Weiss moved to work with The Living Theatre. As we shall see in the work of American, English and Australian companies, the idea of the game as a generative form fed into their work in content, in style and in their attitude towards their audiences

Two of the most significant American theatre companies who used games, exercises and improvisation as part of their devising were The Living Theatre and the Open Theatre. Devised performance became a part of each of these groups' working methods at different points in their trajectory. The Living Theatre's first fully devised performance, *Mysteries and Smaller Pieces* (1964), was made after fifteen years of work, whereas the Open Theatre began life as a workshop group, where devising was part and parcel of the work from its inception in 1962. Both companies emphasised that each production or workshop presentation evolved through slightly differing processes, without a pre-formulated method, and although both companies valued the idea of a stable ensemble of performers, in fact the personnel of each group was in considerable flux. These companies have become the most widely known and taught in part because they were the most publicised and documented at the time, notably through Richard Schechner's editorship of the *Drama Review* from 1962, which was a very effective tool for disseminating information about his own work with The Performance Group from 1967, alongside the work of Grotowski, Barba, Brook, Black American Theatre and other groups who were exploring similar issues.

Julian Beck and Judith Malina's Living Theatre, founded in 1947, initially staged play-texts, which they rehearsed and produced in a relatively traditional manner. They were based in a series of small theatres in Greenwich Village, downtown Manhattan, a centre of experimental excitement in the late 1950s and early 1960s. The location of their work brought them into contact with the alternative artistic community that lived and worked in the area. For example, they rented the fourth floor of their theatre on 14th Street (their home from November 1957 to 1963) to choreographer Merce Cunningham as a rehearsal studio, and John Cage was to perform his durational piece of one-minute Zen parables in the theatre in 1960. From the start, The Living Theatre chose experimental texts from new writers, and poetic works, often drawn from their contemporaries among the young Beat generation of writers, who were pioneering a distinctive American voice in prose and drama. The search for non-naturalistic performance texts led to their excitement about Jack Gelber's *The Connection*, 'a jazz play' which he sent them in 1958. The two-act play was structured as a 'filmed documentary' about a group of heroin addicts waiting for their connection to deliver their fix. Characters told their stories directly to the audience, and a live jazz quartet jammed as response to, and inspiration for, the apparent improvisation of the performers. Like the second play in their 1959 repertoire, Pirandello's *Tonight We Improvise*, *The Connection* had the appearance of improvised performance, but while the rehearsal process had encouraged some limited improvisation from the actors, the language and action of the performance was predominantly set. However, these two plays unleashed an interest in the possibilities of a different creative process, as Julian Beck noted in his diary for 1959:

> I dream of a theatre company, of a company of actors that would stop imitating, but that would by creating a full view of the audience, move that audience in such a way and imbue that audience with ideas and feeling that transformation and genuine transcendence can be achieved. None of the actors know what I'm talking about. (Tytell, 1995, p. 161)

As The Living Theatre at that point did not have a stable company of players and as there was no regular input from actors into the production process, there was no way of realising this dream. The two plays remained in their repertoire for over a year, with casts changing with the impact of commercial pressures on the performers.

Judith Malina's directing style on *The Connection* (1959) and later on *The Brig* (1963) encouraged improvisation and involved the actors in lengthy rehearsals. In preparation for *The Brig*, a loosely structured play with little dialogue, that charted the rituals and routines of a naval correctional institution, rehearsals involved both physically demanding marine exercises, and political education. The Living Theatre actors were drilled in militarised routines for rehearsals of up to seven hours, guided by the writer Kenneth Brown's experiences while serving in Japan. This was similar to the style of rehearsal that Joan Littlewood was using in the 1950s and was an extension of Stanislavskian processes of preparatory improvisation for work on a text; however, both for the Theatre Workshop and for The Living Theatre, there was an additional political element. Not only because of the social and political commentary of the texts themselves but also because the plays had been chosen to reflect an apposite commentary on the social and political moment, the rehearsal processes were laced with political education for director and actor alike. Malina took The Living Theatre actors to protests against the reintroduction of nuclear testing that marked the hotting up of the Cold War in 1963. *The Brig* had a long, successful run in New York, but The Living Theatre's tax difficulties led to a very public eviction from their theatre, and a tour to London and France provided a way out.[8]

The Living Theatre's decision to devise work emerged as much from their pragmatic circumstances as from their ideological commitment to a new kind of theatre. The forced captivity of European 'exile' and touring kept the company of performers together day in and day out. As part of their rehearsal programme the actors had been meditating together, practising yoga and reading Artaud. Asked to give a performance in a barter for rehearsal space in Paris, and disconnected from their source of American poetic writing, for the first time Malina's direction began to lead the company into generating their own text from the rehearsal process (Gottlieb, 1966). *Mysteries and Smaller Pieces* (1964) revealed the structure of its generation, as a collage of nine 'ritual games' that included scenes of meditation, yoga exercises, a series of improvised tableaux or hieroglyphs, and the sound–movement exercise that was the core building block of the

Open Theatre's work, taught to them by an Open Theatre performer, Lee Worley. In this exercise an actor first imitated a noise and gesture made by a fellow performer, before transforming it, performing it and being copied in turn. The influence of Artaud was explicit as the company worked to physicalise one of the poetic metaphors of Artaud's vision for the theatre itself when, in the final game of the performance, the actors choked and died of the 'plague' amongst the audience. The influence of the innumerable demonstrations against the Korean War and nuclear armament, as well as their more parochial battles with the authorities, on the street, in the courtroom and in jail, had brought to Malina and Beck a sense of the importance of theatre as social action. Although the language of the *Mysteries* was limited to a series of expressions of political disquiet and of the nascent pacifist anarchism that the company came to espouse, for the first time the actors actively sought audience involvement and encouraged them to join in the exercises. For example, audience participation was sought halfway through the performance, when the actors formed a standing circle and hummed in communal sound.[9] It is difficult now to understand how unsettling this contact with the audience was, and how challenging the imagery of this performance proved.[10] The dramaturgy of the piece was as radical as anything the European avant-garde had produced. Yet the performance did retain some elements of mainstream theatrical presentation: 'scenes', an interval, climaxes and shifts in dynamic (from comic grotesques in the presentational tableaux to concentrated self-concern in the plague deaths), and the structural logic of these characterless, plotless exercises was to provide a rising series of emotional experiences for an audience.

By the following year the principles of collaborative creation were sufficiently codified that Beck could outline a working proposal as a pitch for a show at the Venice Biennale. He proposed the show *Frankenstein*, explaining:

> there is no text for the play. The action, the words, the effects will all be created by the company working together with the techniques we have developed amongst ourselves ... a work in the tradition of Artaud's concept of a non-literary theatre ... through ritual, horror and spectacle. (Tytell, 1995, p. 208)

Frankenstein was by no means a wordless performance, but Beck's interpretation of Artaud here both reveals the profound influence that Artaud's writing was to have on the development of devised theatre, and is an early example of a much repeated mantra, that devising was an anti-literary form. The Living Theatre now defined themselves as 'a collective, living and working together toward the creation of a new form of nonfictional acting based on the actor's political and physical commitment to using the theater as a medium for furthering social change'.[11] Non-fictional acting, which eschewed traditional ideas of character in order to draw on the actor's own personality and interest, and which challenged the dichotomy between performing and being or doing, shared much with other experiments in performance discussed in Chapter 3.

The evolution of this consciousness of a new form of acting was slow to build through the company's next two pieces. The first was a loose adaptation of *Frankenstein*, which examined the myths of social violence using archetypal figures and little narrative. Gene Gordon, one of the performers, described how the company worked on *Frankenstein*:

> we create our productions together sitting around first and talking about our material, in this case Mary Shelley's book *Frankenstein*, working over every detail, i.e. planning the structure of this play and our other works through communal discussion; verbal, silent, physical, psychic. (Mantegna and Rostagno, 1970, p.123).

The images used in the performance were drawn from contemporary life, from Jungian psychology, and also showed the traces of actor-training exercises, as in the meditation scene that acts as prologue (Croyden, 1974, p. 98). However, The Living Theatre followed *Frankenstein* with a play script, a version of Brecht's *Antigone*. This happy interchange between devising work and performing scripted work is a characteristic of most of the groups we look at here, who start with an interest either in the actor or in the possibilities of actor–audience relationships in the theatre. Devised performance lies on a continuum with script work.

The best known of The Living Theatre's performances, probably because it formed the centrepiece of their return tour to US colleges and conservatoires in late 1968, was *Paradise Now*, a response to the anti-Vietnam War protests, which were reaching their peak that same year. The Living Theatre's European influence had been extended by their involvement with the riots and street activity of May 1968 in Paris and by their work with the radical intellectual Jean-Jacques Lebel, who was a key figure in the radical performance-art arena in

France. As research for *Paradise Now*, members of the company read utopian myths, spiritual writings such as the *I Ching* and Kabbalah, as well as psychologists Wilhelm Reich and R. D. Laing. Jean-Jacques Lebel recorded the working process of the rehearsals, which interspersed long discussions about paradise with meditation and yoga exercises and a series of physical exercises, many of which ended up in the performance (Lebel, 1969). One exercise was designed to break through the defence mechanisms of a personality (using Reichian psychology): a member of the company lay on the floor making a continuous sound, which was then influenced and affected by the other company members manipulating her body or attempting to interact through physical and vocal means. Eventually the performer was lifted above the company's heads and paraded around the space in a kind of funeral procession. This became the sixth Rite of Opposite Forces in the performance. Inspired by Grotowski's performers, and linked to the experiments the group was making with the creative possibilities of drugs, the end of the prologue to *Paradise Now* involved individual actors railing about a forbidden activity, and the script describes how 'the actors go beyond words into a collective scream. This scream is the pre-revolutionary outcry. (Flashout).' A footnote explains: 'Whenever this happens in the play, the actor by the force of his art approaches a transcendent moment in which he is released from all the hangups of the present situation' (Malina and Beck, 1971, p. 16).

Devising supplied a mechanism whereby transformational experience in the workshop, for the actor, could be echoed and carried forward into performance, which it was hoped would then effect a similar transformation in the audience. The political desire for revolution had been central to the rehearsal process and underpinned the company's desire for audience involvement in this piece. This was the performance requiring the most audience participation thus far for the group, including the now notorious Rite Four, of Universal Intercourse, and the final rite where actors and audience were to race out into the street to initiate the rebellion. However, several critics at the time and since have pointed out the limitations of the political impact of The Living Theatre's theatrical images of, and attempts at, collectivity or community.[12]

By 1968, the strains of making communal work were showing within the company, particularly as it had grown so large. Not all members could share coherent ways of working or political ideas. Lebel's account of the making of *Paradise Now* contains many moments when Rufus Collins, one of the black performers, was frustrated by the marginalisation of the fight for black civil rights within the group's discussions. He was later heckled by a group of Black Panthers, when performing in America, for continuing to support the non-violent message of Martin Luther King, after King's assassination (Tytell, 1995, p. 241). Indeed, the demand from Beck and Malina that pacifist anarchism should continue to be the political message of the group was increasingly difficult in the context of the late 1960s. The 'hippie' message of peace had become so common-place that it had turned a show from Café La Mama into the smash-hit musical *Hair*, which opened on Broadway in April 1968. Beck and Malina's increasing concentration on the audience and their desire to teach an audience to take real social action led inevitably towards more community-based work. In 1970 the structure of The Living Theatre as a large group making work together dissolved, and Malina and Beck instead took a small group of actors with them to make theatre on the streets with communities in Brazil.[13] The Living Theatre had travelled a complex journey from poetic plays to collective creation in 1964–8 in the making of the *Mysteries*, *Frankenstein* and *Paradise Now*, to community-based work, some of which used pre-written scripts from members of the company or others. In some ways the *idea* of The Living Theatre was more influential in the development of devising than the actuality of their practice. The devising moment of their work in the late 1960s arose when they were politically activated to be a community, and when the idea of all members contributing, rather than being reliant on a director's authority, felt right politically. Even so, Malina and Beck as director-performers still retained a centrally controlling position within the company.

The same need for a strong directorial figure also characterised another very significant actor ensemble which first developed in The Living Theatre's auditorium space in 1962. The Open Theatre evolved out of workshops on improvisation initiated by a group of actors. Nola Chilton had been teaching acting classes centred around improvisation and transformation techniques, but when she moved to Israel the actors agreed to continue meeting for workshops and Joseph Chaikin and Roberta Sklar slowly became workshop leaders and directors of this loose grouping. Chaikin had performed with The Living Theatre, and he regarded his role in their version of Brecht's *Man is Man* (1962) as a key part of the evolution of his ideas and interest. He had also briefly worked, in Chicago in summer 1963, with Viola Spolin and her son's company, Second City, who had used improvisation and games to build sketch shows.[14] The Open Theatre first presented their work, in a workshop of 'open transformations ... as ensemble improvisations' rather than as a production, at the Sheridan Square Theatre in December 1963 (Pasolli, 1972, p. 21). The programme stated the tenets of the workshop:

> (1) to create a situation in which the actors can play together with a sensitivity to one another required of an ensemble, (2) to explore the specific powers that only live theatre possesses, (3) to concentrate on a theatre of abstraction and illusion (as opposed to a theatre of behavioural or psychological motivation), (4) to discover ways in which the artist can find his expression without money as the determining factor. (Pasolli, 1972, p. 52)

The explicit interest in play as a social and a professional activity was ideologically inflected, and identified the Open Theatre as part of the counter-culture and as resistant to the materialism of the theatre industry. From these initial improvisation exercises examining 'social performance', to their final show, *Nightwalk* (1973), the central investigation of the group was to remain the work of the performer. As Chaikin summarised it, the aim was to 'work as actors on trying to get through initial armour, and trying to get through the initial clichéd ways of performing' (Chaikin, 1975, p. 39). Devising performance, through play, was a means of exploring acting itself and alternatives to psychological realism.

The Open Theatre's relationship to scripts was a complex one that shifted over time, as Chaikin reflected on the closing of the Open Theatre in 1973: 'we don't have any one way of working with a writer. ... Usually the writer is there at the start, so that anybody might initiate a scene, an image, an idea, including the writer' (Chaikin, 1975, p. 39). Initially the group worked with a range of writers, notably Megan Terry and Jean Claude van Itallie, who wrote short plays for the company, some of them linked to or arising from improvisation ideas. The company then performed these alongside improvisation exercises from the workshops. The group also worked on texts from Eliot, John Arden, Brecht and Maria Irene Fornes among others. The first full-length plays which grew from workshop improvisation, although they were not devised, were Terry's *Viet Rock* and van Itallie's *America Hurrah* (1966) (Chaikin, 1972, p. 104). Both were closely connected to contemporary events, express-ing disquiet at the evolution of the Cold War and America's involvement in Vietnam. The commercial success of these productions, as the company toured them, might have pushed the group away from the discoveries being made in the workshop into straightforward rehearsal of pre-written texts, had there not been a grant to the company that paid the actors to undertake a more intensive workshop timetable.

The first production to evolve as directly devised was *The Serpent* in 1967. As with many of the processes of devising, the subject matter that begins a group's investigation does not always survive into the final performance. *The Serpent* began as a series of workshops exploring the life of Christ as a social anarchist. But the stories of the Old Testament lent themselves to the search for archetypal imagery more easily than did the individuated figure of Christ, and the moral themes of Genesis began to interest the company more. Using structured improvisation exercises drawn from Spolin, Stanislavski and those they invented themselves, they evolved images around the narrative of the myth. The mode of working might be exemplified by the company's search for the image of the serpent itself.

> One day in the workshop actor Roy London arranged several actors, including himself into a single creature with five flicking tongues and ten undulating arms and hands. Immediately, the workshop recognized its serpent. They played with the figure for weeks, varying the number of actors before finally settling on a five-part version. ... They also explored different sounds for this beast. In one experiment a serpent-actor read a snake speech from Ginzberg's *Legends of the Jews* while the four other actors 'jammed' along. Then someone tried putting apples into the creature's hands. And it became a bizarre, stunning amalgam of serpent and tree: its arms now were tree limbs as well as creature limbs, its sinuous movement the swaying of the tree in a wind as well as the animal's writhing. (Blumenthal, 1984, p. 149)

In this process of working, different actors contributed to and guided sections of the work, taking responsibility for different activities. All of the actors were involved in research for the performance, in reading and inviting key figures to talk to the group. This produced a strong sense of collective creativity, as evidenced by the moment of collective recognition of an effective theatrical image in the making of the serpent/tree.

However, having worked on the images and structure of *The Serpent* for almost a year, the pressure to mount a public performance and an international tour led Chaikin to invite van Itallie to write a script from the improvisations. This script was at some distance from the workshop ideas. Actors had been asked to suggest an overall structure and their ideas had included an 'LSD trip; black mass; a retreat from the plague ... a presentation of the lives of the actors' (Blumenthal, 1984, p. 134). Ultimately the script van Itallie created interleaved a chorus of contemporary women with the physical images of the Kennedy and King assassinations, the Garden of Eden full of strange animals and the active begetting and growth of the human race. Rehearsals of the script seemed disconnected from the process of generating the initial images, and this caused great tension in the group, especially on the European tour. When the company returned to New York they reshaped and 'reclaimed' the work from van Itallie's script in order to be able to continue to perform it. The conflict between the input of the generating performer and the writer was an ongoing one for Open Theatre, as an anonymous actor described:

> All the things I did in *Terminal* I came in with myself. That's why I always had a resentment of the writers. I would see a text a few years later where it says, such and such a piece by so and so, and the actors aren't even mentioned! Look at *The Mutation Show* as an example. It did not have a writer. I resented the fact that those writers were listed and given credit on the program. (Blumenthal, 1984, p. 147)

The potential conflicts between devising work and written text were exacerbated by the commercial mechanisms of publishing, recording and publicity. Shared credit by a group continues to sit uncomfortably within the traditional economics of publishing practice, where ownership and copyright remain with the named, usually solo, author.

The Open Theatre's production that made least use of a writer was *The Mutation Show* (1971), directed by Roberta Sklar and Joseph Chaikin, and perhaps as a result the piece had far fewer words than other Open Theatre performances. As research, the actors read *Soledad Brother: The Prison Letters of George Jackson* (Jackson had become an icon for the injustice of the treatment of young black men by the judicial system), Richard Wright's *Black Boy*, David Cooper's *Death of the Family*, and Freud and R. D. Laing on learning and the stages of maturity. The original premise of the piece developed from stories of neglected or feral children, such as Kamala the wolf girl (discussed in Singh and Zingg's study, reprinted in 1960 and 1966), or the reawakened interest in Kaspar Hauser. The actors evolved physical types of 'selves' in improvisation: 'acceptable, narcissistic, no bull-shit mask, human animal, male or female self, myself in the world self etc.' (Blumenthal, 1984, p. 150). These ideas owed much to Reichian and Laingian psychology about the habits and accretions of life, which 'gradually harden into a protective but inhibiting shell' (ibid.). These 'selves', begun as animal transformations and improvisations, became the 'freaks' in *The Mutation Show*. The actors played on a variety of levels: as the characters within the play, as professional entertainers who provided all of the sound and music for the piece, and as 'themselves', where in a late scene, the Human Gallery, they revealed autobiographical material as fellow 'mutants'. The actors swapped roles and characters throughout the piece and in the last scene, 'The Mutants Give Testimony', the performers sat on stools around the performance space, shifting focus from one to another, as snippets of the preceding scenes and the differing characters of the 'freak show' passed through them in a kind of chaotic vocal 'jamming', which was a hallmark performance technique.

> At the end of the jamming the actors sat breathing quietly with an awareness of the present space and moment and audience.   (Blumenthal, 1984, p. 166)

The performance's dynamic had moved through chaotic climax to a satisfying close in silence. The ending reinforced the central idea of presence and encounter between actor and audience, and paradoxically, despite the performance's threatening demonstration of the multiplicity of 'selves', suggested a symbolic meeting of real selves, unmasked, the actor behind the acting.

In Australia, a similar interest in the possibilities of actor-based performance influenced the work of the Australian Performing Group (1970). The repercussions of world events had led to the stoning of the US consulate in Melbourne, and huge street protests against 'conscription, American imperialism and the "dirty unwinnable war" in Vietnam' (Radic, 1991, p. 5). There was also a second level of cultural disenchantment with the remaining colonial authority of Britain, which hung over Australian cultural and political life. The early alternative theatre groups were primarily about establishing space for a distinctive Australian 'voice' through playwriting, rather than devising. However, when Betty Burstall established the Australian La Mama Café in Melbourne in 1967, a group of actors used the cheap venue to set up a workshop on Sundays, to improvise together. Graeme Blundell, a founder member, described the activity:

> We got into psychotherapy, group gropes and encounter training ... we
> tried to dissect ensemble playing and the nature of performance ... [using]
> a mixture of the second-hand and the makeshift: a variety of ensemble
> exercises drawn from many sources but adapted to our own situation and
> the beginnings of our own performing vocabulary.   (Blundell, 1970, p. 12)

Underlying much of the improvisation was 'a great notion of the transforming power of play ... [and] improvisation based on the transactional analysis of Erving Goffman, the theatresports of Viola Spolin and the gurus of *TDR*' (Robertson, 2001, pp. 6, 43). In 1970 the actors' workshop formally became the Australian Performing Group (APG). A first attempt at a collaboratively written review was a political satire based on the history of Melbourne 1888–1901 and the personal histories of the actors, *Marvellous Melbourne* (1970–1).[15] However, as the writers generated more and more material from the workshop, the performance moved further from the performers, particularly the women performers, who found that, as so often, the newly emerging Australian 'voice' was white, male and raucous.

It was dissatisfaction with *Marvellous Melbourne* that led to the APG's first devised work, from the female members of the group. In collaboration with Carlton Women's Liberation Group, and created over a period of six months, *Betty Can Jump* (1971), for five women and one man, told the story of women's experience since the settlement of Australia and 'was very much a group-devised show with all of us having an input into the scripts', as Claire Dobbin recalled (Dobbin, 1984, p. 130). Kerry Dwyer was one of the moving forces behind the women's group, which used 'transformation exercises in which the women tried to express in physical terms what they felt it was like to be women living in Australia in the early 70s' (ibid.). Added to this was the historical and documentary research the group had done using letters, diaries, poems and songs to produce a performance that was structured as a series of moving snapshots of women's lives, intermingled with one or two burlesque sketches. The Women's Theatre Group emerged as a concern separate from APG and devised a series of successful shows (*Out of the Frying Pan*, *Women and Children First* and *Add a Grated Laugh or Two*), which emerged from the sharing of personal experience that was funnelled through improvisation into sketches and song.

Similarly to the Australian experience, the content and processes of Halprin, Malina and Beck, and Chaikin's groups were echoed in the work of a UK company, The Freehold. The director, Nancy Meckler, was an American who had worked with La Mama Plexus in New York, a group influenced by Eugenio Barba and Grotowski. Arriving in the UK in 1968, she established The Freehold in 1969. Contemporary commentators judged that 'its emphasis on the highly-disciplined movement and the total physical and emotional involvement of each of its actors in the collective effort made it one of the pioneers ... of an ensemble approach' (Hammond, 1973, p. 38). Meckler recalled the sources of that involvement:

> Everything was collective, that was the emphasis. Even to the point where, when we performed, we never printed what parts the actors were playing. We were all anti anything to do with careers, or anything vaguely materialist. ... These actors were saying 'I don't want to work in conventional theatre, I only want to work in a deeply idealistic way'. They were really turning their back on the Establishment.[16]

The aspiration of the group's rhetoric emphasised the empowerment of the actor, the desire for equality amongst the group, and the resistance to absorption into the existing theatre industry. The physical interaction between the actors in order to create theatrical images was a hallmark of the company's work, emerging from a long improvisatory workshop period. The actors used a series of techniques drawn from The Living Theatre, Open Theatre's verbal 'jamming' exercises, and some of Barba's experimentation drawn from Grotowski's work, alongside material from dramaturgs or brought in from their research (Chambers, 1980, p. 106). Moments of the performance were left open for improvisation and connection with the audience: for example, this was particularly the function of the Chorus in *Antigone* (1969). The Freehold's focus on physical imagery was not conducted in rejection of the writer, indeed most of their productions were based on adaptations, such as Peter Hulton's adaptation of *Antigone*.[17]

The desire for a collective work-ethic did not negate the leading role of Meckler as a director. She articulated the paradox of being responsible for selecting and structuring exercises and guiding the evolution of the performance: 'I was the guide, but I was desperately trying to be totally collaborative, and that's why everyone felt so connected and felt so much ownership'.[18] Meckler's commentary reveals a paradox that runs through almost all of the companies that we examine in this chapter, working in the 1960s and 1970s. Whilst the rhetoric of devising emphasised the collaborative nature of the empowered actor in generating the performance material, the extent to which any of the theatre groups discussed here relinquished the idea of directorial authority is a moot point. Indeed, in many ways the director–auteur of the alternative theatre movement represented the culmination of the rise of the director, which had been initiated by the late nineteenth-century theatre industry. In part this was also a result of pragmatic conditions, as few devising companies were able to maintain a stable core of performers, or wage equality across jobs. None of these early theatre groups worked so collectively as the Judson Church Dance Theatre for example, or its offshoot in the early 1970s, Grand Union (Ramsay, 1991). However, the evolution of the actor as a contributing member of an artistic community was, in the early 1960s, one bred by these artistic communities them-selves, and certainly not by the conventional actor-training institu-tions of the US, UK or Australia. Indeed, the limitations of traditional drama schools for this work was part of the rationale for the estab-lishment of a strand of non-conservatoire, performance arts depart-ments in universities.

Rituals and Encounters

A second context for the evolution of this mode of actor-based devising was the desire for an 'encounter' between actor and audience. Theatrical performance was reconceptualised not as an exercise in illusion or pretence, but as an experiential ritual. Devised perfor-mance was an opportunity for the actors to create new rituals. Peter Schumann's Bread and Puppet Theatre (1962) made explicit allusion to the rituals of the Christian sacrament, by involving the sharing of bread with the audience as part of each performance:

> We would like you to take your shoes off when you come to our puppet show or we would like to bless you with the fiddle bow. The bread shall remind you of the sacrament of eating. We want you to understand that theatre is not yet an established form, not the place of commerce you think it is, where you pay and get something.   (Schumann, 1970, p. 35)

In Open Theatre's *Terminal* (1969/70) the actors embodied a ritual of presence on behalf of the audience, summoning the dead to be present through the bodies of the performers: 'we call upon the dying'. Julian Beck and Judith Malina also wanted 'to aid the audience to become once more what it was destined to be when the first dramas formed themselves on the threshing floor: a congregation led by priests, a choral ecstasy of reading and response' (Beck, 1965, pp. 21–2). Richard Schechner followed Grotowski in characterising the actor as shaman, and pursued his interest in ritual drama and anthropology through the *Drama Review* and his theoretical writing, drawing on metaphors from a different cultural tradition. Of course, the metaphoric roles of priest or shaman imply that the performer acts 'on behalf of' the audience, using a performative stance that militates against activating the audience to direct political activity, a conundrum that was to trouble several groups, as we shall explore later.

The idea of rites and rituals had become a powerful metaphor in post-war sociology and psychology.[19] The development of psychology and psychoanalysis had been crucially affected by World War II, not only in its dissemination, with the emigration of several European psychologists to the US and UK in the 1940s (for example, Fritz Perls, a founding father of Gestalt therapy), but also in its content. *Social* psychology became vital as psychologists attempted to comprehend and respond to the rise of fascism. Authors from the Frankfurt school, perhaps most significantly Theodore Adorno in *The Authoritarian Personality* (1950), linked politics and psychology explicitly in their attempt to understand the individual within social life. A writer whose work drew on the development of new models of psychology as generative and as social was Erving Goffman. His key books, most famously *The Presentation of Self in Everyday Life* (1959), *Encounters* (1961), and *Behaviour in Public Spaces* (1963), used theatrical metaphors to discuss interaction in everyday social life and were deeply influential, running through many popular paperback editions. R. D. Laing, an English psychologist, was a household name in the late 1960s and 1970s with his anti-establishment views of the institutional treatment of mental health patients. He developed Wilhelm Reich's ideas of the 'self' comprising a protective shell and an inner core, and insisted on regarding mental illness as on a continuum with sanity. His two important books, *The Divided Self* (1960, rpt 1970) and *The Politics of Experience* (1967), which extended his attention from the individual to society, went into popular paperback and he became a byword for enlightened thinking, even adorning bumper stickers.

Laing's popularisation of the protected, inner, true self and Goffman's articulation of an increasing sense of 'masked' public life were part of the context for the idea that a theatrical encounter between audience and performer could be therapeutic and that the audience might be positively affected by an encounter with the performer's body as unguarded and transcendentally revealing. Anna Halprin's work with dancers in the 1950s used improvisation to 'eliminate stereotyped ways of reacting ... to release things that were blocked' (Halprin, 1995, p. 77); Grotowski articulated much of the same attitude with his concern that the audience should be brought 'face to' the actor, and the actor 'face to' themselves in a revelatory confrontation. Richard Schechner discussed Goffman in his *Six Axioms for Environmental Theatre* (1973), and acknowledged the impact of psychoanalytical thinking on early experiments at the Performance Group. Indeed, for much of the company's life Schechner was in psychoanalysis himself and the Group met every Thursday for group therapy sessions. Likewise, for Chaikin a performance was 'where the delicate and mysterious encounter takes place. That encounter is not "made" but permitted. It is not performed at that moment, but let be' (Chaikin, 1972, p. 117). The idea of 'meeting', confronting or 'encountering' an audience as a beneficial psychological activity encouraged performers to devise moments of direct address to their audience and to invite a limited engagement within certain structures of the performances. The groups explored here were not, initially at least, as interested in audience participation as many of the Happening artists discussed in the next chapter. For example, Allan Kaprow's piece *Household* (May 1964) had no spectators, only participants in a symbolic battle of the sexes. Instead these actor-focused groups tended to offer their trained, professional, often transgressive bodies in pseudo-religious rituals, on behalf of the audience.

The inspiration for much of the idea of 'encounter' in the theatre was drawn from the gnostic imagination that haunts Artaud's *Theatre and its Double* (English translation, 1958). The expressive breath and body of the performer, before and beyond the text of any play, was increasingly significant as Artaudian ideas inspired a generation of theatre makers. In his essay 'On Affective Athleticism' Artaud called for an integration of the body, breath and emotion of the actor. The audience was to be physically affected, as a curative and purgative experience: 'Theatre is the only place in the world, the last group means we still possess of directly affecting the anatomy' (Artaud, 1974, p. 61). Artaud also rejected the 'idolising of set masterpieces, of middleclass conformity' and theatre that was 'purely descriptive, narrative theatre, narrating psychology' (Artaud, 1974, p. 57). It was partly in response to Artaud's call for a new content for theatre that many of these groups chose to work on myths and epic stories drawn from national mythic history or folklore, or religious texts such as the Bible, the Tibetan Book of the Dead, or Jewish spiritual literature.[20] Such subject matter offered groups both recognisable archetypes and narrative structures from which to devise, and a reservoir of assumed shared cultural reference with their audiences.

One of the first groups to expressly champion and utilise Artaud was the Polish troupe led by Jerzy Grotowski at the Theatre of Thirteen Rows, in Opole (1959), soon renamed the Polish Laboratory Theatre.[21] Grotowski's company initially undertook production of absurdist and poetic plays of the 1950s, in a relatively traditional manner. He had visited the Avignon Festival in 1957, and the discovery of Jean Vilar's work seemed to confirm his choice of repertoire, inflected by existentialism in a Catholic Polish culture. His theatre was concerned with image work, and alongside the constructivist inspiration of Meyerhold and Piscator he was also drawn to the 'ideograms' and images of Indian theatrical traditions and ancient Japanese and Greek forms, particularly after working on Kalidasa's *Sakuntala* (1960). In order to generate such images, his troupe needed additional physical and vocal training, which came to include forms of yoga. Moving from the idea of a traditional theatrical relationship, his search for a 'ritual acting' led the troupe to a different understanding of their relationship to an audience:

> we do not demonstrate action to the viewer; we invite him ... to take part in the 'shamanism' in which the living, immediate presence of the viewer is part of the playacting.   (Osinski, 1985, p. 49)

The rediscovery of traditional Polish rituals was echoed in their performance of Mickiewicz's *Forefathers' Eve* (1961), which they performed from a much-adapted text as a series of sacred games. The level of government subsidy the Polish Laboratory Theatre received meant it was able to maintain a small, stable ensemble and to pursue its interest in actor training, alongside extended rehearsals and preparations for performance. By the early 1960s the troupe were touring to international festivals and university groups, and the teaching and demonstrating of their actor-training methods was almost more popular than their production work.

The significance of the actor as a generator of material, alongside the dramaturg's work on the various texts the company chose, led them to stage *The Hamlet Study* (March 1964), as a public rehearsal of 'a study in the acting methods and collective direction of a production' (Osinski, 1985, p. 78). After performances of adapted texts, Marlowe's *Dr Faustus* (1963) and Slowaki's *The Constant Prince* (1965), their final production, *Apocalypsis cum Figuris* (1968), was devised by the company. One of the actors, Stanislaw Scierski, described the process of this production, which was three years in the making and began from an adaptation of *Samuel Zborowski*:

> We began to do the étude work, both collective and individual, not even using the text of the rough draft, not even 'basing' ourselves on it, but preserving it only on the outskirts of memory. ... One should note that many of the études were improvised. ... [F]rom the études that we performed for Grotowski, and the ones he co-created with us from the beginning, he built a new whole. If there were études which needed a text, both we and Grotowski made some proposals. In addition to Dostoevsky, he added excerpts from Eliot and Simone Weil, writers known and close to all of us. All of this work was an experience that was both thrilling and dramatic and bore a sense of that specific community. ... (Osinski, 1985, p. 111)

The work on études was about generating movements from structured improvisation exercises, but the concentration was on a connection between each movement and exercise and imaginative associations. Grotowski also wrote of the production as part of a different, new development for the company, a real move away from literature, as Artaud had encouraged. 'This was not a montage of texts. We were approaching this during rehearsals, through flashes of insight, through improvisation. Twenty hours of material were accumulated. We had to build something out of this that had its own energy, like a stream. ... We cite no one in what we're doing now' (Osinski, 1985, p. 112). The production premiered in 1968 and was the only truly devised production that the company performed.[22]

Grotowski's interest in actor training and the work of the Polish Laboratory Theatre greatly influenced Richard Schechner's The Performance Group, established at New York University (NYU) in 1967. Grotowski and his Laboratory were hosted at NYU in November 1967 and worked with acting and directing students for a month. The Performance Group's first production, *Dionysus in 69*, became somewhat infamous because of its nudity and audience interaction, and the extensive coverage that Schechner gave it in illustrating his theories of performance.[23] The Performance Group continued this work in the group-devised *Commune* (1970–2), but then returned to staging plays, including Sam Shepard's *Tooth of Crime* (1972–4) and

Brecht's *Mother Courage* (1975). In 1980, the group folded, but the Performing Garage, where the group worked, produced several interesting performance artists and other projects, notably The Wooster Group (see Chapter 7). In the UK, Peter Brook and Charles Marowitz were among the first to experiment with Artaudian demands in their 'Theatre of Cruelty' season, and this led to Brook's first experiment with devising, *US* (1966; discussed further in Chapter 3). Brook briefly pursued his interest in improvisation and Artaudian work in a very different context, with two projects, *The Conference of the Birds* (1972–9) and *The Ik* (1975), where he transported Western actors to African villages in an attempt to prove that the actor's body could be a source of revelatory, communicative experience beyond culture. Christopher Innes's commentary on these projects draws out their place in the tradition of the modernist, European avant-garde and its unhealthy interest in 'primitivism' (Innes, 1993, pp. 141–4).

By contrast, the Black Arts Movement's interest in Africa was part of a political programme that called for an Afrocentric reassessment of black culture, politics and experience. The Black Arts Movement and the championing of the Black Aesthetic was a key part of the Civil Rights Movement of the 1960s.[24] Profound dissatisfaction with the representation of black experience in existing play-texts and the desire for a direct, transformational relationship with its audience contributed to the development of devised performance rituals. Barbara Ann Teer, an actress who had grown increasingly disenchanted with the very limited roles available to her, moved to Harlem and established the National Black Theatre (NBT) in April 1968. For Teer, the Western canon had nothing to offer and what was needed was

the concept of God-conscious art, which is supposedly guided by the creative impulse that emanates from within. Inwardly inspired creativity obliterates artificial boundaries between performer and spectator, between experiences that are lived and those that are imitative. Western art is an accumulation of culturally biased symbols and archetypes that intimidate and inhibit artistic participation by potentially creative Blacks ... a theatre geared toward spiritual and psychological transcendence, a unique form of expression was needed to replace conventional art forms. (M. Williams, 1985, p. 51)

The National Black Theatre performed plays, but mainly engaged, in the early years, in a series of audience encounters they called 'ritualistic revivals'. Rather than actors, the members were 'liberators', and the actor training that Teer introduced was unique:

> The first stage is a form of deprogramming; the term used by NBT is *decrudin*. Realizing that Blacks as a distinct ethnic group in America have been subjected to psychological conditioning to minimize their racial differences ... the specific intention is to return Blacks to their spiritual base so that they can rediscover their individual identities and their collective identity. (M. Williams, 1985, p. 52)

'Decrudin' was a combination of political education and consciousness-raising for actors, offering them a five-stage emergence from a state Teer called 'nigger' and defined as materialistic and self-serving, through negro, militant and nationalist understandings, to achieve revolutionary wholeness. Actors were poorly but equally paid, and the common vision of the group was the essence of the work. The performances that the group devised were built on established rituals from the African diaspora and multiple traditions, particularly Yoruba culture. Rituals included audience participation in song and action. For Teer:

> There is no such thing as a stage, nor such a thing as an audience; only liberators and participants. And you try to remove that psychic distance, that nigger space that separates Black people from each other. In a ritual you mould, meet and merge into one. (Fabre, 1983, p. 231)

The theatre was sometimes dubbed the Temple, and it was developed as a space to celebrate Black life stories and lifestyle.[24]

Barbara Teer's challenge to the inhibiting limits of existing art forms for black creative artists was also a call picked up by many women working within, apparently radical, devising groups. Martha Boesing formed the feminist collective At the Foot of the Mountain (1974), in part because of dissatisfaction with the limitations of the sometime-devising Firehouse Theatre Company, Minnesota:

> The Firehouse called itself a collective, but it was not. It was a very male-dominated dictatorship, and the only way to power for a woman was through the bedroom. (Roth, 1982, p. 5)

At the Foot of the Mountain developed a series of strategies in devising their own performances, which drew on the practices of other devising or experimental companies such as ProVisional or The Palace Theatre,[26] but which turned them to a specifically feminist end. They used a Feeling Circle at the beginning of all rehearsals, where all the actors defined their emotional state, and explored how this would influence the day's work. This was a group-creating exercise, after the model of consciousness-raising, and a political activity to validate emotion, often socially denigrated as weak and feminine, as well as an actor-training exercise: 'The actors were going to follow their feelings – train them as much as they did their bodies and their voices' (Flynn, 1984, p. 96). In their collaborative creation the group used a combination of improvisation with realist scenes and characters, alongside physical-contact improvisation, to produce abstract images. Out of such work, Martha Boesing, the usual director, would write repeated drafts of a script.[27] They defined their performance work as a search for a ritual drama and frequently sought to involve the audience, asking them to express their experience of the themes of the play through 'lighting candles, or naming names or speaking their thoughts out loud, sharing something with a neighbor' (Flynn, 1984, p. 187).[28] As the examples of the National Black Theatre and At the Foot of the Mountain illustrate, to devise their own theatrical rituals was, for many groups, not only an aesthetic or spiritual concern, but also an expressly political one. Both these companies illustrate the limitations of the processes behind the apparently open, collaborative rhetoric and aspiration of the actor-centred devising groups.[29] In many ways these two companies could have been considered under the rubric of 'political theatre' in Chapter 4, and their inclusion here is not in any way an attempt to denude the political aspects of their devising and performance.

The Politics of Popular Forms

As we discussed in Chapter 1, actor-centred groups who were trying to experiment outside and beyond the mechanisms of the cultural establishment were in tune with the rhetoric of participatory democracy and the evidence of the power of massed political protest. The socialist ideal of a workers' cooperative or collective was linked to the recognition of the actors as theatre *workers*, and opened up a discussion about their ownership of the means of production. Several groups had a policy of equal wages, including Théâtre du Soleil, the Australian Performing Group, and The Living Theatre.[30] The very idea of a group was politically nuanced, as Tim Robertson, who worked with the Australian Performing Group, one of Australia's first devising companies, quipped:

a group was something to be, the exemplary organ, a source of power, proven catalyst of revolution and scientific discovery, lever to world fame and wilder sex. (Robertson, 2001, p. 1)

The theatrical tradition of small-scale, popular touring theatre troupes such as those of *commedia dell'arte*, vaudeville, circus or even the Workers' Theatre Movement offered a model that chimed with the aspirations of many of the groups of the 1960s. The romanticised heritage of such troupes seemed to offer many things: a commitment to communicate with a popular, working-class audience; a source of recognisable, lively and accessible material and structuring mechanisms for performance; and a resistance to the commercial, text-based hierarchies of the theatrical establishment.

The broadly anti-establishment commitment of many devising groups led them to consider the empowering possibilities of communicating with a popular audience, in that audience's setting and context. For example, working on the West Coast in the late 1950s and early 1960s, the long-lived RG Davis, later San Francisco, Mime Troupe emerged from the San Francisco Actors' Workshop in 1959. The work of this group sprang from a commitment to actor training in popular performance, particularly *commedia dell'arte*. The performance attention of the Mime Troupe was directed firmly towards political activism in public parks and the streets.[31] Likewise groups like The Pageant Players (1965) set out to radicalise their audiences through their devising.[32] This more politically activist work is discussed more fully in Chapter 4. However, as Baz Kershaw warned, 'to be both oppositional and popular places performance on a knife edge between resistance to, and incorporation into, the status quo' (Kershaw, 1992, p. 8). The use of popular forms did not *per se* guarantee a theatre of political resistance.

Popular forms underpinned the devising methodology of one of the most successful collaborative creating cooperatives in Europe, Théâtre du Soleil.[33] The company was formed as a workers' cooperative by a group of ten young students in Paris in 1964, with its director Ariane Mnouchkine, who studied with Jacques Lecoq in 1966. The political inclinations of the group were clear from the outset, but they did not produce politically didactic work.[34] Initially their work was not collaboratively created, but involved staging texts as diverse as Wesker's *The Kitchen* (1967) and Shakespeare's *A Midsummer Night's Dream* (1968). However, in 1969, the collective nature of the group's ideology, and their investigation of popular forms, led to the devising of *Les Clowns* (1969–70).

Mnouchkine described how she and members of the company experienced 'a kind of weariness under the influence of the enormous suicidal atmosphere that followed in the wake of May 1968' (Williams, 1999, p. 24). There had been no revolution, no theatre text seemed to encapsulate the difficulties France faced, and the company itself was facing financial meltdown. The group retreated to live and work together for two months in a borrowed ex-salt factory in Arc-et-Senans, exploring clowning, *commedia* and chorus work. Each member of the group developed a clown figure and they gave an improvised workshop for the local village at the end of their stay. This period of concentrated work and collective living produced an excitement about the work, and the workshop performance was so successful that the troupe evolved it into a performance. For Mnouchkine:

> our work on *The Clowns* is first of all an attempt to strengthen our abilities as actors, to free us from psychological acting, to get rid of naturalism and everything in us which is too everyday. It is also a first step in that experience which we are undertaking as a collective to find a new form, directly accessible to our contemporaries.   (Kiernander, 1993, pp. 65–6)

In fact, the group devised only four productions, during the late 1960s and 1970s: *Les Clowns* (1969), *1789* (1970–1), *1793* (1972–3) and *L'Age d'Or* (1975–6).

Although each process was slightly different, work on all the devised productions began with the actors involved in extensive research. One actor, who joined the company for *1789*, Louis Samier, described the difference in working for Soleil:

> Not only do I feel like an actor here, but I find myself in tune with what I'm making ... here the actor is required to be a creator in the production. What comes through in the performance stems from what's outside the performance and is intimately connected to the group's life and work. (Williams, 1999, p. 30)

The use of popular forms had a political effect on the generation of Soleil's work, leading their improvisations to develop 'character-types', rather than individual characters. Improvisations were to develop the function of the role in the story, rather than to develop the relationship between the individual actor and the role, as in more traditional, Stanislavskian improvisation.

> We recorded the text of *Les Clowns* and then transcribed it. We distributed
> the good improvisations among the actors, who went back over them and
> reworked them. They often went over what they had already done, modify-
> ing it. This time [on *1789*] we are recording, we are reworking – not in the
> sense of prettying, or finishing, but so as to remove the parasites, to focus
> on the meaning and always after the event.   (Williams, 1999, p. 20)

Describing the decision-making process of the group, Mnouchkine
rejected the idea of the director having the 'last word', and championed the impact of collective intuition in recognising the appropriate theatrical image when it appeared in improvisation (Williams,
1999, p. 219). However, after the production of *L'Age d'Or* (1975),
the group returned to using texts as the basis of productions, with
Mnouchkine firmly established as director, although their improvisational work on staging remains key to their style and purpose.[35]

Clowning, *commedia* and vaudeville theatre techniques allowed
devising companies to draw on pre-existing forms of entertainment
that already carried a popular, political weight. Characters were
presented, rather than lived by actors, and the audience was acknowledged and involved in the performance. Popular traditions offered
ways of structuring performances, through the mechanics of *commedia* scenarios or storytelling. Footsbarn (1971, UK), a Cornish-
based group, had initially written their shows collaboratively, but,
as Théâtre du Soleil did, began experimenting with clowning and this
led them to devise *The Dancing Bear* (1977):

> It was about ourselves really. We kept most of the characters and used them
> as clowns, and we still use those characters although they've moved into a
> different age. Everybody got a good character from *The Dancing Bear*,
> a good clown character.   (Cousin, 1985, p. 106)

Here was a different way of using the popular motifs of clowning or
vaudeville from that of Théâtre du Soleil's political archetypes. For
Footsbarn, as for many other devising companies, devising lent itself
to the use of the actual dynamics, experiences and preoccupations of a
group of actors, rather than forcing them into presenting predeter-
mined 'characters'.[36]

The use of the clown or trickster figure in order to discuss personal
and popular native stories was a key part of the development of
Spiderwoman Theater (1975), a multi-racial, feminist group. The
company, initially composed of Native American and European-
heritage American actresses, were inspired to devise in part through

Muriel Miguel's time with the Open Theatre. The first performance, *Women in Violence* (1976), a piece about domestic and social
violence, was built through improvisation using personal story as
'a healing process' and clowning techniques, in order to create a direct
connection with the audience:

> You might have an idea for a story, or you might have a story, so you tell the
> story. We try to repeat it back to you. ... Some of us went home and would
> write, some of us did it on our feet. Some of it was suggested and some was
> improvisation and writing.   (Abbott, 1996, pp. 172–3)

The original company membership split (Lois Weaver and Peggy
Shaw developed the lesbian performance company Split Britches),
but Spiderwoman Theater has continued to explore the political
implications of Native identity, class and gender through the use of
popular oral traditions, storytelling and clown/trickster personae
(Haugo, 2002).

Some groups were less concerned with the political value of their
devising, and chose strategies that emphasised the accessibility and
entertainment value of their engagement with an audience. Vaudeville
offered a structure and content to one of the key devised shows from
the Australian Performing Group, *The Hills Family Show* (1975). The
impetus for this performance came from actor Max Gillies, who 'felt
an urge to liberate himself from the written word. He proposed a
comedy workshop in which performers would develop their own
comic personae' (Robertson, 2001, p. 77). The actors became the
theatrical Hills family, a touring troupe of strange variety acts on its
last legs. The eventual typescript of the scenario read 'a bare outline
of the happening ... merely a guideline. Improvisational skills are
needed ... certain acts may need to be changed depending on the
talents of the cast available' (Robertson, 2001, p. 82). Audience
engagement began when they were greeted in the foyer by the
unprepared vaudevillians, and continued through the troupe's doomed
attempt to demonstrate their acts and perform a play, *The Accidental
Poke*, whilst continuing long-established family feuds. One of the
many brief turns involved Winston, a terrible lounge croon act, who
battled Granny Fanny, a sometimes wheelchair-bound equestrienne:

> Through the life of the show his *lazzi* with Granny became more extended
> and extreme. In deepest Gippsland the audience was led out of the
> community hall towards a level crossing where he threatened to abandon

her. At Bondi pavilion he trundled her over the sands towards the surf and shark attack.   (Robertson, 2001, p. 84)

Both the theatrical personae drawn from the popular tradition and the vaudeville structure had given a form to the group's devising. The piecemeal nature of the performance was bound together by the over-arching theatrical conceit. The engagement with popular forms had also prompted the decision to turn to devising itself.[37]

Clowning, *commedia* and the actor-training exercises that empha-sised transformation fed the devising strategy of a British storytelling group, Shared Experience (1975), directed by Mike Alfreds. Initially, the company created collectively from the scenarios of texts that they adapted, producing a three-part version of *Arabian Nights* (1975), and a four-part adaptation of *Bleak House* (1977). The company set out to:

reexplore the function of the narrative ... and the specific nature of the individual actor's contribution towards shaping the performance, not only through the technical skills he/she has and can develop, but also through his/her own personality, standing as a complex human being in a social situation.   (Alfreds and Barker, 1981, p. 12)

In evolving a physical storytelling technique, using plenty of direct audience address, the members of the company 'shared the narrative, swapped roles and even played the scenery'.[38] The company became so proficient at improvised storytelling that they evolved a completely improvised performance, *Science Fictions* (1978), a fully formed play, which had a series of optional scenarios providing a loose structure. Mike Alfreds described how the production had begun with a set scenario, but as the actors rehearsed and performed:

there was no starting 'ploy' which got the action going, [but] a whole repertoire of initiating points which might or might not be used, and a choice of endings. Some nights were zany, some were cruel, some were quite moving. The company improvised together daily in rehearsal, and in performance for the best part of a year.   (Alfreds and Barker, 1981, p. 13)

Like Shared Experience's other early work, this piece was initially based on *commedia*, and the group had evolved clown characters in order to carry them through the demands of live improvisation. Using the idea of the touring theatrical family, the *commedia* troupe or the clowning group as thematic content as well as methodology offered devising companies a model of a cultural alternative to the theatrical establishment, even if only some groups also made use of the model as political resistance.

Conclusion

Devising emerged as part of the desire of groups of actors to establish collaborative companies that reflected an anti-establishment and anti-hierarchy ethos that was in keeping with the more radical trends of the 1960s and early 1970s. And the content of much of the work that the groups produced chose to address social issues of their moment – the Vietnam War, trade unionism, racial identity, terrorism, the rise of feminism, Civil Rights, institutional violence and the Cold War. Despite their resistance to conventional hierarchies, many groups had strong directors, figures who displaced the authority of the writer. Richard Schechner made this tendency most apparent when he announced the 'Death of the avant-garde', arguing that the end of the avant-garde had arrived with the 1980s when actors rebelled against directors, like himself (Schechner, 1981). Arnold Aronson sardonically noted that 'most groups functioned more on the model of the totalitarian phase of communism: there was a collective of actors, but the groups tended to have autocratic, even dictatorial, leaders in the form of visionary directors, who, in essence, replaced the playwright as the creative fount for texts' (Aronson, 2000, p. 80). Other commentators, however, have seen the benefits of collaborative work for the actor. For Colin Chambers:

> ironically, it was the notion and practice of the collective that allowed the individual to flower rather than the ailing market system, which claimed to be based on individual freedom while putting a few on a pedestal for a time and dumping the rest on the scrap-heap. Likewise, it was radical, egalitarian cooperation that allowed the individual actor to be more expressive and creative rather than the authoritarian relationships of the conventional theatre.   (Chambers, 1980, p. 106)

The apparently Artaudian challenge to the supremacy of language in the theatre had been picked up by many of these groups. However, many of them also moved back to scripts. The process of generating actor-centred performance by groups with an actor-training focus was not very far divorced from the traditional processes of mainstream theatre production, and it is perhaps not surprising that the writer/ director nexus reasserted itself.[39]

However, there were more radical differences for some groups. The devised performances of these groups often bore the hallmarks of their generative processes in the disjunctive, piecemeal structure of games and exercises. It is difficult now to recapture the sense of excitement surrounding the use of games as performance, since these games have become canonised within actor training at university and drama school. For example, Clive Barker, an English actor/academic, wrote about his work with Littlewood's Theatre Workshop and suggests many games and exercises for devising in his helpful workbook *Theatre Games* (1977). In it he offers the plague game, 'a general theatre training game which has also been used in performance', which is drawn directly from the culminating scene of The Living Theatre's performance *Mysteries and Smaller Pieces* (Barker, 1977, p. 104).[40] This volume and the exercise has been very widely used for years, but the exercise instructions cannot convey, and perhaps wisely do not encourage readers to attempt, the Artaudian-inspired, extremely disrupted breathing which brought the original performers to froth at the mouth, writhe in pain, and reach an altered state, the 'death point', in order to affect the audience with an experience of visceral need.

Devised performance generated by actor-centred groups reconfigured the rituals of theatre-going, fed by the contemporary cultural interest in psychology and social responsibility. The body and persona of the actor provided both the measure of the imagery and the content of a performance, and the basis of its engagement with the audience. Devising strategies, drawn from improvisation, provided actors with a means of having a direct effect upon their audiences. And the development of devising strategies themselves extended the rationale of existing actor-training mechanisms into new kinds of improvisation. The possibilities of using personal story and personal belief both as source for, and within, performance contributed to the political aspects of the performances in an era that was discovering that 'the personal was political'.

3 Devising and Visual Performance

Many of the companies explored in this chapter were committed to a primarily visual sensibility in relation to the composition of their devised work, thereby placing it on a continuum with other art forms, including painting and sculpture. Of course, the difference of performance from other art forms is its liveness – its temporal quality and ephemerality; and it was these unique features that were part of its appeal. The 'eventness' of performance – something happens here and now – made performance ideally suited to the times, a tool by which to liberate both the artist and the spectator who shared time and space. In the devised work explored here, the liveness of performance led often to a focus on action rather than on acting, and performing equated with doing rather than pretending. Perhaps paradoxically, live performance offered the potential for authentic activity and within this frame, representation might best be reconsidered as presentation. As this chapter will trace, the notion of theatre as art also emphasises the visual potential of theatre. The People Show, founded in 1966, have from their inception realised the imagistic qualities of theatre. Discussing the aesthetics at the heart of their work, co-founder Mark Long's insights are more widely applicable:

I believe very strongly that theatre is definitely a very visual form and I think this has been denied for a long, long time. I don't think it was always the case, but it has generally become a verbal art form. I don't reject this but I also don't believe that it is the only thing that the theatre is about. It is not necessarily a carrier of ideas, it is very much a thing people look at. (Long, 1981–2, p. 8)

Whilst not being 'anti-literary', the move away from a verbal art form towards a visual one challenged the authority or dominance of the written text, and arguably the means then of authoring a text.

Happening Times

The radical political context of the late 1950s and 1960s demanded art and performance practices that aimed, like the counter-cultural interventions, to resist the effects of repression in order to liberate the alienated individual. Just as the Futurists, Dadaists and Surrealists had forged new forms and new languages appropriate to their times, so theatre practitioner Ken Dewey recognised that 'We need new methods and new techniques of articulation: ways in which people can articulate themselves' (Dewey, 1995 (1965), p. 208). The 'Happening' was considered one such 'method'; a form of performance that was 'art but seems closer to life' (Kaprow, 1966b, p. 3). Allan Kaprow, credited by many as being the 'originator' of the Happening, having coined the term in 1959, insisted that 'the line between art and life should be kept as fluid, and perhaps indistinct, as possible ...' (Kaprow, 1966a, p. 189).

Though the term 'Happening' was loosely and often problematically applied to a vast array of different live performance events,[1] the majority of activities gathered under that term focused on performance as non-matrixed action; Happenings were not structured according to the principles of plot development, narrative, or character.[2] In the Happening, since all properties – performer, objects, time, space, place – were accorded equal status, the mode of devising used was 'compositional', the juxtaposition of 'diverse materials' (Kaprow, 1966a, p. 162). For Kaprow, the Happening was an extension in time and space of the earlier Environment and Assemblage techniques: 'that is, it is evolved as a collage of events in certain spans of time and in certain space' (ibid., p. 198). Stressing the 'organic' nature of 'composition', Kaprow insisted that composition should not be reduced simply to the arrangement or organisation of materials. Rather, the specific or unique properties of the materials generated or suggested the form of the Happening; form was not imposed upon the materials as an external structuring principle: 'let the form emerge from what the materials can do' (ibid., p. 202).

The live aspect of these performed events encouraged a sensitivity towards time and space, leading to an awareness of the contingent or 'the accidental', and in particular the effect and potential of chance. The introduction of deliberate chance procedures provided further means for juxtaposing different materials, prompting new and unexpected meanings to arise from unusual relationships. In devising a Happening, then, artists might employ chance techniques to generate both the material and its structuring. A roulette wheel or a thrown dice might determine 'how many persons ... will be part of the compositional activity. ... Materials may be obtained by cutting up all the items listed in a random selection of pages from the "Yellow Pages"' (ibid., p. 177). For Kaprow, chance did not erase the possible imputation of meaning to relationships between seemingly disparate materials but rather the results of chance freed 'one from *customary* relationships' (ibid., p. 207).

> As a point of view and a technique, chance methodology is not only refreshing in the best sense of the word; it is extremely useful in dispersing and breaking up knots of 'knowables,' of groupings, relationships, and larger structures which have become obsolete and habitual through overuse. Everything, the stuff of art, of daily life, the working of one's mind, gets thrown into sudden and startling patterns, so that if old values are destroyed, new experiences are revealed. (Kaprow, 1966a, p. 181)

The unpredictability of chance fitted well with the ephemerality of the Happening form, both seeming to reflect lived experience. If reality was 'understood as *constant metamorphosis*' (ibid., p. 169), constantly in a process of flux, or change, then 'art work must be free to articulate this on levels beyond the conceptual. There is no fundamental reason why it should be a fixed, enduring object to be placed in a locked case' (ibid., p. 168). As Richard Schechner similarly noted, 'Being in the world, the artist reciprocates and tries to make his Happening an image of that world, particularly of its busy-ness. The multifocus complexity of these pieces is astounding' (Schechner, 1995 (1965), pp. 217–18).

French Happening artist Jean-Jacques Lebel, a frequent visitor to the UK, insisted on the Happening form's political potential, specifically within the cultural arena, where it enacted a challenge to 'this mercantile, state-controlled conception of culture' (Berghaus, 1995, p. 353). Lebel was passionate in his reconfiguring of the purpose of art in a transformed society.

Paris Postscript, May/June 1968.

Something has changed ... No more theatre or expensive spectacles for a passive audience of consumers – but a truly *collective* enterprise in political and artistic research. A new type of relationship between the 'doers' and the 'lookers' is being experimented with. Perhaps we will succeed in helping hundreds of thousands more to let go of their alienated social roles, to be free of mental Stalinism, to become the political and creative doers they dream of being. ... Today more than ever the emphasis is on getting things done. ... The sooner everyone realizes ART I$ SHIT, the better. From then on, it's spontaneity.

[Signed] Jean-Jacques Lebel.   (Sandford, 1995 (1968), p. 283)

Lebel's pronouncement made particular sense when placed in the context of Paris 1968, which, as one commentator noted, 'was a producer's dream, an enormous street happening: everything was theatrical, and there was no need for theatres' (Anon., 1971, p. 63). Wolf Vostell's 'manifesto' on the 'Happening' (1964), like Kaprow's, similarly linked directly to the Dadaist and Surrealist desire to minimise the gap between art and life, and instead to render the everyday an aesthetic experience. Within the context of the 1960s, the turn towards the 'everyday', away from narrative and fiction, was perceived as a political turn towards the 'authentic', with the 'authentic' frequently located in real action, rather than in acting. Art, like life, should become or be made real, should enable or encourage experience rather than contemplation, should be authentic rather than mimetic. This position was directly opposed to the presumed autonomy of modernist art, as well as the presumed 'authority' of a director and writer. If art was life, then anyone and everyone had the right to make it. The aim of transfiguring life into art, and art into life, was an undoubtedly political act.

happening = life − life as art − no retreat from but *into* reality − making it possible to experience and live its essence − not to abandon the world but to find a new relation to it − to let the participant experience himself consciously in the happening − to shift the environment into new contexts − to create new meanings by breaking up the old − let the participant experience indeterminacy as a creative force − to uncover and let uncover nonsense in sense − lack of purpose as purpose − open form as form − eccentricity − participants and performers instead of spectators − simultaneousness through juxtaposition of contradictory elements − new combination and absurd use of everyday objects.   (Vostell, in Berghaus, 1995, p. 325)

In an era marked by a demand for wide-scale 'participatory democracy', it was little wonder that such ideals were applied to the status of the spectator, going further than The Living Theatre's 'interactions' discussed in the previous chapter. The spectator was, ideally, an equal participant. Kaprow's 'rules-of-thumb' for Happenings recommended that 'audiences should be eliminated entirely'. Through the integration of 'all the elements – people, space, the particular materials and character of the environment, time', the 'last shred of theatrical convention disappears' (Kaprow, 1966a, pp. 195–6). For Lebel, similarly, the Happening was a participatory art, a means of 'overcoming art, of leaving theatre behind, and of arriving at life' (Berghaus, 1995, p. 352). Like Dada, then, it was anti-art or anti-theatre. The demand for participatory action aimed to make life thoroughly sensuous and aesthetic.

Happenings and Theatre

Though the emergence of the Happening has been credited to Kaprow, this attribution is somewhat problematic. Kaprow's 'first' named Happening in 1959, *18 Happenings in 6 Parts*, was preceded by John Cage's untitled theatre event of 1952 at Black Mountain College, ostensibly a Happening that, according to Sally Banes, was 'inspired by futurist and dada events' (Banes, 2000, p. 229).[3] Cage himself also admitted to earlier influences; the ideas of Huang Po, Artaud and Duchamp 'all fused together into the possibility of making a theatrical event in which the things that took place were not causally related to one another – but in which there is a penetration, anything that happened after that happened in the observer himself' (Aronson, 2000, p. 39). Notably, Cage had also attended Tadashi Suzuki's lectures for three years, and claimed that his 'testing of art against life' was one outcome of this (Kostelanetz, 1980, p. 52).[4] Cage taught Kaprow, as well as Dick Higgins and Jackson MacLow, at the New School in New York. Ken Dewey has similarly suggested that 'the causes of Happenings have been "in the air" for at least fifty years, probably longer' (Kostelanetz, 1980, p. 10). Such 'causes', recognised also by Banes and implicitly by Cage, included Futurism, Dadaism and Surrealism with their various explorations in the use of simultaneity, automatism, the found 'object', and 'chance' as a generative process.[5]

Histories of the Happening most typically locate it within an art trajectory. Kaprow, as we have seen, traced the Happening directly to the Environments and Assemblage techniques. Artist Jeff Nuttall proposed a link between the Happening form and the abstract expressionist movement of the 1940s. In the latter, 'The painter didn't make the splash of paint, he allowed it to happen, and then "found" it' (Nuttall, 1968, p. 118). For Nuttall, the 'Happenings' was an art of found 'human action'. Gunter Berghaus, meanwhile, considered the Happenings 'a natural outcome of the [European] Pop artists' concern with the problems of representation and with the connections between art and life' (Berghaus, 1995). Claes Oldenburg located the emergence of the Happening in that moment 'when painters and sculptors crossed into theatre taking with them their way of looking and doing things' (cited in Dewey, 1995 (1965), p. 206).

There are undoubtedly links between or across various develop-ments in art and the Happening form; but we should also recognise that when artists crossed *into* theatre they confronted an already existent field that had its own histories, practices and potentials. The tendency to historicise the Happening solely from within an 'art world' context ignores not only the activities of theatre, but also the inevitable interdisciplinary relationship forged between theatre and art when art turned to 'action'. As Dewey recognised, the Happenings were a hybrid form, 'the products of some kind of fusion' (Dewey, 1995 (1965), p. 206). Cage certainly referenced Artaud and Suzuki as influential practitioners. And John Calder, a British radical publisher, proposed theatrical precedents rather than artistic ones, in particular earlier challenges to the forms of 'play texts', suggesting that the Happenings 'developed naturally from the absurd tradition of Jarry, Artaud, and Ionesco and others' (Calder, 1967, p. 7). As should also be apparent from preceding citations, theatrical forms and their relationship to the performance activities of Happenings were often addressed. Michael Kirby, critic, Happening artist and The Wooster Group collaborator used conventional theatrical dramatur-gical structures as his primary point of reference when explaining the Happening:

> Happenings have abandoned the plot or story structure that is the foundation of our traditional theatre. Gone are the clichés of exposition, development, climax and conclusion. ... Gone are all elements needed for the presentation of a cause-and-effect plot or even the simple sequence of events that would tell a story. In their place, Happenings employ a struc-ture that could be called ... *compartmented* ... based on the arrangement and contiguity of theatrical units that are completely self-contained and hermetic.   (Kirby, 1995 (1965), p. 4)

Equally, though Kaprow warned against the Happening becoming 'stage theater', he also recognised that the term 'theatre' was open to redefinition: 'The definition of theatre need not be limited to the stage, scripts, actors. The theatre can include rodeos, TV commercials, excursions – and 101 other things that have a performance function' (Schechner, 1995b (1968), p. 229). Theatre practitioners explicitly engaged with the Happening form specifically to challenge and reject the conventions of dominant theatre practice at the time. For Richard Schechner, the Happenings challenged 'theatre people to re-examine the stage (should there be a stage?), focus, and the relationship to the audience (should there be an audience?)' (Schechner, 1995a, p. 218). Arnold Aronson similarly credited the Happenings with calling 'into question the basis of Western drama' (Aronson, 2000, p. 68).

One theatre practitioner to realise the potential of the Happening as a new form of theatre practice, in relation to both product and process, was Ken Dewey. Dewey claimed to have made a Happening 'somewhere around' 1957 or 1958, on the subject of the Sputnik (Dewey, 1977, p. 5). In 1963 Dewey collaborated with Allan Kaprow, Mark Boyle, Charles Marowitz and Carrol Baker on the notorious Edinburgh Happening.[6] *In Memory of Big Ed* was commissioned by John Calder for the Edinburgh Festival International Writer's Conference, and was intended to introduce this 'theatre of the future' to conference delegates. Prior to this event, Dewey had already worked with Anna Halprin, and was also familiar with many of the Happening artists in New York. Nevertheless, in Dewey's opinion, *In Memory of Big Ed* first brought the form specifically to the attention of *theatre practitioners*: 'Cage has confronted the music community with his music, Kaprow had confronted the art community, Halprin had confronted the dance world, and this was the time I confronted the theatre world' (ibid., p. 33). Dewey's claim might not have been too far fetched; 1500 delegates attended the 1963 Writer's Conference, including Peter Brook, Arnold Wesker, Laurence Olivier, Peter Shaffer, Jan Kott, John Arden, Harold Pinter, Edward Albee, Wole Soyinka, Joan Littlewood, William Burroughs, Alexander Trocchi and Peter Hall.

Dewey's 'background' had been in theatre, and where Cage, Kaprow and Halprin were all defining, working with, or testing the limits of the unique qualities of their practices, Dewey was similarly focusing on the essential elements of theatre.

My adventure was completely different. ... I was trapped, literally in the notion of all the formalities of theatre – the script, the rehearsal process and the architecture. The script defining what you were going to do, the rehearsal process defining how you were going to do it. My problem was to break myself loose from those dependencies – develop new methods in each of the three areas.   (Dewey, 1977, p. 13)

Dewey aimed to 'find a non-literary base for composing in theatre', where each component or material had 'its own identity' relating to its material presence rather than to its function (ibid., pp. 6, 11). Performances were composed from available materials, or environments, and according to the particular situation (ibid., p. 8). Influenced by working with Robert Whitman, Dewey was interested in all materials being treated as art objects and as enabling potential experiences or encounters, typically actions. Moreover, Dewey considered all components equal in relation to each other, although he also acknowledged that the person was 'the conscious element', the 'one who can be most active in the situation and can activate' (ibid., pp. 31–2). Thus, 'there was a relationship of one-to-one between director and performer. One-to-one between performer and material' (ibid., p. 11). Recognising the specific possibilities of theatre practice, Dewey noted that most of his Happening colleagues

don't have my commitment to collaboration. The painters and sculptors come from an individual image-art; so they ask people to come in and participate with them. ... Now, theatre has been a collective form from the beginning; and to stabilize various interests, it seeks out a common denominator.   (Kostelanetz, 1980, p. 182)

Dewey wanted to challenge the hierarchical structure typically encoded in theatrical processes where one person would assume leadership. To this end he was 'very much involved with collaboration and the distribution of responsibility', aiming to define a 'theatre form for a democracy' (ibid.). His aim of enabling each component within any performance to retain its own identity was very much part of this idea of 'democracy' (Dewey, 1977, p. 11). Dewey's exploration inevitably led him away from his earlier role as a playwright (an individual activity) towards devising performances (a collaborative event):

My whole approach has been to try to form a rapport among the people, and then among the materials and then among the situation in which they can relate directly without me. ... The piece sort of gradually takes over and begins to compose itself. Things present themselves. ... You ... work with a provocation, a catalytic thing, which starts somebody else's imagination going. You know it's a nuclear principle really, where you start the reaction and then it takes over.   (Dewey, 1977, pp. 13–14)

Asked whether he had any words to describe the material, content or realm offered in his work, Dewey responded: 'Generally, it's themselves, where we are, the physical characteristics of the place. It's the process rather than the result. ... The way of doing it rather than fixating on what was to be done' (ibid., p. 15).

Dewey's sensibility, relating to the moment, to the here and now, and to action within the moment, is one shared by many Happening artists. The early performance works of UK artist Mark Boyle, fellow collaborator on *Big Ed*, were similarly representative of performance experiments that sought to reconfigure the place and form of 'theatre'. In 1964 Boyle created *Street*.[7] The 'audience' were led through a door marked 'Theatre' and then seated in a kitchen, in front of a curtain. When the curtains opened, they were confronted with an actual street. Erasing the gap between art and life, the window framed the street as 'theatre', the actions in the street as 'performance', and the people observed as 'actors'. There was no pretence here; an everyday scene was simply made visible through a different framing. Boyle's *Suddenly The Last Supper*, presented the same year, also incorporated real actions executed in real time and in real space – Boyle's own flat. Slides of Botticelli's *Birth of Venus* were projected onto a naked woman, who enacted the same poses, while Boyle and his friends completely emptied the flat of all of his possessions. Notably, this performance coincided with the real-life event that the Boyle family were facing – eviction from their home.

The People Show's first performance, *The People Show* (1966), similarly challenged the boundary between art and life, while also mounting an implicit critique of the commodified art object. The show was, literally, a people show, which is how the company arrived at its name. In the basement of Better Books the performers

presented ourselves as sculptures. One wall of the basement forms three alcoves. These we screened off with cardboard. We cut holes in the cardboard and through these carefully cut holes we displayed bits of us – my belly, Mark's feet. ... Syd was masked on a pedestal. The other people came in and wandered round prodding us.   (Nuttall, 1979, p. 30)

When the company moved to Jim Haynes's newly opened Arts Laboratory in Drury Lane in 1967, one of their first shows continued this exploration of the 'real' versus the 'as if', the presumed 'authentic' rather than 'enacted', and the performer/spectator divide. During the performance, each member of the audience was to be interrogated in turn, with each interrogation being 'something of an ordeal'. There was also to be a real telephone at hand, in order that people could ring witnesses (ibid., p. 34).

Boyle's and the People Show's performances were also exemplary in that they were presented in unconventional spaces. Art which managed to escape the walls of the galleries by becoming live, or performances located in non-theatre spaces, were felt to escape the repressions of those 'bourgeois' environments, and of capitalism more generally. Given the existence, in our own time, of well-established 'experimental' performance venues and the presence of a University 'touring circuit', it is easy to forget that in the 1960s there were absolutely no spaces available for showing work that did not fit the typical format, in terms of content or of form. Boyle's decision to construct a performance for/from his own home might as equally have been pragmatic as aesthetic or political. Mark Long made clear the scarcity of opportunity at this time:

> Initially there was not a studio theatre in this country, there was not a pub theatre in this country, there was no such thing as a small touring group. The only touring thing you'd get was the big, big touring company doing the musicals. (Long, 1981–2, p. 36)

The 1960s and early 1970s witnessed the development of art centres in the UK. For example, Bristol's Arnolfini, originally located above a bookshop, was established in 1961; Better Books in London opened in 1964, and the Drury Lane Arts Lab, supported by the counter-cultural/new-leftist newspaper the *International Times*, opened in 1967. The underground club UFO, another *International Times* endeavour, also opened in 1967, where, alongside appearances of the Floyd and The Soft Machine, there were light shows by Mark Boyle and Joan Hill, and Happenings staged by David Medalla's Exploding Galaxy and the People Show. Lancaster's Nuffield Theatre opened in 1969 and Cardiff's Chapter Arts Centre in 1971. The establishment of arts centres would continue into the 1980s, for example Manchester's Greenroom opened in 1983, and Hull Time Based Arts emerged in 1984.

'Happenings' and the 'Theatre' of Art Schools

Evident in recollections from the period, in both the USA and the UK, were the web-like interconnections and collaborations between performers, with people coming together for different projects, and then separating again and transposing the experiences into other realms, addressing related or different concerns. Gunter Berghaus, cognisant of theatre practitioners as well as artist practitioners in Britain, proposed that the 'scandal' of *In Memory of Big Ed* 'brought the potential of Happenings as a means of protest and provocation to the attention of many nonconformist writers and dramatists' (Berghaus, 1995, p. 368). As a result, 'the next years saw a mush-rooming of groups who combined the inspiration they had received from the Happenings genre with their artistic training and/or literary and dramatic interests'. The word *group* is to be noted and the list that Berghaus then offered, as evidence, is impressive:

> Welfare State, the People Show, John Bull's Puncture Repair Kit, the Yorkshire Gnomes, Cyclamen Cyclists, New Fol-de-Rols: a large number of early British fringe and experimental touring companies evolved from the Happenings scene. (Berghaus, 1995, p. 369)

Many of the 'personnel' of the companies listed were connected to Bradford and Leeds art schools, a situation which contributed to the creative collaboration between artists. Albert Hunt taught at Bradford College of Art, whilst Jeff Nuttall taught at Leeds College of Art and both invited many other practitioners to work with their students.

Albert Hunt also collaborated with Peter Brook on *US*, an interesting example of the speed with which the 'radical' can be subsumed into the 'mainstream'. *US*, described as a 'group-happening-collaborative spectacle', was presented by the RSC in 1966 (Williams, 1988, p. 73). As David Williams noted, the research for *US* included 'close group study of "happenings"', of which Brook 'admired the spontaneity and poetry of the best' (ibid., p. 75). Having been one of the delegates at the Edinburgh International Writers' Conference, Brook would have witnessed *In Memory of Big Ed* at first hand. In one section of the performance of *US* the influence of action paint-ing, Happenings and perhaps even of Yves Klein's 'live paintings', *Anthropometries*, could be detected:

> the top half of the painter's body was painted one colour, the bottom half another. He was further flicked and sprayed with a variety of colours,

> leaving him with a violently lacerated appearance. Finally he writhed in pain
> on a sheet of paper which was then torn in two – graphic dismemberment
> of a nation. (Williams, 1988)

The ending of *US* conjured another reference from the Happening
milieu: white butterflies were released from a box into the auditorium.
American composer La Monte Young, himself influenced by John
Cage, had created a piece in 1960 called 'COMPOSITION 5', the
score for which read:

> Turn a butterfly (or any number of butterflies) loose in the performance
> area. When the composition is over, be sure to allow the butterfly to fly
> away outside. The composition may be any length, but if an unlimited
> amount of time is available, the doors and windows may be opened –
> the composition may be considered finished when the butterfly flies away.
> (Henri, 1974, p. 157)

US adapted this piece to its own political ends; following the release
of the butterflies into the auditorium, the actor reached into the box
and removed what appeared to be one last butterfly, which he then
burnt.[8] Charles Marowitz, acknowledging also the 'destruction art' of
Gustav Metzger and John Latham, accused the piece of being 'studded
with dazzling little thefts from old happenings and contemporary
destructivist exercises' (Marowitz, in Williams, 1988, p. 106).[9]

Albert Hunt's reflections on *US* suggested that because of its
location, its intended politics were bound to fail: 'I'd been conscious
that we weren't really talking to anybody in particular – that the
Aldwych audience had no common code of interest to which our
communication could be directed' (Hunt, 1978, p. 104). Hunt's
political intentions for his students at Bradford College of Art were,
by contrast, consciously located in and aimed at the context of education. Hunt hoped to transport the desired (or demanded) 'authenticity' and participatory potential of the Happening and related
performance forms (such as Fluxus) into the realm of education,
which he perceived as another 'state'-controlled institution in need
of radical intervention. His tract *Hopes for Great Happenings:
Alternatives in Education and Theatre* (1978) is indicative of Hunt's
commitment towards the new forms, and the creative freedom he
perceived in them.

As early as 1965, Hunt and his students created *Performance*,
which, like other events at the time, used the 'actual' rather than
acting, and was constructed out of a game that gradually developed

into a fully devised piece. In November 1967, the streets of Bradford were famously transformed into St Petersburg, not in order to re-enact the October Revolution so much as to set up a city-wide participatory game, using the Revolution as a source. Very much aware of the processes of the time, and of their historical precedents, Hunt also produced a Festival of Chance at the college:

> each day a different visitor created a chance event. John Latham brought an abstract film: we made a sound-track, banging tins, chairs, anything that made a noise. ... Robin Page experimented with sense in which somebody read an article from a newspaper, while somebody else performed actions at random. ... Cornelius Cardew made what he called music by moving all the objects from one half of the room into the other half, including the window frames and doors.   (Hunt, 1978, p. 73)

Arising from their performance explorations, Hunt and his students developed a collage technique which distilled 'hours of improvisatory work – on war scenes, circus acts, the telling of fables ... taking single lines from several improvisations, and juxtaposing them' (ibid., p. 81). In 1968, they devised *The Destruction of Dresden*, adapted from a piece created by Robin Page. Hunt recollected that this was 'the last show we staged which was more of a happening than an entertainment' (ibid., p. 95).[10] In the performance, an account of a battle scene was narrated, followed by the entrance of five men dressed in RAF outfits who each chose a different way to destroy cardboard boxes. These actions were juxtaposed with the simultaneous playing of a game of Monopoly and the painting of aeroplanes onto maps. The performance lasted for eighteen minutes, the exact length of the first actual raid, and ended when an alarm clock rang. In this way, real time was introduced into the event, combining it with real (task based) action, in a non-linear structure.

Though Hunt was the primary tutor in the college, he invited many other artists to work with him. Nuttall, at nearby Leeds Art College, did the same. Nuttall's and Hunt's recollections depicted a vibrant, creative environment which included John Fox, Robin Page, George Brecht, Al Beach, Mick Banks, John Darling, Ulli McCarthy, Diz Willis, Bruce Lacey, the People Show, Roland Miller, Adrian Mitchell, Cornelius Cardew and Tony Earnshaw (Nuttall, 1979, p. 71; Hunt, 1978, p. 78).[11] Mirroring the connections between artists in the USA, many of the companies that formed in the UK in the late 1960s–70s, and even into the 1980s, arose out of this mix of artists. For example, Al Beach and Mick Banks, founders of the Northern

Open Workshop in Halifax in 1970, formed John Bull's Puncture Repair Kit, and Mick Banks later joined the Natural Theatre Company, and then founded British Events (1980). Roland Miller joined the People Show briefly (which he left in 1970), as well as starting the New Fol-de-Rols with his partner Shirley Cameron and Jeff Nuttall, and the Cyclamen Cyclists. John Darling formed his own group, The Yorkshire Gnomes, with Mick Banks, Al Beach and Diz Willis, and also became a member of the People Show, and later a collaborator with Hesitate and Demonstrate. John Fox and Roger Coleman started Welfare State, initially a pop band, which transformed into 'a creative tribe with an alternative life-style' (Nuttall, 1979, p. 72). This split after a few years, with the breakaway group becoming IOU. Cornelius Cardew, influenced by John Cage, founded the Scratch Orchestra, often using improvised or found instruments, including saucepans, to make music (Henri, 1974, p. 161).

Most important in relation to the practice of devising were the People Show, considered by playwright David Pomerance as the

> high point of that period. ... The People Show pioneered forms of communication, theatrical forms, that were absolutely extraordinary and which no writer could duplicate, and yet which many writers learnt from. (Pomerance, in Rees, 1992, p. 57)

The genesis of the company is to be found in a Happening that Nuttall had written for the 1966 Notting Hill Gate Festival; he managed to persuade Sid Palmer, Laura Gilbert, John Darling and Mark Long, who were also staying at the Abbey Arts Centre, to perform it (Nuttall, 1979, p. 21). The event consisted of a number of fragmented actions that impacted quite literally on the audience since at the start they were covered in a polythene sheet. Long and Darling 'sold newspapers smeared with strawberry jam' (notably, Allan Kaprow also used jam in his Happening, *Birds* (1964) (Kaprow, 1966b, p. 4)), Nuttall called names from the stage, accompanied by a drum, while an accomplice planted in the audience fled screaming.

Given that the People Show are the longest-standing devising company in the UK, and continue to devise without a designated writer, it is interesting to learn that initially Nuttall's role was scriptwriter. We are again reminded that in 1966 there were no readily-available models of devising that could be easily adopted. Companies had to discover the practice of devising, and then develop it through experience. The experiments in 'live art' were, in this context, undoubtedly influential. Nuttall, deeply interested in the Happening form, unsurprisingly produced scripts that were far from conventional, and included real actions, alongside real confrontations with the audience. He intended his texts 'as mere hooks on which to hang the disparate vocabulary, visual, obtuse, abstract, absurd, of the happening' (Nuttall, 1979, pp. 39–40). As Mark Long noted of their first show in the Better Books basement, 'there was a script with a lot of improvisation room in it' (Long, 1981–2, p. 3). Long also reported that not all of the People Show's early works were written.

> I think the first four were. Then we started doing our own thing as well, and we started mixing them as well. Every other one was Jeff's and every other one was ours with Jeff. And Jeff was performing in them sometimes. (Long, 1981–2)

People Show #23, *Tennis* (1968/9), is described by Nuttall as 'the last of the extensively scripted shows'. People Show #26, appropriately titled *Changes*, 'was scripted differently' (Nuttall, 1979, p. 46). In fact, the script was more a 'score' of timed action sequences produced for each of the performers, which left room for them to 'invent' their own script. Miller's 'part' read:

×2 10 mins.	Brings a packet of chips and roe/haggis/black pudding/ baloney or whatever and eats them, trying to share with audience ...
10 mins.	Mimics Laura or Mark.
10 mins.	Being a rubber ball in a story about a dog, a tree and a ball ...
5 mins.	An introverted monologue about mothers in general with some song snatches, ending with a reference to his own mother – Where is she?

(Nuttall, 1979, p. 43)

Long and Gilbert also had their own script, and all three carried out their actions simultaneously. The show was structured every night according to the roll of a dice. Nuttall liked this show 'because it forced the performers to be creative rather than interpretive'. He then added, recognising that a new process was developing, 'I wasn't to know that I was writing myself out of the business' (ibid., p. 46). As he predicted, the People Show began to devise their work collaboratively from scratch, using the skills and particular interests of whoever was involved in creating the show.

One difficulty of writing about devising processes is that they are precisely that, *processes*, and as such they are fluid. Moreover, they are located in specific times and places. In light of this it becomes problematic and disingenuous to propose the existence of 'models'. Even those groups who have existed for many years, such as the People Show, deny any set model of devising, instead working with different processes appropriate to different contexts and to different collaborations. For example, though the People Show have been cited for their enduring refusal to use a designated director in the devising of their work, in their recent performance *Play Dead* (2004), a director was employed. However, it is claimed that this 'shift' in the working process is specific to this production. As producer Emma Haughton commented, following the company's evaluation of their preceding production Christine Entwisle was invited to be an 'outside' eye. Retaining commitment to the collective process and the idea of the 'creative artist', Haughton insisted that 'the People Show makes work that is artist led. A People Show is led by the people in it and they will choose to work with different processes and tools, as required, in devising the work.' Moreover, 'The People Show does not and will not have an Artistic Director'.[12]

An additional problem in writing about devising is that processes are not easily defined; this is perhaps particularly the case for those companies who construct what might be called a 'visual score' or a 'visual composition'. For People Show company member Jose Nova, 'You can't really describe how the group works. Words are irrelevant' (Kirby, 1974, p. 66). The People Show might 'begin' a show from a found object (a dentist's chair), an idea of one company member, a painting (Edward Hopper's *Night Hawks*), a form of theatre (*commedia dell'arte*), a scene from an earlier People Show, a pre-viously discarded idea. The relationship to such catalysts is not one of 'why', but 'how' or 'what': 'How can we use these?' 'What can we do?' In an interview from 1974, Mark Long related the process, where company members would work on their own ideas, their own characters, their own props, etc.:

> Right now we're working on a new show that will come out of three ideas. Derek has this idea for Edwardian boating. I have this idea for a Charlie Chan private detective who takes a shower every two minutes in the show. Jose has this idea of man who's trying to pull down the Chinese wall and finds Rome behind it and gets attacked by a snake and a monster. Now that sounds bizarre, but there is actually ground on which those three ideas will go together.   (Kirby, 1974)

In all of their works a collage effect is constructed, with the juxta-position of many different layers. However, one can nevertheless sense a story or stories in the performance; there is a sense of unity – 'of set, character, time, sound and light' (Long, 1981–2, p. 9). Thus, in People Show #112, *Art of Escape* (2003), though there was a discernible 'romance narrative', there was also an enduring sense of the narrative being nudged off-track; connections between events, characters, place and action could be sensed, but in the end, they would not add up into a neat whole. A disembodied, speaking beard, almost a 'virtual' Greek oracle, threatened any narrative assumptions and the juxtapositions of surrealism prevailed. The People Show's worlds are both familiar and unsettling.

The dramaturgy of the performances is primarily dictated by pacing and by images, what Long referred to as a show's 'dynamics' (ibid., p. 16). Structural decisions, then, are often pragmatic: slow sections are contrasted with chaotic sections; loud with quiet; vertical use of space with horizontal use; the expected with the surprise, or the known with mystery. The question of 'how' also results in other pragmatic deci-sions: 'How can we get this prop to this place?' Or 'How can Laura get to this part of the stage?' In addition to practical demands, the com-pany is also responsive to chance and accidental events. For example, when Mike Figgis accidentally kicked a metal bucket during a perform-ance, the champagne bottle that was in it began to rock back and forth. Figgis 'was immediately aware of the sound and began to rock back and forth in time to the bucket's beat. The show was suspended in this way until the bucket came to a complete stop' (Kirby, 1974, p. 65).

Though Long insisted on the unity implicit in the People Show's work, he also observed that all members of the group have their own personal versions of what a piece is about: 'Everybody has a very different interpretation, they have their line through it, and that is probably their own interpretation of the general meaning of the piece, and is coloured by their line in it' (ibid., p. 34). Members of the group are individual artists in their own right, each with their own ideas. According to Long, 'there has never been a group idea of a show, there has never been a common denominator' (ibid.).

Visual Styles: Painterly, Formalist, Sculptural

Throughout the 1970s, indicative of the collapsing space between art and theatre, various kinds of visual performance 'styles' were developing. One exemplary company were Hesitate and Demonstrate, founded in 1975 by Geraldine Pilgrim and Janet Goddard, students at Leeds College of Art from 1972 (where they were two of only four women in a class of 36). Their decision to work in performance, rather than in sculpture or fine art, was politically located, and acknowledged the live and therefore ephemeral nature of performance. Pilgrim insisted:

> The reason why we started doing it is that I'm of a generation where we did not want to work in galleries, we did not want our work to be sold, we did not want our work to be collected and put on walls, and we did not want to be trapped. Therefore we believed in work that existed for each particular moment, and then passed off into the world.   (Pilgrim)[13]

The aim, as befits the political context of the time, was to 'get out of galleries'.

Representative of the sphere of influence, during her time at Leeds Pilgrim was taught by John Darling, John Fox, Roland Miller, Shirley Cameron, Mike Westbrook and Jeff Nuttall, worked with John Bull Puncture Repair Kit, Welfare State, Ian Hinchcliffe and his Matchbox Purveyors and also performed in Nuttall's jazz band. Nuttall 'taught us about Happenings' (Pilgrim), while Adrian Henri, who had just published his book *Environments and Happenings* (1974), was their external examiner. As Pilgrim recollected, her tutors 'very subtly inspired us. We never knew we were doing Happenings when we were doing Happenings' (Pilgrim). The company's name referred to a unique performance style developed by Pilgrim and Goddard, which arose from their fascination with Muybridge's 'motion-sequence' still photographs, translated by Pilgrim and Goddard into a slight hesitation. This, combined with the two women's love of demonstrations, ranging from make-up to cookery, suggested both the name and the form, Hesitate and Demonstrate.

Notably, Hesitate and Demonstrate's work was not devised in a studio space, but was 'devised by talking' (Pilgrim). Pilgrim and Goddard would discuss visual images and make sketches of them; every idea was written down, and then an image was drawn in order to explore it. The 'picture' would be built up in this way, and simply through talking and drawing was 'scored to the absolute detailed second' (Pilgrim). The company did not rehearse their work until they had actually constructed an environment in space, and it was only once they were within this that they would work out how to physically do the piece. This working process was born out of necessity rather than from any artistic agenda; the company could not afford to rent a rehearsal space and so their studio was effectively a café. However, their process towards making performance work, sketching rather than rehearsing, was also testimony to their art training.

Hesitate and Demonstrate's work has been described as 'kinetic painting' (Sobieski, 1994, p. 102). Their early performances, like much of the People Show's work at this time, had little or no spoken text, being primarily composed as moving visual pictures, 'paintings coming to life' (Pilgrim). The company created dense layers of ideas, or condensed various sources; for example, a book of photographs of New Orleans prostitutes, which Goddard and Pilgrim were fascinated by, became transposed to a Woolworth's building, under the imaginative premise that the site of Woolworth's was originally the site of the photography studio. The ghosts of these prostitutes inhabited the Woolworth's shop girls. Despite such complexity, Pilgrim stressed that there was always a strong storyline in the performances, at least for the company, even if this were far from linear: 'We always know some sense of the beginning, middle and end. It may be all juggled up and juxtaposed but there's always a very strong storyline, a narrative line' (Pilgrim, 1982, p. 13).

When Goddard left Hesitate and Demonstrate in 1979, Pilgrim became Artistic Director and, in her words, 'the one with the vision'. Admitting this, Pilgrim also insisted that because she chose her collaborators carefully, there was never any moment when she imposed her ideas on them. However, Pilgrim did believe that in the end someone had to say 'yes' or 'no', and that to pretend there was no person who filled that role would be disingenuous. 'If a decision had to be made, that we didn't all agree with, I would be the one that made it. And that's why I was known as Artistic Director' (Pilgrim).

Though no video recordings exist of the company's works, contemporary reviews capture their visual impact. *Good Night Ladies* (1981) was described as a 'cinematic dream montage' that 'eludes precise definition' (Dixon, 1982a, p. 13). The performance 'proceeds by a series of disclosures and transformations: a train-compartment door swings back to reveal a hotel bedroom; a vacated café table is suddenly illuminated by a toy train chugging around its perimeter' (Hornick, 1982, pp. 15–16). As early as 1979, a *Time Out* critic commented that Hesitate and Demonstrate, 'Like Robert Wilson ... have poise ... a tight, sophisticated, widely referential approach, essentially literary and imagistic, very much concerned with the visual potency of their tableaux' (in Sobieski, 1994, p. 102). This review also makes apparent the comparisons that were being made across performances. The work of Robert Wilson and Tadeusz Kantor, though employing modes of performance-making very different from the collaborative companies we have covered here (they are typically thought of as 'auteurs'), have exerted considerable influence on the devising performance scene. The structural properties of their performances are recognisable (Kantor was also a painter, while Wilson first trained as an architect), and it is perhaps not coincidental that both were connected to the earlier Happening movements. In 1963, Kantor wrote about the possibility of 'non-acting', asking whether such a state were possible. In his 'poetic' form of writing, he revealed his

> wish for a situation
> in which one could discard so-called acting
> (supposedly the only way for an actor to behave 'on stage'),
> which is nothing more than
> naïve pretence,
> exulted mannerism,
> irresponsible illusion!
>
> (Kobialka, 1993, p. 64)[14]

One company which shared Kantor's concerns over the status of acting, whilst also admitting the influence of Minimal Art, Fluxus and the early performances of Robert Wilson, such as *Deafman Glance* (1970), were the Theatre of Mistakes. The Theatre of Mistakes shared with many companies a focus on task- and formula-based drama-turgy, but added chance into the devising/performing process in order to create performances that resembled 'games', a technique also used by Hunt with his students at Bradford and within actor-training environments, as discussed in the preceding chapter. The Theatre of Mistakes, initially a workshop enterprise, was founded in 1974 by Anthony Howell. Howell, previously a dancer with the Royal Ballet, was by the late 1960s a published poet and teacher of creative writing. Howell's performance experiments with Theatre of Mistakes extended his earlier writing explorations:

> I had carried abstract writing to the extreme of writing 'instruction recipes' for poems under the influence of [Minimalist artist] Sol LeWitt, who would write instruction recipes for wall drawings. Having started creating such recipes for poems it became obvious to me that one could also make them for actions.   (Howell, in Kaye, 1996, p. 129)

Bearing some similarity to the practices of the Open Theatre, discussed in Chapter 2, the workshop explorations 'created a body of exercises which we referred to for the next few years as a "body of thought", a gymnasium of performance exercises' (ibid., p. 130). Performances had a 'Minimalist dynamic organising the system' whereby 'the performances were created rather like you order a meal in a Chinese restaurant – from a vast array of exercises' (ibid.). Their published text, *Elements of Performance Art* (1977), the result of workshop explorations, is a useful summary of some of the wider concerns circulating with regards to a theatre form in which 'acting' had been replaced by 'performing', and was certainly related to Kantor's thoughts on 'non-acting'. In their work, The Theatre of Mistakes performers undertook functional action; they did not act 'as if'. Thus, in the section 'Being, Not Acting', we are informed that

> instead of acting, the performers use exercises to create the possibility of extending their own behaviour into the arena of the action presented to the public – thus the only drama the performers are involved in is that of their real lives at the time of the performance. (Howell and Templeton, 1977, p. 12)

The Street (1975), devised by the core company Fiona Templeton, Michael Greenall and Patricia Murphy, put the theory of *Elements* into practice, in the creation of what Templeton called 'trigger-based pedestrian choreography'.[15] The performance took place on Ascham Street in London, where residents re-situated their internal living spaces into the external space of the street (Kaye, 1996, p. 131). As Howell recorded, a number of performers inhabited first-floor rooms, and whenever a passer-by walked up the left-hand pavement, the windows would be closed, which would in turn trigger performers in the street to collapse to the ground. Similarly, when someone walked up the right-hand pavement, the windows would open. The performers at the windows performed as a 'chorus', reciting snippets of conversation heard from the street below, which were then 'repeated additively in instant, repetitive sonnet forms'. The performance involved approximately sixty performers, including local children who, in slow motion, 'followed a slow motion ice-cream van into the deepening twilight'.[16]

As suggested by their name, the company were also interested in the generative possibilities of performance 'mistakes' and 'accidents', using these as a structural component in their devising. For *Going*

(1977), 'the entire structure had come out of a set of rules where accidents would indeed happen and mistakes caused forfeits and signals' (Howell, in Kaye, 1996, p. 141). This was not live improvisational performance, however, as these initial mistakes were then rehearsed in preparation for the 'resolved piece' (ibid.). Notably connecting with many of the companies explored in both Chapter 2 and Chapter 4, Howell drew explicit attention to the 'politics' of their devising systems, understood to employ democratic structures. Thus, 'if you produced a piece like *Going*, which had five characters, each character was given an absolutely equal status. Nobody was a star, nobody was a subsidiary performer' (ibid., p. 137). Employing structural rules, such as the use of chance, mistakes and accidents as performance 'triggers' which dictate performers' activities, potentially enables more democratic participation as the outcomes of such formalist structures are ostensibly 'objective'. They also reduce the opportunities for individualistic demands – the desire to evade the ego of the performer was a primary reason for John Cage's use of chance in his compositions. Each performer is equally and only a player in a game with pre-established rules, the outcome of which cannot be predicted or known in advance.

One performer with The Theatre of Mistakes, Julian Maynard Smith, went on to found Station House Opera in 1980. While at art school, Maynard Smith participated in a workshop led by Fiona Templeton. During the workshop,

> we were doing extremely gruelling endurance performances, repeating the same thing over and over for hours on end. It was a sculptural way of dealing with performance, a sculptural way of dealing with bodies in space and time.   (Maynard Smith, in Kaye, 1996, p. 194)

Early Station House Opera performances bore similarity with The Theatre of Mistakes' events, although Maynard Smith suggested that they were less tightly ruled (ibid.). In *Sex and Death* (1981), for example, the sculptural and formalist style was evident. All the performers were dressed in blue, and all the objects used were also blue. The piece was configured according to the total number of exits and entrances that were possible with six performers. *A Split Second of Paradise* (1985), *Cuckoo* (1987) and *The Bastille Dance* (1989), though visually stunning, were primarily action-based. Whilst there may have been fragments and hints of narratives, there was also often a 'job' to be done, involving real effort, whether that was building a sculpture from breeze blocks, attempting to sing while breeze blocks were placed on your chest, or cutting up a wardrobe in order to transform it into another usable object. As Tim Etchells wrote in a review of *Cuckoo*, 'Whilst it is rich with stories and recognisable moments from British domesticity the show remains itself. It always remains only Station House Opera working on stage, making things' (Etchells, 1987, p. 42).

During the 1980s, the 'hybrid' status of much performance work – between art and theatre – was epitomised in newly coined categories including 'performance art theatre', 'image theatre' and 'visual theatre'. Naseem Khan described groups such as the People Show and Welfare State as 'visually based performance art' (Khan, 1983, p. 8); Susan Burt and Clive Barker regarded IOU as 'one of the most widely-respected performance art companies' (Burt and Barker, 1980, p. 70). In a summary of IOU's work in 1982, critic Mike Laye positioned them in 'that "no man's land" between the theatre and the plastic arts' (Laye, 1982, p. 18). Rational Theatre equally epitomised this hybrid form. Founded in 1978 by Peter Godfrey (having emerged from the earlier Phantom Captain), their performance *Orders of Obedience* (1983) made the focus on sculptural composition explicit by taking the work of sculptor Malcolm Poynter as its starting point (Godfrey, 1983, p. 24). The company also prepared for the performance by working with a Japanese *Butoh* dance company, Sankai Juki (ibid.). Godfrey recorded that 'shortly after this the cast shaved their heads and work began on interpreting in moving flesh and blood the feelings expressed in Poynter's sculptures' (ibid). Alluding to the *Butoh* influence, the performers were also semi-naked and painted white for the performance. Descriptions of the work suggest that Rational Theatre might sit as comfortably within the various modes of performance explored in Chapter 2 (see Hyde, 1983, p. 25). However, Rational Theatre also consciously mixed various materials, without prioritising any over the others:

> The focus of the work is on the 'mix' of theatrical elements: words do not get overdue emphasis, but neither do they get anathematised as repressive. Designer, musicians, performers, director, writer, sculptor, choreographer and even lighting designer are involved during the creative process and feed off each other. The material that is generated by this collaborative process is then assembled into the show. (Godfrey, 1983, p. 24)

Orders of Obedience was followed with *Hidden Grin*, regarded by Rob La Frenais as 'a more co-operative effort' (La Frenais,

1985, p. 7). In fact, the company changed its name to Hidden Grin, and La Frenais's review of their next piece, *Overseen, Overheard, Overlooked* (1985), performed at the Performance Art Platform, mapped their shift in practice from 'theatre' towards 'performance art', or from 'acting' to 'doing'.[17] Though devised two decades ago, this piece appears to share much with many of the performances discussed in Chapter 7. Durational in form, it incorporated video screens and microphones; performers were blindfolded and subjected to a 'sensory deprivation experiment' and 'a volley of personality-test question[s]. Sexual, social and philosophical' (ibid., p. 8). La Frenais initially perceived the performance as 'cold and above all performed. I mean *acted*' (ibid.). However, by the end of the performance the performers were 'beginning to stop "performing"' (ibid., p. 10), and during its second staging at Brighton 'things seriously started to change for them'. Their performance space had become a 'working environment':

> Newspaper headlines on the wall, items from their lives in glass cages. 'Confessions' spewing out of a computer terminal. That day's copy of the *Sun* had just been pasted up on the wall: 'Budgie Roasted Alive in Microwave'. Its pertinence to the piece was uncanny. The 'technicians' now acknowledged the presence of the public when they walked in. They were moving around the space in 'real time' not acted time.   (La Frenais, 1985)

One might certainly discern some threads between this performance and Forced Entertainment's confessional piece *Speak Bitterness* (1994), and their durational performance *Quizoola* (1996); Forced Entertainment, in fact, performed at the same Performance Art Platform with *The Set Up* (1985).

A company that presented an unusual form of 'hybridity' in that they worked across not only art and theatre, but also aesthetics and politics, were Blood Group. Founded in 1980 by Anna Furse and Suzy Gilmour, their company policy made clear both their feminist and artistic concerns:

> Most productions are devised, exploring strong themes with a primarily visual and physical narrative. The company is committed to working with women wherever possible and appropriate. Blood Group seeks, through collaboration with women from diverse theatrical and artistic fields, to provoke a closer relationship between theatre and other art forms.

Though consciously feminist in their agenda, their concerns were presented through striking visual imagery, choreographed movement and a montage dramaturgical structure. As one company document stated, Blood Group positioned themselves as a 'research company' that sought 'to combine political issues with explorations in form'. Coinciding with the theories of Hélène Cixous, but as yet unaware of *l'écriture féminine*, director Anna Furse was keen to explore the possibility of a 'feminine' theatre language.[18] In Furse's opinion, while the 1970s had seen an increase in the representation of women by women, there was little interest in new forms. Furse's performance training, crossed with her feminist consciousness and experiences as a female performer, led to her focus on the potential 'language' of the (female) body (rather than literal textual language). After extensive study in ballet, Furse spent a year at Peter Brook's International Centre of Theatre Research; prior to founding Blood Group she also participated in Grotowski's paratheatrical workshops and worked with the new dance collective, X6 (where she met Suzy Gilmour), and Reflex Action, a company indebted to Grotowski and other European companies that had visited Cardiff Chapter Arts Centre. Given this background, Furse's need 'to work theatre through the body' is understandable (Furse).[19] It is also worth noting that Furse was the only woman in Reflex Action.[20]

The first Blood Group performance, *Barricade of Flowers* (1981), took Genet's *The Maids* as its starting point and used simple visual imagery to explore gendered binary structures – throughout the piece, Furse and co-founder Suzy Gilmour were tied together with a piece of red cloth symbolising an umbilical cord – as well as women's often-problematic relationships to food. An influential text was Mary Daly's *Gyn/ecology* (1979). The performance also acknowledged the exchange between audience and performer; Furse and Gilmour watched the spectators intently as they entered. Their next performance, *DIRT* (1983), focused more centrally on this issue of exchange, exploring the line between acting in the sex industry and acting in the theatre (or at the very least asked whether there was any difference). Throughout the performance, each of the three female performers would dress and undress within her own red light/dressing area, changing her costume for each phase of the show.[21] At one moment, while the performers were naked, a slide message in three parts was projected: 'We know you are looking.' 'We know you are looking at us.' 'Do you know we're looking at you looking at us?' As with Hidden Grin's *Overseen, Overheard, Overlooked*, *DIRT* shared concerns and features with more contemporary performances.[22]

Surveying performance reviews from the early 1980s it becomes apparent that a new visual language or style could be detected in many devised performances, a style that directly referenced other popular cultural forms. Hesitate and Demonstrate's *Horrid Things*, for example, staged a 'Gothic Horror', whilst their *Good Night Ladies* cited the iconography of 'early Hitchcock and *film noir*' (Dixon, 1982a, p. 13). One reviewer suggested that 'Movie buffs will be thrilled by visual echoes of such films as *The Lady Vanishes*' (Hornick, 1982, pp. 15–16). The filmic atmosphere noted here was to be found in other works from the same time. Pure Monkeys' *Death by Kissing* (1981), for example, compiled 'a definitive pastiche of the B movie feature film' which challenged 'celluloid myths, debunking machismo and upsetting stereotypes' (Hill, 1981a, p. 21). The performance included an orphaned heroine, a diamond fortune, a cocktail lounge, and a 'fatal denouement by the waterside' (ibid.). As evidenced in these examples, the conjured filmic atmosphere was also often that of the clichéd historical environment. The time might have been Victorian or Edwardian, and the place was often 'exotic' or dangerous – Egypt, the Amazon, a war-zone. *Ancient Sights* (1983), the fourth show by Optik Theatre, was set on the banks of the Nile, at the end of the British Empire. Hesitate and Demonstrate's *Good Night Ladies* evoked Europe in the 1920s while *Shangri-La* (1984) was set in a seedy, depressed seaside resort of the 1930s.

Such filmic, 'historical' atmospheres also seem to have been apparent in the work of another influential company, Impact Theatre Cooperative, founded in 1979. Originating, like Hesitate and Demonstrate, from Leeds, Impact were considered at the time 'to be amongst the most interesting of current visual theatre groups' (Dixon, 1982b, p. 24). Co-founders Pete Brooks and Claire MacDonald, somewhat unusually, were studying English literature. Arguably, the work of Impact arose very much from this intellectual context of literary and linguistic criticism; early Impact work was concerned with narratives and metanarratives, and their 'process' of devising was one rooted as much in discussion as in trying things out in the studio. Steve Rogers, writing about the company in 1983, noted that there were three strands involved in developing a new piece of work. First, the company established 'a cultural milieu', Berlin, French café, etc.; secondly, they established 'a philosophy, what is it they want to say'; and finally, they determined 'the performance style' (Rogers, 1983, pp. 5–8). The actual performance was a collaborative composition, with different people taking responsibility for different elements, such as sound and music, or text, out of which the performance would then be structured.[23]

Reflecting the interests of its co-founders, Impact constructed idiosyncratic languages: cod-French for their first devised show, *The Undersea World of Eric Satie* (1980), cod-German for *Dammerungstrasse 55* (1981), and a hybrid language – the discourse of anthropologist Claude Lévi-Strauss crossed with East End gangland slang – in *Useful Vices* (1982). Whilst Impact utilised spoken text in the form of complex linguistic structures, text was simply another element within an assemblage of elements, and was therefore considered to have its own structural possibilities. Text understood as 'form' could be placed in equal relation to all the other 'compositional' materials used – light, sound, music, *mise-en-scène*, and movement. The text, then, was not used to drive the narrative, but served to provide various other textures to the performance; in addition to the invented languages, text would be juxtaposed, cut up, repeated, spoken through microphones, or pre-recorded. The text might be the result of an improvisation, or a piece of found material, or written by Claire MacDonald.

Though early Impact shows employed narratives, reviews made clear that such narratives did not utilise a linear structure; in fact, most reviews focused on the imagistic quality of the works. In *The Undersea World of Eric Satie*, 'a mesmerising collage of post-impressionist images' (ibid., p. 5), a café waiter watched Jacques Cousteau through the windows; the windows then became the glass sides of an aquarium, which was in turn reversed so that the café became the aquarium. This performance, as its name suggested, was surreal in its representations. Moments in the performance bore homage not only to the French composer, but also, perhaps with a sense of irony, to earlier work. The piece was interrupted, for example, by someone planted in the audience who 'Unable to take any more pretentious twaddle ... sighs with annoyance and stomps out only to return with a saxophone, occupying centre stage and jamming away ...' (Dixon, 1980, p. 26). Notably, as in performances by the People Show and Hesitate and Demonstrate, a taped montage of sounds played throughout the performance, providing a continuous score (ibid, p. 24).

The visual power of *Dammerungstrasse 55* was also noted in contemporary reviews. In this show, primarily set in a railway station, 'a pervading sense of ennui is punctuated by searing visual images' (ibid.). *Useful Vices*, meanwhile, like other performances, conjured a particular historical atmosphere. It had 'a feel of the '50s', with Perspex and neon.

> The ending was a real visual coup. The space, by now devoid of natural light, filled with smoke. The audience, blistered with heat behind, frozen with wind in front, watched as naked Indians loomed through the lit smoke to sacrifice a brother who had killed in error a member of the family.   (Dixon, 1982a, p. 25)

No Weapons for Mourning (1983) appeared to draw on Raymond Chandler's novels, although there was 'also a tantalising whiff of the Ray Bradburys, an otherworldliness that casts a cool shadow over the proceedings' (Hall, 1983, p. 30). Reviewer Stella Hall made the further revealing observation that she sometimes 'felt more as though I were in a cinema than a theatre', explaining this with reference to the accompanying soundtrack and the use of atmospheric light and shade.

Such repeated references in reviews to 'filmic' atmospheres points to the vast shift in performance 'style' that had occurred over the previous two decades. The deliberately 'unprofessional', often chaotic and certainly unpredictable events of Happenings and early performances of the People Show and John Bull's Puncture Repair Kit, for example, seem far removed from these accomplished, cinematic stage pictures, which required a large amount of visual flair and, on occasion, technical skill.[24]

David Gale, co-founder with Hilary Westlake of the company Lumiere & Son, in a review titled 'Against Slowness', defined what he considered had become the orthodoxy of performance at this time, which far from being innovative was 'sodden' with 'nostalgia and sentimentality' (Gale, 1985, p. 25). Gale considered the majority of performance

> Dull, vapid, superficial, decorative, comfortable, polite, repetition, humourless, fashionable, nostalgic, twee ... mournful, melancholic, angst-ridden, trapped in impossible pasts ... the 50's, the 40's, the 30's, Edwardiana, Victoriana ... the romance of the cigarette, the languor of the smoke plume, the moustache ... nice little past things, the past movies, whose perfect lighting, perfect costumes, perfect strengths, perfect weaknesses ... and so forth and so on. It's a catalogue.   (Gale, 1985, p. 23)

The pervasiveness of this visual style detected by Gale might partly be explained through the existence of a European touring circuit, the centre of which was arguably the Mickery Theatre, an old farmhouse outside Amsterdam run by Ritsaert ten Cate. According to Geraldine Pilgrim, financial support and encouragement for Hesitate and Demonstrate, and the work they wanted to make, came more from here than from the UK. Many British 'visual performance' companies shared venues with each other, and also with other experimental performance makers, including Laurie Anderson, Robert Wilson, The Wooster Group and Pina Bausch. An element of cross-fertilisation and borrowing was likely, if not inevitable. Pilgrim, reminiscing about her first experience of Pina Bausch's work in the early 1980s, passionately insisted that she would 'never forget it ... and my life has never been the same since' (Pilgrim). Pete Brooks has recognised the impact and influence of the European touring circuit on Impact's later work. This circuit understandably preferred visual, non-textual performances that could communicate across language differences. Impact's *A Place in Europe* (1983) indicated an interesting shift in the company's *oeuvre*. In place of their 'hybridised language', which would demand an intimate knowledge of, and a high level of proficiency in, English, this piece used only short, repeated fragments of text (spoken into a microphone). The scale of the stage, and the haunting, repetitive, live musical score, accompanied by continual physical action, also seemed indebted to the choreographed, repetitive and serial movement of Pina Bausch's work. Impact's shift away from text was arguably a pragmatic response to the demands and needs of European touring.[25]

Recognising the frequent 'citing' or reciting of film genres and narratives in performances, we might also consider the impact on aesthetic sensibilities of various developments in media throughout the 1970s and 1980s. From 1972, television stations in the UK could begin to broadcast whenever they wanted, day and night, leading to increased production and consumption of television programmes. According to Andrew Crisell, 775,000 colour television sets had been purchased up to 1970; by 1973 this figure had leapt to 6 million (Crisell, 1997, p. 150). Crisell further recorded that from 1961 to 1986, 'average weekly viewing doubled from 13.5 to 26 hours' (ibid., p. 151). By 1986, 'nearly 80 per cent of people watched television at some point during the day' (ibid.). Video may also have had some influence. In 1976 there were only about 40,000 VCRs in use in the UK; by the end of 1985 this figure had risen to 8.5 million, with almost 40 per cent of the UK population owning a video recorder (Abercrombie and Warde, 2000, p. 340). It was also during the 1980s that, with the use of digital and satellite technology, television became a global rather than a 'merely regional and national activity' (Crisell,

1997, p. 211). Live Aid, broadcast on 7 July 1985, 'the biggest media event since the first moon landing', was indicative; 59 per cent of the UK population, and one and a half billion people from over 160 countries, watched the live broadcast of concerts staged simultaneously in London and Philadelphia (ibid., p. 226).

Significantly, the 1980s was also the decade for the appearance, and increasingly widespread use, of the personal computer. Though many in the West now take for granted the use of personal computers and information technology, the accessibility of this technology is fairly recent. In 1983, *Time* magazine prophesied the impact that the PC would have, selecting it as its 'Man of the Year' (Campbell-Kelly and Aspray, 1996, p. 1). Russell Hoban, science fiction writer and collaborator with Impact Theatre on their penultimate performance, *The Carrier Frequency* (1984),[26] also recognised the shifting sensibilities belonging to these times:

> Never before has the human brain been compelled to take in so much at once and in so many different modes; our minds move in sweeps and scans of words, pictures, noise, emotions and sensations with a flickering speed foreign even to our childhoods let alone the mental life of those who saw the plays of Shakespeare or Molière or even Strindberg. (Hoban, 1984, p. 11)

This expansion in visual materials offered for consumption in the contemporary world necessitated in turn an increase in the speed of consumption. It was within this context that Hoban regarded Impact's shows as being 'not realistic but hyper-real, a syntax of image and sound, speech and movement that is not of the printed page but of the exploding mind'.[27] Impact's approach 'draws its energy from the same speed and fragmentation, the same lighting circuitry that makes computer technology possible' (ibid.). Hoban astutely comprehended that a different way of understanding, representing and interacting with the 'world' had transpired.

Conclusion

Throughout the 1960s and 1970s, processes of devising performances intersected with various artistic developments relating to conceptual matters and formal concerns, resulting in performances that had a 'hybrid' status – between theatre and art. Arguably, these developments were themselves connected with the earlier avant-garde explorations in art and performance forms, in particular the use of 'chance' procedures and non-linear, simultaneous representations. Apparent in the work of many companies was an interest in exploring the particular art form of theatre, or the specific potentials afforded by theatre; in fact, this seems to have been almost a research imperative for much of the work devised in the 1960s and 1970s.

Our argument has also been that the social context was as much a catalyst as aesthetic concerns or questions. The counter-cultural movement led many artists and performers to seek alternatives to the prescribed, dominant practices and institutions, affecting both the processes of production and their outcomes. In large measure, the desire to circumvent the commodification of the art object resulted in a focus on process over product, on participation over consumption, on ephemerality over permanence, and on indeterminacy over certainty. In a context in which, for many, global events suggested a bankruptcy of ethics and morals, the 'liveness' of the performance moment was one feature that separated it from other artistic mediums; it was its liveness that held out the promise of 'authenticity', evidenced in the use of chance, of found objects, of one-off perform-ances, and of 'audience' participation. In the absence of already existing models of devising in theatre, the various experiments in 'live art' offered a variety of practices and modes available for transla-tion into collaborative activity as befits theatre practice. Equally, the specificities accruing to theatre practice, an art composed of all the other arts, as Kantor might have said, provided opportunities for further development of these explorations.

As the political and cultural context changed throughout the 1970s and into the 1980s, the hybrid status of performances allowed a focus on the visual potential of theatre – a representational medium. Retaining the dramaturgical 'interruptions' to narrative evidenced in earlier work, the dominant model of 'experimental performance' in the 1980s was of carefully constructed stage pictures, heavy on cine-matic atmosphere. Coinciding with the demise of any belief in, or commitment to, the ideals of an 'alternative society', technological developments – in particular in media and the widespread consump-tion of television and home videos – undoubtedly had an impact on live performance. Where the work in the 1960s and 1970s had tended to be deliberately 'rough', 'chaotic' and/or provocative, often aiming to involve the spectator in a visceral or emotive experience, by the 1980s it had become visually polished and marketable, and often a product for the European theatre circuit.

As we shall argue in Chapter 7, the slickness of visual performance did not necessarily make it easily consumable; some performances still aimed to have a tangible impact on the spectators, drawing attention, as Blood Group did in 1984, to the activity of spectatorship. Impact Theatre Cooperative's *The Carrier Frequency* appeared to bridge earlier performance forms with the visual finesse expected in the 1980s. Steve Rogers' description of the show as 'total theatre', where 'what you see is real, actually happening, and not a representation', seems curiously reminiscent of 1960s aims (Rogers, 1985, p. 28). In 1986 Claire MacDonald, co-founder of Impact, asked, 'How do you have an art which is humane, which is rooted in social and political issues, but which is not about them? An art which is not "for" something but which "is" something?' (Rogers, 1986b, p. 18). Though the forms might seem to have travelled a fair distance from the 1960s to the mid-1980s, they carried with them early concerns and explorations; and MacDonald's question is not really so far removed from the earlier impassioned rhetoric of Jean-Jacques Lebel.

4 Devising and Political Theatre

The focus of this chapter is the use of devising in the creation of political theatre. We understand the politics of theatre here to embrace not only the explicit political content of devised works, but also the structures and processes employed. As John McGrath, co-founder of the socialist theatre company 7:84, wrote,

> It is important ... to see theatre not just as plays, but as a means of production, with bosses, workers, and unemployed, with structural relationships. ... It is through its structures as much as through its product that theatre expresses the dominant bourgeois ideology. (McGrath, 1984, p. 44)

The work explored in this chapter arose out of and was informed by the specific historical and political context of the 1960s and the New Left politics of the 1970s, which necessitated organisational structures and working processes that matched certain ideological beliefs. The increasing politicisation of society could be seen in the rising trade union membership in the UK, from '9½ million at the end of the 1950s to over 11 million by 1970' (Davies, 1987, p. 163). The election of a Conservative government in 1970 motivated further political activity, particularly in light of new anti-workers legislation such as Edward Heath's Industrial Relations Act. As David Edgar reflected, 'millions of workers became involved in industrial and political struggle who had never been involved before' (Edgar, 1979, p. 27).

Against this political background, many theatre workers throughout the 1970s actively sought to create organisations that did not promote or support bourgeois ideology, in particular the hierarchical structure of boss and workers. This desire to implement models that ideally enabled the practice of 'participatory democracy' initially led, in most cases at least, to the use of devising as a means of production.

In a culture in which models of devising are now commonplace, it is important to remember that in the 1960s and 1970s there were no models available to be appropriated. Reflections by practitioners throughout this period reveal an ongoing search, often characterised as a painful struggle, for *new* working practices appropriate to the political and ideological needs and aims of the time. When the ideological needs and aims shifted, so too did the practices.

Forms and Processes

Arising directly from the political ferment of the time, the catalyst for the founding of many of the best known political theatre companies was often to be located in political protest. Prior even to attempts to develop appropriate working practices, theatrical forms and working processes were often arrived at accidentally or through pragmatic decision-making in light of immediate pressures and concerns, including the intentions of the work and the performance conditions of the proposed playing environment.

The 'genesis' of the Chicano company El Teatro Campesino is instructive here. Its founder Luis Valdez wanted to use theatre to support the striking farm workers of Delano, California (his own father was a grape picker).[1] In 1965, broaching the idea to the strikers, he realised that in order to convince them of theatre's potential he would need to connect it to the workers' own experiences. He hung some signs – Scab, Striker, Grower, and Contractor – around workers' necks, and invited them to 'enact the characteristics of their signs. The results far exceeded his expectations' (Harrop and Huerta, 1975, p. 31).

> The scab didn't want to at first, because it was a dirty word at that time, but he did so in good spirits. Then the two strikers started shouting at him, and everybody started cracking up. All of a sudden people started coming ... they filled up the whole kitchen. We started changing signs around, and people started volunteering ... imitating all kinds of things. We ran for two hours just doing that. Thus was El Teatro Campesino born.   (Harrop and Huerta, 1975)

Valdez did not approach the workers with a ready-made script, supportive of the strike. Instead, the 'form' realised here was developed from within a context of necessity – how to convince the workers of theatre's radical potential, when theatre was considered an alien, bourgeois activity. Connecting theatre to the real lives and real struggles of the workers necessitated drawing on the workers' own experiences, and using these experiences in the devising of the performances. The workers themselves both suggested the content and enacted the pieces, extending the sense of ownership and therefore relevance.

The circumstances surrounding the form developed by CAST (Cartoon Archetypical Slogan Theatre) proved equally productive. Ejected from the 'legitimate' left-wing Unity Theatre for attempting to introduce non-traditional political matters, such as anti-nuclear and anti-apartheid sentiments, the founding members of CAST

> found ourselves sitting in a hired pub room in Camden Town, dreaming of changing the world and theatre along with it. None of us had previously considered ourselves actors, we had in fact been theatre technicians. (Muldoon, 1976, p. 40)

As they undertook 'exploratory exercises' in the hired room it dawned on them that 'on other nights [this is] where our potential audience sat' (ibid.). In devising their work, CAST members realised that, given the context of its presentation – a pub or club – they needed an approach that was dynamic, and that would grab attention. They quickly learned that 'we had to work fast, cut fast, to get at least a laugh a minute, if we were to stop the bastards going for a beer in the middle of it' (ibid., p. 41). Recognising the mass appeal of other cultural forms, including rock music, cinema and television, co-founder Roland Muldoon understood that

> if I was going to be in theatre with the idea that it must be popular culture and have the attraction of rock 'n' roll, then I had to invent a style for that theatre. Twenty, twenty five minutes long, totally compressed, totally dynamic, cut, cut, cut, speed. So much so, that we could move faster than you could think ... (Rees, 1992, p. 70)

The aims of this 'fast cut' approach appeared to have been realised, as one critic reported that their work was, even as early as 1973, 'readily appreciated by younger audiences brought up on television and commercials' (Hammond, 1973, p. 46). CAST, describing its approach as 'agit pop' rather than 'agit-prop', considered itself a 'group with a gang ideology', more a rock 'n' roll theatre group than a collective. Notably, then, the politics of production did not, at first, influence the working process of the first socialist theatre company. As Muldoon admitted, 'All that collectivism came later' (Itzin, 1980, p. 41).

The Agitprop Street Players, founded in 1968 and re-named Red Ladder in 1971, similarly devised a form in response to a particular context, in this instance a request for help from a Tenants' Action Committee who were striking against imposed rent increases. Company member Chris Rawlence recollected that about half a dozen people got together 'and made the simplest of little sketches, a seven-minute thing saying basically: shall we pay the rents, no we won't' (ibid.). Richard Seyd, meanwhile, recalled that they made 'a 15-minute play. The result was a primitive – and not very well acted – "cloak and dagger" account of the rent fight up to that date. It used the traditions of melodrama and the music-hall.' In spite of any shortcomings, the sketch 'worked – and was booked for a dozen meetings' (Seyd, 1975, p. 36).

The important facts here are that the group were responding to an initial request, and that their 'play' was made for a specific group (a Tenants' Association), a specific place (Tenants' group meetings) and with a specific purpose (to support striking tenants). The form and content were dictated by political and physical context, and the criterion was simply, as Kathleen McCreery stated, 'did it help the struggle or not?' (Itzin, 1980, p. 41). This synergetic relationship between 'product' and context is further evidenced by the fact that the sketch developed as the real events altered. Seven plays, responding to the strike, were devised in total.

The 'model' proposed by the Agitprop Street Players, which connected performance to real workers' struggles, was one practised by a number of socialist theatre companies. The issue of rent increases, for example, was also at the root of North West Spanner's genesis. Originally it was a children's company; parents asked the group if they could support their rent strike in 1972, resulting in their first play for adults, *The Rents Play*. Similarly, The General Will's play *Rent, or Caught in the Act* (1972) was also 'devised for and played to tenants' groups, giving them information ... in an entertaining way' (ibid., p. 141). Unlike the other companies, The General Will actually had a company playwright, David Edgar, who was involved from the outset in the devising of the pieces.

Agit-Prop Form

The Agitprop Street Players' play *The Industrial Relations Act*, also known as *The Cake Play* is illustrative of the agit-prop form developed during the early 1970s. It was performed at a Trade Union demonstration in Hyde Park in February 1971, the context again necessitating a short, attention-grabbing performance. Cognisant of this, the company composed a series of memorable symbolic or meta-phoric images accompanied by simple, sloganeering text, intended to represent clearly the political message. The central images used, for example, were the 'national cake' and a set of ladders.

> The workers are bakers who bake the national cake, the strike is seen as a knife which cuts into the cake; the myth of the national cake is exploded visually because it is the capitalist who sits on top of the cake, the workers purchase the cake to eat, the cake itself is a visualisation of the class structure in society, etc. (Seyd, 1975, p. 39)

Judith Condon provided a detailed account of the performances at the Hyde Park demo:

> There were massive columns of men and women lined up behind the banners, rank after rank, and the players set up their props at the end of each line, giving performance after performance. There are three bakers' workers, men and women, in overalls, and the boss stands on a ladder looking rich and greedy. The workers produce a big section of pink cake, and stand it up against the boss's ladder. The boss looks pleased. He gives them their wage and they give it back to him in return for their slice of the cake: it isn't very much. (Lambert, 1977, p. 26)[2]

Using imagistic techniques to show the effect of the Industrial Relations Act, the play ended with the workers combining their strength to pick up the cake knife and 'strike off the heads of Heath and the Boss'. As member Richard Seyd explained, the aim of the play was to make tangible and comprehensible the invisible forces that create and impact on our lived experiences 'so that they can be grasped and, hopefully, acted upon' (Seyd, 1975, p. 39). Indicative of the rousing intention of agit-prop work, the final slogan shouted by the workers was 'We don't want a slice of the cake. We want the bloody bakery.' Capturing the atmosphere at Hyde Park, and the enthusiasm with which the play was met, Condon reported that 'Everyone had been joining in the workers' shouts, and at [the last line] we gave a great shout' (Lambert, 1977, p. 26). Such a response substantiates Seyd's claim that 'agit-prop is an effective, perhaps the best, theatrical method of mobilising support' (Seyd, 1975, p. 40). However, as Condon also noted, the play would only have had an impact on those already convinced of its arguments; the simplistic content demanded by agit-prop might mobilise already existing support then, but it would be unlikely to persuade the not-yet-converted.

Luis Valdez of El Teatro Campesino, developing the fortuitously 'found' method whereby worker-actors simply wore archetypal characters' names around their necks, devised a similar form to agit-prop, called *actos*. The *actos*, like the agit-prop plays of the Agitprop Street Players, were intended to

> inspire the audience to social action. Illuminate specific points about social problems. Satirize the opposition. Show or hint at solutions. Express what people are feeling.   (Kanellos, 1987, p. 20)

Actos, similarly determined by the context of their performance, were short, humorous scenes that presented clearly the facts relating to political situations. Scenarios were developed from improvisations enacted by the farm worker-actors, drawing on their real experiences (ibid., p. 18). *The Two Faces of the Boss*, a typical *acto* presented in 1965, aimed to erase the intimidation workers felt, by revealing the boss to be simply a man, like them. In the *acto* the boss initially wore a pig facemask, carried a whip and smoked a cigar. Attempting to persuade the worker that he would not want the trials that attended his life, the boss swapped his mask, whip and cigar for the worker's shears and hat and sign. The worker, confronted by the unmasked boss, laughed in response, saying, 'Patron, you look like me' (Kourilsky, 1972, p. 48). In addition to the appropriateness of the form in relation to its political intentions (simple and clear messages), agit-prop and *actos* were 'practicable' – cheap to produce and able to be performed anywhere (DiCenzo, 1996, p. 44). They were also capable of being adapted quickly in response to real events. This is one advantage of the devised script; having been devised and performed by the group, it could quickly be revised and kept up to date.

The agit-prop form used in the 1960s and early 1970s was felt to be one that could be mastered by anyone, and was not considered the preserve of the professional theatre maker. In fact, this model of practice aligned itself with the perceived primary function of *political* performance – its political intentions – rather than with any aesthetic concerns. Theatre was considered a tool. Thus, as a Red Ladder programme from 1972 stressed, 'Theatre is not our end; it is our means. A way of putting across ideas. ... A means of stimulating thought, discussion and even action, on issues of critical importance to the working class' (Shank, 1978, p. 52). Luis Valdez, in very similar tones, declared in 1967 that his company 'shouldn't be judged as a theater. We're really part of a cause' (Elam, 1997, p. 19).[3] This focus on politics rather than aesthetics rendered possible the ideological stance of anti-professionalisation, itself tied to a general desire to democratise the arts, making them accessible to all. 'Devising', the creation of a 'product' from scratch, enabled by everyone's contribution, was considered a potential model of democratic arts practice.

The Mode of Production

Aligning political ideologies with working practices led many companies to develop collective structures. Rather than one person assuming a position of ultimate control over the theatrical product (the director), and over those who created it (the performers), political companies most often attempted to operate collectively. Initially, collective practice was equated with everyone having an equal say, decision-making operating via discussion and consensus, all jobs being undertaken by everyone (either randomly or on a rotating basis), and all jobs considered as equally important. The collective model insisted on shared and equal responsibility for all aspects of the production. As we will soon see, different companies evolved their own different collective models, partly responding to the actual experiences of working collectively.

What was also apparent in many companies operating at this time was their own ongoing consciousness-raising and political education. Red Ladder, for example,

> would read Lenin and Marx and other theorists every week and have a discussion about it. The political discussion was also about how to organise the group. For many years they were an absolute model of democracy. ... They had weekly meetings, a whole afternoon to discuss the group, to ensure that everybody had an equal role, that all work was rotated, including the Chairman of the Day.   (Itzin, 1980, p. 47)

The reflective writings of theatre practitioners at this time are evidence of their theoretical training, illustrated and substantiated with statements from the 'canon' of radical politics, from Chairman Mao to Lenin to Brecht.[4]

The lesbian collective Siren Theatre Company, founded in 1979 in Brighton, also bore testimony to this process of group education and the focus on political clarity over aesthetic sophistication. Member Jane Boston 'recalled that the discussion and the clarification of political positions seemed to be more important than its theatrical expression' (Freeman, 1997, p. 49). Like Blood Group, Siren's discussions were prompted by Mary Daly's *Gyn/ecology*. Interestingly, Sandra Freeman noted that because of members' different experiences of class and background, there was no emergence of a 'collective mind, rather a reconciliation of individual differences' (ibid.).

The Bradford Art College Theatre Group, founded by Albert Hunt and his students, which developed from the 'Happening' performances discussed in Chapter 3, also provides an interesting example of the relationship between political ideas and collective organisations. Hunt's description of their devising process is certainly similar to that of other political companies, but there is also some resonance with other less explicitly political groups, such as the People Show. The Theatre Group

> works as a collective, putting together ideas in discussion and improvisation: but it's made up of individuals, each of whom might have his own descriptions and definitions of what we are trying to do. We work together because we respond to each other's ideas and attitudes and inventions – and not because we've sat down and hammered out a manifesto and an ideological line.   (Hunt, 1971, p. 47)

That said, it is clear that the company did practise consciousness-raising, or what Hunt calls 'political discovery', during the creation of their plays (Hunt, 1975, p. 6). The group did not begin by already knowing the answers to political questions. Instead, like Red Ladder, they 'discovered the content as we worked. ... As we put our plays together, we were trying, not to parrot simple slogans, but to examine, scrutinise, question our own received ideas – and to invite our audiences to do the same' (ibid.).

In an article written in 1975, Hunt posed a question to all those engaged in political theatre at that time: 'why theatre? At this moment? Why not other forms of political agitation or activity? Why not social action?' Hunt's own answer insisted on the politics of production: 'In the first place, the theatre, at its simplest level, that of small groups of people coming together to work, offers a concrete form for creating new, collective working relationships' (ibid.). The process of devising, without any pre-existing script, potentially enabled greater collective practices.

The desire and aim for shared and equal creative responsibility needs also to be read within the particular context of dominant theatre practice – a practice marked by hierarchical structures. By the 1950s the director occupied the apex of the theatrical hierarchy, and – as Dan Rebellato has argued – the role of the playwright had by this time also received professional recognition. Both of these shifts were indicative of 'the lure of professionalism', which 'was extremely strong in the forties and fifties' (Rebellato, 1999, p. 83). As Rebellato summarised, such professionalisation 'sharply delimited the creative freedom of all but a select few theatre workers' (ibid., p. 85). The political theatre 'movement' of the 1960s could be read as a deliberate refusal of this 'lure of professionalism'.

As the ideology of 'participatory democracy' took international root, it was evident that for theatre to play its role in the formation of any new society, the praxis of participatory democracy should also be implemented. Set beside the model of hierarchy, specialisation and increased professionalisation, devising as a collaborative process offered a politically acceptable alternative. According to Theodore Shank, alternative methods of theatre creation developed in part

> as a reaction against the psychic fragmentation the artists experienced in the technocratic society which believed that human needs could be satisfied by technical means requiring a huge degree of specialization. Instead of the individual specialists of the established theatre, the typical member of an alternative theatre has broad creative responsibilities. (Shank, 1982, p. 2)

Devising a Play

Strike While the Iron is Hot, or *A Woman's Work is Never Done* (1974) was one of Red Ladder's best known plays. Responding to certain political shifts of the time, not least the impact of the burgeoning feminist movement, this play moved Red Ladder, for the first time, from its singular focus on socialism. Complementing this widening of focus, the form of the play attempted a more socialist-realist style in place of the crude agit-prop form of earlier work (albeit interrupted in places with more expressionist language). Though the usefully illustrative visual metaphors used in their agit-prop plays were retained, they were placed within a framework of realism. For example, in one scene the principles of Equal Pay were explained to the main character, Helen, using quantities of beer in pint glasses. This explanation was given while the characters were in a pub, therefore making the use of beer as a visual prop probable within the overall structure of the play.

The word 'play' is significant here; where the agit-prop performances were more like 'sketches' in their form, *Strike* developed into a full-length piece, and deliberately attempted to construct realistic characters, situations and exchanges. Though the words and images used in agit-prop had always to be precise in order to be clear in their ideological message, the devising of a full-length play, aiming for a socialist-realist form, complete with plot and dialogue in place of sound bites or slogans accompanied by images, might arguably demand a different process of play construction. Where the agit-prop sketch lent itself easily to a fragmented script, the socialist-realist form required a greater narrative unity (even if presented episodically). In this example, we can see the interrelation between form and process; as the one shifted, so too did the other.

Richard Seyd's article 'The Theatre of Red Ladder' provided a full account of the 'play-making process'. Though this relates to *Strike While the Iron is Hot*, it nevertheless proposes one model of devising a play, a complicated and ostensibly 'careful' model that Red Ladder arrived at through six years of previous experience collectively devising agit-prop performances. According to Seyd, the total process, from the beginning to the opening of the play, took about nine months (Seyd, 1975, pp. 38–9). This model also reveals the company's organisational structure. The collaboration of all members, alongside the delegation of different responsibilities, matches and reflects the company's ideological beliefs.

The group's decision to make a play focusing on feminist concerns arose out of post-show audience discussions following previous performances, and members' own concerns. Once the subject matter had been agreed upon, one person undertook primary research, which included interviewing a variety of people, while the whole group continued to discuss the subject for a further three months. As the group worked its way towards its own understanding of the issues, an element of consciousness-raising was inevitable, during which members of the group confronted their own actions and behaviour. The group worked out a series of components that four people then used in order to plan the play's structure, which took two months work. This dramaturgical skeleton was presented to the whole group for discussion, changes, or even total rejection. Improvisations based on the material that had been agreed were used to find ways in which the content could be made as clear as possible, and the different characters were also devised during these improvisations. Following the improvisation work, the play was again distributed amongst different people in order that a rough script could be prepared from the material that had been generated. The whole group again discussed the results, and further changes were made. Two people were finally given the responsibility of providing a stylistic unity to the entire script. The play was cast according to the principle that all members should have the opportunity to play different types of parts in each of the company's productions. The script was further developed during rehearsals, and would continue to evolve whilst touring, in response to audience feedback (ibid.).

Other companies shared many of the features evident in the process used by Red Ladder. For example, the Women's Theatre Group's first performance, *My Mother Says I Never Should* (1975), similarly involved group discussion in order to determine the focus of the piece. The subject matter – sex and contraception – was then collectively researched. As the intended audience was young women, the company members talked to girls, parents and teachers. This information was then pooled, and through group improvisation characters and plot were created. Finally, company members formed small sub-groups in order to write and rewrite the script (Wandor, 1980, p. 115).

Organisational Structures

Many reflections by practitioners on their modes of production focused on the struggles experienced in attempting both to determine and then to practise a collective model. This would obviously have repercussions on the methods of devising that were adopted; different models resulted in different methods. For Seyd, developing an appropriate working structure 'has been perhaps the most problematical part of the work, relating, as it does, to the creation of an organisational structure that is at the same time democratic, productive, and non-oppressive to the individuals working within the collective' (Seyd, 1975, p. 42). Seyd's next comment is revealing:

> The major problem was that we made an idealistic analysis of the nature and practice of democracy. We worked in what we would now call an ultra-egalitarian structure. (Seyd, 1975, p. 42)

One effect of this collective structure was, ironically, that it created an 'anarchic tyranny of structurelessness' (ibid.).

John McGrath similarly used the word 'anarchy' to describe certain collective models. Referring to the differences in aims between himself and his former 7:84 colleague Gavin Richards, McGrath claimed to have distrusted the actuality, if not the concept, of the 'liberation of the performer'. For McGrath, such 'liberation' was 'a kind of anarchism', whereas he was 'interested in a Socialist theatre, not an anarchist theatre' (McGrath, 1975a, p. 50). Richards in fact broke away from 7:84 in order to found another socialist company, Belt and Braces. McGrath's experiences of mounting a joint production with Belt and Braces, *The Great Money Trick* (1976), substantiated his suspicions, at least in McGrath's opinion,

> there was a total decentralization, a total exchange of roles. Everybody was a writer, everybody was a bureaucrat, everybody could do anything on the show. It was total chaos. The gigs got all fucked up because somebody didn't tell somebody that they'd made an arrangement to ring somebody back, because one day they were organising the gigs and the next day they were rushing around finding props.   (McGrath, 1975a)

Collective decision-making also, in practice, often fell short of the ideal. Red Ladder initially employed a model of unanimous agreement. However, Seyd revealed that such 'unanimity' might in fact be the result of the most dominant members of the group – typically the men – getting their way, rather than there being actual agreement with all proposals. As nothing could progress until a unanimous agreement had been reached, 'those in a minority would eventually put up their hands and make the decision unanimous ... just so the work could continue' (Seyd, 1975, p. 42). It was only when the company began to work on *Strike While the Iron is Hot* that members of the group confronted their own oppressive behaviour. As one member, Glen Park, recalled, the preparatory discussions for the play involved examining personal histories of being men and women, 'and for the first time making conscious the ways in which male oppression took place within the group. Everyone was very shaken up by that' (Wandor, 1986, p. 96).

Another potential danger of the collective model was that, as Lizbeth Goodman recognised, the very structure of collective organisation often ironically prompted a non-agreed hierarchy to be imposed. In order for a play to progress, it was often necessary for someone to step in and take control; in the 1970s, that someone (a necessarily confident figure) would typically be a man (Goodman, 1993, p. 55). Gillian Hanna, founding member of the feminist company Monstrous Regiment, similarly referred to the 'hidden hierarchy that can lie beneath the surface of a group' (Hanna, 1991, p. xx).[5]

Equally damaging to companies was an unquestioned faith in the democratic model. When Red Ladder deployed the collective structure but then experienced resentment and tension, explanations for such failure were sought in 'individual personalities and psychologies', rather than in the process. As Seyd stressed, one effect of this collective method was, paradoxically, the individualisation of everything (Seyd, 1975, p. 42). Responding to such experiences, by 1975 the model favoured by Red Ladder had shifted to one of 'majority' rather than unanimity.

The organisational history of the San Francisco Mime Troupe is an instructive example of the struggle to find a mode of production that is both ideologically acceptable and practicably workable. Though the Troupe was founded and directed by Ronnie Davis, the context of the group's work (San Francisco in the 1960s), and its increasingly political focus, created a tension with the hierarchical structure, the 'one-or-two-person-lead [sic] group' (Davis, 1975a, p. 114). As the company grew, 'others wanted a chance to direct, perform and do the creating' (ibid.). One alternative model that was implemented was a Gerontocracy, 'whereby the oldest members became a committee of decision-makers' (ibid., pp. 98–9). This structure did not work, however, since these members did not want the responsibility of running a company and were not involved in the day-to-day organisation of it. Two members of the company then proposed an alternative structure: five members of the group would be elected by the company to form an 'Inner core', which would 'decide on the direction and policy of the company' (ibid, p. 99). The practice of this group, in relation to decision-making, was as ineffectual as the Gerontocracy, resulting in the group being voted out. This then led to the creation of what Davis termed a 'loosely ordered collective', a development that prompted Davis to leave the company. Davis considered that 'requiring people to be all things at all times (actors are writers, directors are actors, technicians are theoreticians, and so on) hampers the wholesale improvement of the work' (Davis, 1975b, p. 26). Further, in Davis's opinion, participatory democracy 'is not likely to lead to revolutionary work nor sustained revolutionary activity. In the theatre, it is likely to lead in the opposite direction – congratulatory participation, amateurism and bourgeois choice' (Davis, 1975a, p. 124).

Evident here is a tension between 'politics' and 'aesthetics', and process and product, and Davis suggested that such tension was also tangible between performers who were professionals and those who were amateurs, when both had an equal voice in meetings. In presenting his critique of collective theatre processes, Davis included the informed reflections of Sandy Archer, his former colleague (who also left the Troupe a few months after Davis). Archer proposed that, as divisions of labour were erased, so too was 'the trust and respect that was associated' with them. In Archer's opinion,

> while this can bring out innovative ideas or techniques, it primarily focuses on breaking down identities built upon what we would call experienced or professional wisdom. In this way, anyone's opinions become as valid as anyone else's. The extreme result of this would be *individualism*, i.e., total expression of each in all areas.　(Davis, 1975a, pp. 125–6)

In place of this model, Archer instead envisioned a cooperative, where each would use their specific skills and experience for the benefit of the total production (ibid.). Archer's cooperative ideal would in fact be a model pursued and practised by various companies seeking a mode of production that would overcome the problems identified above, including the 'hidden hierarchies'. Such a model of cooperative practice was not, however, the one favoured by the San Francisco Mime Troupe at this time.

Though some of the San Francisco Mime Troupe's productions, such as *A Minstrel Show, or Civil Rights in a Cracker Barrel* (1965), developed under Davis's leadership, were considered by the company to be 'collective' productions, the collective process became more conscious following Davis's and Archer's departure. Company member Joan Holden referred to the collective model as 'group production', first explicitly experienced in the making of *Seize the Time* (1970) (Holden, 1975, p. 28). Holden's account of the process revealed that there was still a division of labour – there were writers, directors, and actors, for example; however, the aim of the company was to 'allow more people to play those roles'. It is evident from Holden's account that the writers used work generated by performers, and in this sense, the production might be considered a collectively devised piece. In *Seize the Time* there were two writers, and two directors who 'assembled the show from the fragments of style and staging produced by the workshops' (ibid., p. 30). The ideas for the play also came from the whole group. The collective process was signified in the programmes by the lack of company members' names; no one person was credited with any specific task.

In spite of the new model of collectivism instituted at the San Francisco Mime Troupe, an article by Theodore Shank, written two years after Joan Holden's 'positive' appraisal of collective play-making, revealed that the company was still working through what might be a 'hidden hierarchy'. The fact that Holden had published an article about the company does suggest that she held a certain amount of power. Shank's account of the making of *False Promises* (1976) rendered explicit the difficulties of collectively arriving at a subject matter, and then of writing a script for this. Joan Holden eventually wrote the play. Given that she was the most prolific writer in the group to date, having written *Independent Female* (1970) and *Frijoles* (1975), as well as being a writer for *The Dragon Lady's Revenge* (1971), the company policy of rotating creative tasks did not appear to be holding. As Shank reported, tensions within the group were evident:

> About seven weeks after the play had opened, a meeting was held to discuss the process by which it had come about. There was still dissatisfaction about how the play had been written because the company had begun with the idea that it would be developed at all stages by the entire group. These dissatisfactions needed to be talked about openly. (Shank, 1977, p. 48)

The meeting also acknowledged that every play so far presented had been created differently – no 'perfect' model had yet offered itself. One note from this meeting captured well the potential tension that arises from a collective process and a model of equal and shared responsibility: 'The group's commitment to collective process is unanimous. ... However, those participating must maintain concentration and energy during the discussion to realize fully the benefits of collective playmaking' (ibid.).

The Role of the Writer

Although the focus of this chapter is primarily political devised theatre, in most cases the form of this theatre was 'text-based', and as such, the problematic relationship of writing to devising cannot be ignored. In distinction to those performances that might be 'scored' or 'composed' from visual images or physical actions enacted by the group, the plays explored here are usually textually scripted, although the means of producing that script is, as we have already seen, varied. In this context, Lizbeth Goodman's supposition that 'one of the primary difficulties of devising is a definitional one: that of distinguishing between "writing" and "devising"' (Goodman, 1993, p. 101), is one that the reader would do well to bear in mind, although it is a conundrum not easily resolved.

In the production of agit-prop plays, with their emphasis on unambiguous political messages, the accompanying text was necessarily sparse. This was particularly so given the performance environment – often outside, often programmed as part of another event, and often with limited time available for performing. There was no attempt at characterisation, story line, or any sequential unfolding of plot in time and place (Seyd, 1975, p. 39). The form of agit-prop would more readily lend itself to a group devising process provided the group was in agreement about politics. As we have seen, group discussion involving much personal consciousness-raising around the issues to be addressed was a large part of the devising process.

However, as the agit-prop sketch gave way to socialist-realist plays, complete with narrative structure or plot and a degree of character psychology, the process of devising the material also shifted. We have already seen one example of this in Red Ladder's *Strike While the Iron is Hot*, where specific members were given the responsibility of writing the text. The process of producing *Mother Country*, a play by Mutable Theatre (1975) that explored the interconnections between class oppression and racism, is also instructive. The group adopted the by-now familiar model, beginning with a research period which involved reading various materials and holding discussions with appropriate different individuals and organisations, and then sharing this information with all members of the group. The company then met to discuss what they had learned – a process of consciousness-raising. This was followed by a period of improvisatory workshops, after which one company member took responsibility for writing up a script, using the devised material as the basis. The written script was then further discussed and revised by the whole group (Shank, 1978, p. 57).

It is notable from this example that it was finally one person who took responsibility for writing the play-text. Responding to the various strains produced by a collective model, in the mid-1970s many companies in the UK developed a cooperative structure, matching Sandy Archer's ideal form of collaboration. Aiming to retain the ideological foundations of the collective, companies would typically insist that all skills were equally valuable. Important to our survey of the devising process is the fact that one specific skill recognised by the mid-1970s was that of writing. John McGrath had always been passionate in his defence of the professional writers' skills, and although 7:84 was considered a socialist theatre company, McGrath maintained a powerful position during his time in the Scottish company as its writer and director. For McGrath, though the process of writing was open to discussion by all members of the company, nevertheless 'writing a play can never be a totally democratic process. They are skills which need aptitude, long experience, self-discipline and a certain mental disposition in one individual' (McGrath, 1975b, p. 9).[6] In a neat sound bite, McGrath's aim was 'to de-mystify the role, without castrating the talent' (ibid.). The purpose of opening up to discussion the process of writing was intended to give all company members a sense of shared ownership over the play, even if the act of writing remained an individual task. Members should feel 'part of the creation of the show, not alienated from it or the mere instruments of it' (ibid.). The making of *Boom* (1974) began with the company involved in discussion, followed by ideas 'of all kinds, from all directions. ... The whole company was throwing in their ideas which were taken up, knocked down, analysed by everyone else and fed into the growing pool of unrealised material that was to be the basis of the show itself' (ibid., p. 10).

The published introduction to 7:84 (Scotland)'s *The Cheviot, the Stag, and the Black, Black Oil* (1973) provided further insight to the company's working process and McGrath's position within that. McGrath stated bluntly, 'Obviously I, as a writer, had a very clear idea of exactly how I wanted the show to be. I knew who it was for, and I knew what I wanted to say and how I wanted to say it' (McGrath, 1981, p. ix). Aligning the production process with his ideological beliefs, McGrath tempered this blow of individualism by insisting that even though 'this wasn't to be a free-for-all, utopian fantasy: I wouldn't expect to play Allan Ross's fiddle, or to sing in Gaelic, or act', the hierarchies of theatre could be smashed by giving equal respect to each individual's skills, whilst still keeping the processes of each open to 'collective discussion and advice' (ibid., p. x).

McGrath's unequivocal designation as 'playwright' makes it difficult to claim that 7:84 was a devising company at that time. Yet in practice their process during the 1970s does not appear to be that dissimilar to other companies which might be thought to employ a devising model. Michael Patterson's conclusion that 'it is not the writing that is a collaborative process but the research that precedes it' seems, however, too easy a separation when placed against the evidence of the actual creative methods used (Patterson, 2003, p. 129).

The impetus for many political companies throughout the 1970s and 1980s was the observable lack of plays that addressed the concerns of many people. In order that the experiences of gay men, lesbians, disabled people and women, for example, were represented on stage, companies such as Siren Theatre Company, Gay Sweatshop, the Women's Theatre Group, Graeae Theatre Company and Monstrous Regiment realised that they would need to generate their own texts.

Monstrous Regiment, a feminist collective founded in 1975, were from the outset clear about their need for a writer. Recognising the assumption that a collective company should employ a collective method of devising scripts, and therefore aware of the potential tension that having a designated writing role might cause in such an organisation, co-founder Gillian Hanna asked:

> Wouldn't it be more democratic to write scripts collectively? If you were working in a collective, how could one voice represent the ideas of the whole? We acknowledged some truth in this, but there were some areas where we recognised it as bunk. Enough of us (and I was one of them) had been through the painful experience of writing shows collectively in other groups to know that the skill of playwriting was one we wanted to acknowledge.   (Hanna, 1991, p. xxxiii)

However, aiming to maintain the ideal of a collective organisation, Monstrous Regiment hoped to develop a 'collective relationship with the writer'. Like the Mime Troupe, in the absence of any already existing model for this, each of their ventures was to employ a different model, and not all of these could be considered successful. The company's first play, *SCUM: Death, Destruction and Dirty Washing* (1976), was written by Chris Bond and Claire Luckham. The original intention of holding discussions from which Bond and Luckham would then write the play, or of the play being written first and then opened to discussion, was never realised. The writing was mostly done from a distance and when Monstrous Regiment received the script, they decided to collectively revise those elements they considered to be 'still in an unresolved state' (ibid., p. xxxiv).

> Under Susan's direction, we improvised, we discussed, we argued, we went away and wrote scenes and bits of scenes. We also added more songs. It's impossible now to say who did what. ... Everybody wrote something. (Hanna, 1991)

In this example, then, an originally commissioned script was adapted through a collective devising process. In a later project, Monstrous Regiment attempted to devise their own script, adapting *Gentlemen Prefer Blondes*. Hanna described this new venture as 'a disastrous foray into the grave labelled devised writing' (ibid., p. xlviii). Though *Scum* had been a great success, 'Claire and Chris had created a substantial basis of structure and narrative, a vision from which we worked' (ibid.). In Hanna's opinion, the totally devised work, by contrast, was 'incoherent. Too many people had a hand in writing it' (ibid.).

Claire Grove, a member of the Women's Theatre Group, addressing the collective devising process, similarly found problems with collective writing. She reflected that:

> Quite often it completely cut against what you wanted to say, because having set up a structure like that there's a feeling that everyone can contribute ... and you ended up with a sort of gap in the middle of a group of people that was the play. All your intentions were right and the play was dreadful. (Goodman, 1993, p. 54).[7]

It was perhaps an awareness of such a gap in the middle of *Care and Control* that prompted Gay Sweatshop to invite Michelene Wandor to assist with the production of the final script. Gay Sweatshop's first play, *Mister X* (1975), was scripted by Roger Baker and Drew Griffiths, with the text being reworked in rehearsals through discussions and improvisations (Osment, 1989, p. xix). *Care and Control* was the first play to arise from the women's section of Gay Sweatshop, founded in 1977. Following an established model, the women of the company first undertook group research and used interviews with women as primary material that was then drawn upon during workshops. A scenario, and then a more detailed synopsis, was developed out of improvisations, which were in turn transcribed by some members of the cast (Wandor, 1980, p. 63). However, having undertaken this process, the group 'arrived at a point where we had a lot of material, but felt we could not produce an adequate script ourselves' (ibid). As a result, the group invited Michelene Wandor to 'come in and script it'. Wandor's revisions consisted of 'editing and tightening and reorganising' what was already there, and also adding new material where needed, all of which involved discussion with the company. Nancy Diuguid's description of *Care and Control* as being 'a collaborative effort, a collaborative piece' that 'Gay Sweatshop collectively wrote' is unequivocal (Goodman, 1993, p. 95). Wandor, similarly, did not claim the status of 'author' of the play. As she explained, 'The company researched and devised the play and I scripted it (which is not the same as writing)' (ibid., p. 96). This distinction between scripting and writing is an important one that recognises collaborative creation. The difficulty of defining the status or practice of 'writing' in relation to collaborative models of devising remains in contemporary examples. Companies that employ a writer, but which also want to acknowledge the collaborative contribution of others, such as the Scottish company Suspect Culture, or the New York company The Civilians, replace the term 'playwright' with that of 'dramaturg', or 'text by ...'.[8] Both of these work against the assumed individualism or autonomy of the writer, whilst still recognising that writing demands its own particular skills and/ or experience.

The model used by Gay Sweatshop could be contrasted with that employed by The General Will in its early years. David Edgar was, from the start, the company's playwright, collaborating on *The State of Emergency, Rent, or Caught in the Act* (1972) and *The Dunkirk Spirit* (1974). Where Wandor was brought into the process late in its development, Edgar was involved in the discussions from the outset. Edgar would write scenes that arose from 'day-to-day discussion and/ or improvisation', which he would then bring back to the group to try out, and for further discussion. In this process, Edgar was 'writing a scene a day' (Itzin, 1980, p. 140).

Graeae Theatre Company, founded in 1980, employed a similar devising process. Speaking of the genesis of the company, co-founder and actor Nabil Shaban recollected that in 1980 there were no opportunities in theatre for disabled actors: 'even local amateur dramatic societies at that time looked askance at having disabled people on stage'.[9] Further, there was little representation of people with disabilities, and what did exist was written by observers of disability rather than those who directly experienced it. The co-founder and director of Graeae, Richard Tomlinson, set out to redress this invisibility.[10] Like other companies discussed here, Graeae adopted a devising process in which the actors would improvise in workshops and Tomlinson would then take this material and translate it into a dramatic script. For Shaban:

> Devising is an attractive process because it offers the opportunity to make a piece that is as 'authentic' as possible. Robert couldn't hope to be able to create what disabled people felt and experienced. However, he used his professional theatre craftsmanship to turn what was developed during workshops into a credible piece of theatre.[11]

Importantly, the early shows of Graeae, including *Sideshow* (1980) and *3D* (1981), were very much determined by and dependent upon the people who performed in them. As cast members changed, so too did the script. In this sense, the 'product' was always in 'process' and the play was always 'owned' by those contributing to it. By 1983, both Shaban and Tomlinson had left Graeae; that year the company presented *The Endless Variety Show*, a performance written by Geoff Armstrong which indicated a shift in the working process of the company.

The early work of Joint Stock Theatre Company also raises the difficulty in determining the relationship of the 'writer' to our concept of 'devising'. The impetus for the foundation of Joint Stock is to be found in some of the companies covered in Chapter 2. Inspired by a visit of Café La Mama to Jim Haynes's new project, the Traverse Theatre, Max Stafford Clark had set up a workshop there (1968–72) and in 1974, with writer David Hare and David Aukin (from Freehold), he established the touring company, Joint Stock. Actors once again undertook research and generated improvisational material, but a writer worked with them on a project from the beginning and generated a script that was then rehearsed as a traditional production. The pace and activity of the workshop discoveries fed into the scripts and performances that the company produced. The material that the group worked on was often factual, and actors were involved in gathering research in order to generate the performances, as in *Speakers* (1974), *Fanshen* (1975) and *Yesterday's News* (1976). The script for Caryl Churchill's *Cloud Nine* (1979) was conditioned by the interests of the actors, and their desires for equality of parts.[12] Nabil Shaban, Gillian Hanna and others have identified this desire for equality of parts as a potential problem shared by many collective companies. Reflecting on the experiences of Graeae, and its shift towards the employment of a writer and commissioned scripts, Shaban suggested that 'The danger with a devised piece [by a collective company] was the attempt or desire to please everyone, and the attempt to give everyone equal parts, resulting in a homogenous piece'.[13] Shaban's insights suggest an attention to product over process.

Politics vs Aesthetics

It is apparent, from the examples so far offered, that by the mid-1970s there was a move away from a singular focus on the political function of theatre, and the primary importance of that, and a move towards prioritising theatre as an aesthetic form. This focus on the production, over process, implies an equal or greater degree of concern with the cultural value of the work than with its political impact, or at the least, it suggests a different way of relating 'politics' to 'product' by suggesting that practitioners were becoming more critical of the forms through which politics were being presented. In its early years, members of Red Ladder had insisted on the primacy of its politics over any aesthetic concerns, but by 1975 Seyd was writing that the 'disrespect and mechanical relegation of the forms used do a disservice to the ideas being communicated. No craftsman would disregard the tools of their trade to the extent that socialist theatre workers often disregard theirs' (Seyd, 1975, p. 39). This sentiment was supported by a quotation from Mao Tse Tung: 'Works of art which lack artistic quality have no force, however progressive they are politically' (ibid., p. 41). By this time, members of Red Ladder were taking 'on their own shoulders areas of the group's work – in other words we have a division of labour' (ibid., p. 42). Like the San Francisco Mime Troupe model, rotation of the different tasks was intended, so that 'no one job is the preserve of any one individual'. However, Seyd admitted that some jobs had to be occupied for at least a year, 'otherwise swapping around does become counter-productive' (ibid.).

El Teatro Campesino represents an early instance of the shift from explicit politics toward aesthetic concerns. In September 1967, Valdez relocated the company to Del Rey, thereby breaking the previously exclusive bond that it had with the Delano strikers. Valdez commented:

> We found we had to back away from Delano to be a theatre. Do you serve the moment by being just kind of half-assed, getting together whenever there's a chance, or do you really hone your theatre down into an effective weapon?   (Harrop and Huerta, 1975, p. 31)

Valdez suggested here that the 'professionalisation' of his theatre would enable it to be an even greater political tool; more sustained focus on the production values of the performance did not then, in his opinion, render its political import any less significant. However, the geographical move was matched by a move in political sensibilities, with politics being read from a broader cultural perspective rather than a socialist one. Valdez now identified more with a Chicano identity than with worker identity, and the purpose of the work was to strengthen Chicanos' sense of, and pride in, their own culture, history and traditions. As Harrop and Huerta documented, in order to approach these 'broader and abstract issues his theatre would require a greater technical sophistication on the part of the actors' (ibid., p. 32). A new training programme was developed, bearing resemblance to other ensemble training of the time, in particular that of Joseph Chaikin (discussed in Chapter 2). Such a training programme was far removed from the devised *actos* of the unskilled farm worker-actors. Perhaps unsurprisingly, from 1971 Valdez replaced the *actos* with *mitos*, 'the playing and singing of a narrative drama' (ibid., p. 34). *Mitos* were written and directed by Valdez himself. Again, we witness in this example the symbiotic relationship between form and process. As the form shifted, so too did the means of attaining it. Indicating the dramatic shifts in both practice and content, in 1974 Valdez commented, 'Now our acts are the acts of human beings living and working on this earth. ... We are still very much the political theatre, but our politics are the politics of the spirit – not of the flesh but of the heart' (ibid., p. 34).[14]

As suggested in the example of El Teatro Campesino, the move away from politics to aesthetics, and from collective models towards cooperative ones, correlates with a re-professionalisation of practice. Though undoubtedly some companies encouraged radical forms of writing, there was nevertheless some notion of 'good' theatre being applied (even if that were 'good popular entertainment'). In the 1980s, plays written for those collaborative companies that still survived certainly approached the conditions of more conventional – or bourgeois – theatre. It was perhaps not unsurprising that such plays were written using more conventional methods, for a different approach to producing written texts would arguably be likely to result in a different form of text (such as those that are discussed in Chapter 3 and Chapter 7). Any 'gap' perceived in the play, then, might well have resulted not from the process of collectively devising the play, but because the type of play being aimed for – social-realist with naturalist dialogue, narrative-driven with a linear plot, and structural unity and coherence, for example – could not easily be made using a collective devising process.

By the 1980s any explicit political signifiers that remained were to be found not in radical modes of production but instead in the content of plays, although by now these politics were far removed from the socialist politics of work produced in the 1970s. Though many companies did attempt to retain their difference from mainstream theatre by at least insisting on a collective, rather than a hierarchical model, even this practice was to be challenged by the new economic pressures of the 1980s.

Shifting Economics

So far we have explained the move away from processes of collectively devising political productions by recognising the growing concern of companies with 'aesthetics'. However, another major (and related) factor in the shift away from collective and collaborative models is that of subsidy for the arts. If the economic climate does not support, in general, collective modes of production, then a collectively devised process becomes difficult to sustain.

The issue of state subsidy in relation to political theatre has always been somewhat contentious: can a theatre company which attempts to challenge the status quo be simultaneously supported by an institution seen to be a cog in, and an emblem of, that dominant culture? Seeking to secure funding from the Arts Council, and then retain it, companies would inevitably 'become more interested in professional survival than in revolutionary action' (Birchall, 1978).[15] The focus shifts to financial matters rather than political objectives (Davis, 1975a, p. 16). This argument coincides with the debate between politics and aesthetics; as companies became professionalised, working in political theatre might have been considered a career option rather than a political passion (Birchall, 1978, p. 39). Though funding provided some stability, in Ronnie Davis's opinion this resulted in a dangerous cycle of events: professional status brought with it increased overheads and larger production costs, necessitating the securing of further funding in order to survive, and so on (Davis, 1975a, p. 16).

Any changes in arts policy would most affect those companies who depended on arts subsidy. After taking office in 1979, Margaret Thatcher revoked the Labour government's arts budget by cutting

£1.1 million from the previously agreed Arts Council funding. In 1981 the Arts Council instituted its first-ever series of cuts. By 1983/ 4 there was a 1 per cent fall in the Arts Council budget (DiCenzo, 1996, p. 69; Kershaw, 1992, p. 170). The 1986 Cork Inquiry into Professional Theatre in England noted that while, between 1975 and 1980, eleven new companies were granted Arts Council annual revenue funding, between 1981 and 1986, only two additional com- panies were funded, whilst thirteen lost their funding (Brown, Brannen, and Brown, 2000, p. 380).[16] Though the Arts Council is meant to operate at arms length from the government, as Baz Kershaw noted, by 1985 it 'increasingly looked like a central government clone' adopting the same language as its 'paymaster'. There is no mistak- ing the ventriloquism of the then Chairman of the Arts Council, William Rees-Mogg:

> The qualities required for survival in this age are the qualities of the age itself. They include self-reliance, imagination, a sense of opportunity, range of choice, and the entrepreneurial action of small professional groups. The state should continue to help the arts, but the arts should first look to themselves, and to their audiences for their future and their growth. (Kershaw, 1992, p. 170)

The concept of 'cost-effectiveness' inevitably had an impact on year-round employment of collective company members. Cost- effectiveness referred also to programming choices in relation to maximum box office returns. As funding schemes began to insist that applicants secure match-funding, the majority of companies were also forced to seek private sponsorship. In such a climate, the survival of those companies seemingly pushing marginal or radical political agendas, or employing non-traditional modes of production, was threatened. Elaine Aston, in relation to feminist theatre, summarised the situation:

> For many professional feminist practitioners the economic squeeze on political theatre in the 1980s was in part responsible for the displacement of issue-based, political theatre and the rise of a theatre which prioritised style over (political) content.   (Aston, 1999, p. 14)

Ian Milton (of Pirate Jenny and 7:84 England) further noted that the conservative Arts Council's preferred organisational structure was that of a limited company with an artistic director, a structure which emulated private business but which was diametrically opposed to the practices and ideals of many non-hierarchical collectives that were still in existence (Goodman, 1993, p. 56).

Experiences of many companies operating throughout the 1980s indicated clearly the difficulty of attempting to operate a collective model that would employ a devising process. For example, in 1975 Monstrous Regiment were organised as a collective, with eleven members. By 1989 they had a management structure composed of five people (Hanna, 1991, p. lix). The number of collective members had reduced partly because some wanted or financially needed to work with other companies, or could not accommodate the arduous touring schedules that were required to prove the company's 'value for money'. This inevitably led to a weakening of the collective structure and the need for some alternative.

In relation to 'product', though the company had 'continued to commission and champion women's work of all kinds ... economic conditions force us into a conservative position' (ibid., p. lxxii). The output of this conservative position was the staging of 'safe plays', since programmers were not prepared to take risks in a competitive market. According to Hanna, the reliance on already existing scripts was a response to 'the changing political climate, theatres were beginning to want to read the script of a show before they would book it' (ibid., p. lxvi). Such a situation obviously worked against the devised play script. Notably, the devised 'visual theatre' performance was, at the same time, becoming increasingly supported, a situation not lost on Hanna, who designated the 1980s as 'the decade of style' and 'de-politicised' work (ibid., p. 65). The portfolio of companies such as Monstrous Regiment would not have been considered 'experimental' enough for the performance venue circuit, even if the company had continued to utilise a devising mode of production. Monstrous Regiment lost its funding in 1994, in spite of its new management structure.

The Women's Theatre Group (WTG) provide another example. Like Monstrous Regiment, they began to commission scripts extensively, rather than devise their own. Also like Monstrous Regiment, they began as a collective but by 1989 they too had reorganised into a management team, with a board of directors. More radically, in 1991 they 're-branded' themselves as Sphinx Theatre Company. The company had tried and failed, on numerous occasions, to attract sponsorship. As their administrator in 1990 stated, the WTG 'is not what the sponsors want to fund' (Goodman, 1993, p. 67). Sue Parrish, artistic director of Sphinx, justified this new name:

[a] survey had revealed the company name to be no longer an essential call sign to the radical faithful, but a fossilised slogan turning away audiences, potential and stalwart. Feminism had moved on, and the company needed to forge a new 'take' on the world, and its place in it.[17]

Though the company's focus on supporting women writers remains central to their policy, an element of 'safe' programming is evident in their output. Replicating a trend evidenced across the UK, in the past few years Sphinx have produced, in addition to new plays, a number of adaptations, including Jouho and Juha Turkkas's *Cherished Disappointments in Love* (2001), adapted by Bryony Lavery. Less radical in terms of writing, if not in terms of staging, was a production of Shakespeare's *As You Like It* (2003). Sphinx's recent show is an adaptation by Pam Gems of Hans Christian Anderson's *Little Mermaid* (2004), aimed at audiences of 7 years old and above. It is also to be noted that recently the company has produced only one play a year.

Re-branding and repositioning is not unusual in a competitive art's market. The Black Theatre Co-operative, founded in 1978/79 by Mustapha Matura, was primarily a producer of conventionally scripted plays, such as those by Matura, Farrukh Dhondy and Edgar White. It too has recently changed its name to Nitro, and now markets itself as a producer of black musicals, although its conception of these at least suggests a willingness to experiment with the form: 'Encouraging Black artists working in film, video, music, live art, visual art, fashion, digital media, poetry and rap to join us in expanding the boundaries of Musical Theatre' (Nitro).[18] This move into contemporary musical form might, in fact, in opposition to the trend we have identified, offer further opportunities for a devising process. A recent production, *Catwalk* (2002), was described as 'A story told in a series of monologues with recorded music and sounds mixed live by a DJ; projected video and digital imagery and set in the world of fashion, fabulous costumes and "beautiful people"'.[19] There would appear to be certain similarities here with some of the work covered in Chapter 7. Notably, no playwright is credited; instead, we are told that the 'Text [is] by Malika Booker'. As the work moves away from the production of a conventional 'play script', the process appears to open itself up again to devising practices.

Red Ladder, whilst not changing its name, has nevertheless undergone dramatic shifts in direction. In the 1980s, the company changed from a cooperative to a hierarchically organised structure, complete with an artistic director and board of management. It also changed its focus, making work for young people, and it now describes itself as 'one of Britain's leading new writing companies for youth audiences'.[20] The company no longer devises work, instead commissioning plays from both new and experienced writers, and – along with Sphinx and many other companies – spreads its production costs by entering into collaborations or mounting co-productions with other organisations, such as Manchester's Contact Theatre and the Half Moon Young People's Theatre. A unique development of Red Ladder is its establishment of an Asian Theatre School.

Red Ladder, it would seem, has managed to survive by redirecting its attention towards a specific market. As Chapter 5 will argue, the targeted focus and agendas of the political companies that all but disappeared throughout the 1980s have, to some extent, been redirected into community theatre, where they are more likely to receive some form of subsidy. Given that, initially, political companies were closely tied to what might be thought of as 'political communities', such as striking tenants, this shift is perhaps not so large as we might initially think. The work is less visible because political activity is, generally, less visible. The case of 7:84 Theatre Company (Scotland) is instructive in that, though it now most typically commissions new writing, it also has a 'community' arm, which works with specifically targeted 'communities' for particular projects. It is through this that the process of devising is maintained, with participants frequently contributing to the scripting of a play, as well as performing in it. The Chicago-based About Face Theatre, a gay and lesbian company founded in 1995, is similarly illustrative. Though their programme consists of the presentation of scripted work, their About Face Youth Theatre very specifically devises plays with young people, explaining this with the same rhetoric of empowerment as that employed by companies discussed in the next chapter.

> We believe that engaging youth in the rigorous process of creating and performing an ensemble-based play in a dynamic collaboration with a community of accomplished adult artists encourages youth development and supports youth to become agents for change in their communities.[21]

Shifting Politics

The demise of companies using a collective, devising model in order to make political theatre is also, of course, connected to a general demise of visible, collective political activity. Though trade union figures in the UK continued to rise throughout the 1970s, peaking in 1979 with a total of 55 per cent of all employees belonging to a union (Abercrombie and Warde, 2000, pp. 86–7), it is certainly the case that throughout the later 1970s, socialism became less a primary or even an equal concern in the work of devising groups. The increase in companies representing 'new ideological formations' (Kershaw, 1992, p. 134) was as dramatic as the increase in socialist companies during the first half of the 1970s, rising from about 5 in 1975 to approximately 20 in 1980: 'fifteen women's, two gay and three black' (ibid., p. 139).[22] For Kershaw, this shift in focus from socialist to multiple causes 'led to the ideological fragmentation of the *movement*' (ibid., p. 252). Kershaw perceived that from 1968 to 1975, there was a political (socialist) theatre *movement* in Britain, and that this movement, like any political movement, aimed towards widespread social change. Any 'collective determination' fractured in the face of a more pluralist politics; and a fragmented movement was, arguably, no movement at all.[23]

Another factor impacting on concerted political activity in the UK was the consistent attack on organised union activity. Between 1980 and 1993 the Conservative government introduced eight major acts which 'outlawed the closed shop, curbed picketing ... made all secondary industrial action illegal, imposed the use of secret and postal ballots ... and rendered unions liable to be sued for a wide range of unlawful activities' (Abercrombie and Warde, 2000, p. 85). Thatcher's monetarist policies, which prioritised the free-market economy and led to the privatisation of nationalised industries, inevitably also affected the labour movement, as did the closure of previously heavily unionised industries, including coal mining. By the end of the 1970s, unemployment in the UK had doubled to over 2 million. The failure of the year-long, bitter and difficult miners' strike of 1984 did nothing to instil confidence in the unions (ibid.).

The impact of such a combination of factors can be seen in the falling union membership throughout the last decades of the twentieth century. A Workplace Survey, conducted in 1990, gathered evidence from over 2000 British workplaces and found that 36 per cent of these had not one single union member. Further, 'the proportion of employees who were union members in all the workplaces fell from 58% to 48% between 1984 and 1990' (ibid., p. 90). While 55 per cent of the working population were union members in 1979, by 2000, this had fallen to 30 per cent (ibid., p. 95). Arguably, then, the socialist theatre movement all but disappeared during the 1980s because the socialist movement disappeared.

At the end of the twentieth century and in the early years of the twenty-first century, there is undoubtedly a widespread apathy towards party politics, as reflected in the decreasing election turn-outs across western Europe. Though the 2004 elections in the USA recorded the highest election turnout since 1968 (more than 60% of the population), the fact that 78 million people did not vote remains significant. Within the context of diminishing traditional industry and increasing service industry, alignments between class and political party have weakened dramatically. Further, as cred-ible concepts of a radical left have diminished, it is difficult for any political theatre to find a position with which it might align itself, and it is equally difficult to find a supportive base from which it might issue political challenges. As Peter Dahlgren has written, any 'atmosphere of anti-politics must be understood as the consequence of the inability of the political system to meet social expectations and an absence of an alternative and compelling political vision' (Dahlgren, 2001, p. 67).

However, we must not confuse party political apathy with a lack of politics. The 1990s and beyond have witnessed an upsurge in eco-politics, and massive international demonstrations directed against global capitalism and the continuing oppression and exploitation of 'Third World' countries. Thousands of demonstrators, worldwide, recently took to the streets to protest against the second invasion of Iraq, a war initiated by the USA and the UK in 2003. Not all political activity can be deemed to belong to the typical 'left' either. Recent massive protests in the UK have been against the ban on fox-hunting, causing unexpected alliances between various groups, for example, the rural working class and landowners. Sociologist Anthony Giddens has referred to these political activities as signalling a 'life politics', political engagements outside of the parliamentary system (ibid., p. 68). As Dahlgren suggested,

> [people] are in the process of redefining just what constitutes the political, often within the context of social movements. The boundaries between politics, cultural values, identity processes and local self-reliance measures become fluid; civil and political society become less differentiated from each other. ... This new politics is characterized by personalized rather than collective engagements and a stronger emphasis on single issues than on overarching platforms or ideologies.   (Dahlgren, 2001)

Though the political theatre seeded in the 1970s seems, as Itzin feared, to have 'simply become a chapter in a book' (Itzin, 1980, p. 339), if we take 'life politics' as our identifier then arguably political theatre persists. The docudramas so successfully produced by London's Tricycle Theatre, for example, such as those of the Stephen Lawrence inquiry, *The Colour of Justice* (1999), and the most recent, *Guantanamo: Honor Bound to Defend Freedom* (2004), were indisputably 'political', as was the Chicago-based Tectonic Theatre Project's *The Laramie Project* (2000), a play based on the homophobic, brutal murder of Matthew Shepard in 1998, scripted from interviews conducted by Moisés Kaufman and company members. David Hare's play *The Permanent Way* (2003), produced by Out of Joint (a reincarnation of Joint Stock), took as its foundation transcript materials relating to the state of British transport in light of recent rail accidents, while David Edgar's double-bill, *Continental Divide*, which premiered in Oregon in 2003, was the most broadly political, exploring the attitudes of America's political left and right.

Admittedly, none of this detracts from the plain fact that the practice of devising in the production of a political theatre, however that is designated, remains almost non-existent. One exception is Theatre Workshop in Edinburgh, which became, in 2000, a fully inclusive producing theatre. Robert Rae, director since 1995, has continued to use a devising model to create ostensibly political, contemporary performance. *The Jasmine Road* (2003), for example, a play that addressed both the Palestinian and Israeli conflict and the experiences of refugees in Scotland, was written through the collaboration of the director Rae, the two performers, Nabil Shaban and Marnie Baxter, and the writer Ghazzi Hussein. Credits for an earlier Theatre Workshop production, *D.A.R.E.* (1997), similarly attributed the play-text to Rae and all of the performers. Nabil Shaban, again one of the performers, recalled creating nearly everything his character said in *D.A.R.E.*[24] Theatre Workshop have published a statement that indicates a commitment to this devising process: 'The work we perform is produced at the theatre through a process of devising with our main company. This allows actors, musicians and designers a fuller role in the creative process'.[25] Notably, however, the most recent Theatre Workshop production, *The Threepenny Opera* (2004), has started with an already written text, perhaps signalling a shift in both direction and process similar to that experienced by Graeae over twenty years earlier.

In the early twenty-first century, the theatre market continues to be a market. Even if, as Brown, Brannen and Brown have suggested, subsidy from 1986 to 1998 increased in real terms, such subsidy is nevertheless continually threatened, and the field remains competitive. During this time, an additional 19 companies were awarded revenue funding. The nature of the recipients suggested that there appeared to be an emphasis 'on new work of various kinds, primarily on black and children's theatre' (Brown, Brannen and Brown, 2000, p. 384). Three of the companies who lost their funding during this period, Joint Stock, Monstrous Regiment and Foco Novo (and soon after, Gay Sweatshop), 'may be seen as traditionally political'. However, for Brown et al., given that Graeae, Tara Arts, and Gloria were awarded funding, it would be 'vain to argue that such companies ... are not political', though they may be defined as 'personal/political'. That this may be the case does not, however, explain why Monstrous Regiment, a feminist company, or Gay Sweatshop, a gay company, had their funding withdrawn, since they were also arguably 'personal/ political'. If one were to be more cynical, an alternative analysis of the awards might suggest that the awarding or withdrawal of funding was dependent both on 'quotas', and on what issues or sectors were considered 'hot', 'worthy' or 'needy' at any particular time. According to Barnaby King, by 2000 there were still only four 'black' (African-Caribbean and Asian) professional companies working in the UK (Tara Arts, Tamasha, Temba and Nitro) (King, 2000, p. 28). Arts Council England's own survey for 2001/02 also reported that from a sample of 503 organisations in receipt of regular or fixed-term funding, only four companies from the drama section (from a total of 50) described their work as 'African, Caribbean, Chinese or Asian led'.[26] It is also to be noted that funding in drama for this period decreased by 1 per cent (£2.5 million).

In an environment where funding is dependent on continual appraisal, and can be withdrawn at any time, or where project-funding applications can be refused, there is little encouragement towards experimentation or risk taking, either in production methods or in form and content. An already written script, by an already recognised or 'sponsored' writer (for example, a 'young writer from the Royal Court'), is an altogether more bankable option than an, as yet, literally immaterial script. Further, though funding does exist for devised productions, it tends to be channelled into community-devised projects or 'cross-art-form', 'experimental' performances. In all cases, where a company has to rely on project funding – and this is the most typical source – collective organisation remains extremely difficult, as companies cannot be guaranteed an income from one project to another, having to continually reapply for funding for each project. As this chapter has shown, devising processes are arrived at through experience, and the garnering of experience takes time. Project funding does not permit companies to consolidate their experience or their practices.

Post-script

Though the organisation of this book suggests clearly defined categories, the practices themselves do not obey the imposed rules of such neat divisions. In spite of any such divisions implied by critics' methodologies, including this one, there are in fact many crossovers between oft-separated practices, and a substantial sharing of people, space, and form. The work undertaken by Albert Hunt and his students at Bradford College of Art is instructive in its clear merging of the aesthetic avant-garde and the explicitly political. Alongside the Festival of Chance, explored in the previous chapter, students could participate in 'The Strike Game', itself a follow-on from the 'Vietnam War Game'.

> We shall pretend that we are involved in an industrial enterprise which has labour troubles. A crisis will be invented, which will lead to an unofficial strike. There will be teams representing the strikers, the official Trades Unions, the management and the Government. We shall also need people to run a daily newssheet, and a broadcasting service. (Hunt, 1978, p. 182)[27]

Hunt, John Fox and their students also created an environment to accompany CAST's performance of *Harold Muggins is a Martyr* (1968), itself a collaboration with playwrights John Arden and Margaretta d'Arcy.[28] The San Francisco Mime Troupe's early performance explorations included a foray into Happenings, and one 'helper' at these was Ken Dewey, who would later stage the notorious Happening in Edinburgh (Davis, 1975a, p. 20).[29]

Perhaps more problematically, the focus of this chapter – the use of devising in the creation of political theatre – suggests that work discussed in other chapters is not, therefore, political. It is, of course, impossible to ignore the political intent of The Living Theatre's work of the 1960s, or indeed the work of Stalker or DV8. A liberal position would also suggest that all theatre is political: 'even the silliest farce or most innocuous musical will reflect some ideology, usually that of the Establishment. In this sense, all theatre is political' (Patterson, 2003, p. 3). Typically, theatre may be divided into alternative theatre – understood as a cultural movement rather than a sector of the theatre industry (Kershaw, 1992) – which is explicit in its political agenda, and theatre that ideologically (even if inadvertently) supports the status quo. This division assumes that political theatre must be explicit in its aims. Though such a certainty might have been possible in a cultural context in which there was a shared understanding of what constituted oppositional political activity, or even some sense of the existence of a shared oppositional culture, contemporary times – multinational capitalism, globalisation, postmodernity – make concepts of the 'political', 'political activity' and 'political opposition' contested. The pluralist 'politics of postmodernism', for example, would resist promoting the idea of a 'single' political solution, such as Socialism.

Much existing devised 'visual performance', defined by Baz Kershaw as 'neo-expressionist', does not appear to be explicitly political when held beside the 'political devised theatre' arising throughout the 1960s and 1970s, or the feminist, gay or black theatre of the 1980s. However, many contemporary practitioners would in fact insist upon the politically intended nature of their work, in spite of (or indeed because of) the fact that its 'ideological orientations were opaque or even invisible' (Kershaw, 1992, p. 178). Is a visible ideological orientation of a work necessary for it to be perceived as 'political'? The context and potential politics of other contemporary devised performances will be further discussed in Chapter 7.

Conclusion

As this chapter has argued, the political devising companies that proliferated during the late 1960s and early 1970s were very much of that time; their means of production were aligned to their political ideologies and aspirations, and in most cases this led initially to a collective devising process. As the political and economic context changed, alongside the aims of the companies, so too did the organisational structure, and therefore the creative processes. As the devised plays moved further towards more traditional play scripts, the collective devising process diminished. Similarly, when the organisational structures shifted towards more conventional models of production, the opportunities for collective devising processes also lessened. Finally, as explicit and visible political activity decreased, along with any sense of a political socialist movement and a related political theatre movement, the explicitly political content of devised plays also became negligible. From this, one might argue that political theatre companies who forged devising processes were only ever politically reactive, arising from the given, politically favourable, conditions of the late 1960s and early 1970s. Though feminist, gay or black political theatre endured throughout the mid-1980s, by the 1990s this too had become threatened by economic pressures, and also by challenges to ideas of fixed and knowable 'communities' and 'identity' politics. Where the companies of the 1980s might, for example, argue for 'gay rights', in the 1990s the term 'gay', and our assumptions of what that meant, would itself be taken as the ground to be challenged.

In 2004, there appears to be a dearth of politically devised theatre that is distinct from 'community theatre'. There remain, however, some hopeful examples, such as a recently formed Scottish company, Reader. Committed to a model of 'shared authorship through processes of collaboration',[30] Reader's recent work-in-progress, *Songs from the Burning Bed: Selected Songs* (2004), shied clear of constructing a 'play', and instead used a cabaret structure, presenting humorous 'sketches' that involved a great deal of audience collaboration, a device that served to provide a unifying non-textual frame. We would argue that this structure lent itself more readily to 'shared authorship' than the construction of a more 'traditional' play script. Throughout the performance, the group mined a contemporary political vein, raising into public view a number of troubling contemporary social events, including the imprisonment of terrorist suspects without trial or formal charges. Reader's form was almost a hybrid-hybrid, blending the implicitly hybrid practice of 'live art' or 'performance theatre' with an unusually blatant nod towards political injustices and oppressions. Perhaps Reader is the CAST of the twenty-first century; and perhaps, in spite of the forty-year gap, it is not that far removed from its predecessors.

5 Devising and Communities

Devising emerged as a core feature and methodology within the burgeoning field of community arts in the 1960s. The passions, ideology and contradictions of the emergent community arts movement produced a distinctive set of devising strategies, and the movement itself was informed by the possibilities of devising. This chapter examines the relationship and distinction between community arts and the politically-activist companies discussed in Chapter 4. The evolution of radical pedagogy in the mid-century underpinned the emergence of Theatre-in-Education, which championed participation in the processes of devising. The political, social or personal benefits arising from involvement in devising processes for unskilled participants has remained a central debate within the field of community arts throughout the period we look at here.

Devising and Community Arts

Early on, devising within community arts was closely allied to the more political, alternative theatre discussed in the previous chapter. Many of the British companies considered in Chapter 4 were also part of The Association of Community Theatres (TACT), established in 1973, which envisaged community theatre 'as part of the larger class struggle and as a means of changing dominant concepts of culture' (Itzin, 1980, p. 176). Baz Kershaw has argued for community theatre to be viewed as part of the alternative theatre movement, which saw theatre as more than simply cultural intervention, seeing it as a way to oppose and change mainstream politics (Kershaw, 1992). Certainly, early community arts were part of a movement towards the 'democratization of culture' and a desire to reach different audiences from those the existing commercial theatre attracted (Giesekam, 2000). Drawing on the principles of the Workers' Theatre Movement of the 1920s and 1930s, and the Federal Theatre Project, the widespread re-politicisation of the arts world in the late 1950s and 1960s produced a new wave of practitioners and educationalists who envisaged a liberation politics and a liberational art (see Chapter 4). Devising appealed as part of this agenda because of its 'democratic' process – an apparent equality of participation in the production of theatre – and because of the need to deal with topics of immediate relevance to community audiences rarely addressed by existing, written plays.

Who the 'communities' of community arts were and how they have been defined and imagined has shifted fundamentally over the last forty years. In the 1950s and 1960s 'community' was most often viewed as a static, utopian ideal of neighbourliness and locality, and its absence was mourned. The mediatisation of national and global concerns through the increased visibility of television and the overflow of infor-mation in the face of which the individual seemed powerless, as McLuhan identified in *War and Peace in the Global Village* (1968), prompted a backlash of desire for the local and for 'authentic experi-ence'. Anthropologists such as Victor Turner were happy to oblige with studies of small-scale groups in 'Third World' contexts, and offered romantic views of tribal or village communities who experi-enced 'spontaneous communitas' (Turner, 1972, p. 1100). In Amer-ica, Paul Goodman's influential *Growing Up Absurd* (1960) berated schools and social institutions for 'The Missing Community'. How-ever, there was a competing idea of community that had influenced the working-class, socialist theatre movements since the 1930s; a dynamic understanding of the formation of class-consciousness which offered an alternative and dynamic model of community-conscious-ness. As E. P. Thompson, an historian of the British working class, pointed out, class was not a structure nor a category 'but something which in fact happens in human relationships' (Thompson, 1963, preface). David Watt argued that the same is true of a community:

> the interactions within a group of people who choose to see themselves as a community continually alter the nature of that community, so that it is always in a state of 'becoming', and therefore, growing, and thus avoids the stasis of a 'thing' to be serviced.   (Watt, 1991, p. 61)

Paulo Freire's notion of 'conscientization', widely circulated in the 1970s, articulated this principle clearly – that communities of interest, rather than locality, can be forged. During the late 1970s and early 1980s the idea of community as 'a set of shared social meanings which are constantly created and mutated through the actions and interactions of its members, and through their interaction with wider society', implied that the activity of community intervention could be very powerful (Kelly, 1984, p. 50).

This active model of community being forged through action and interaction led to an increased concern with the participation of communities in the making of an artwork. Indeed, for Naseem Khan, the defining characteristic of community theatre was participation (Khan, 1980). And the use of devising strategies might seem a natural mode for achieving community participation and animation. For Eugene van Erven such work first started to evolve in South America, where devising or the collaborative creation of theatre with a community was the essence of the South and Latin American tradition of *creación colectiva* (van Erven, 2001). This mode of working emerged from experimental popular theatre groups all over South and Latin America during the 1950s and 1960s. Liberation politics underpinned the work of groups as diverse as Enrique Buenaventura and Cáli Experimental Theatre (TEC) from the 1950s, Santiago García's collective La Candalaria (founded in Bogotá, Columbia, 1957), and the Cuban Teatro Escambray (1968).[1] Although diverse modes of working evolved, the component principles of the work were:

> music, carefully researched themes that correspond to the interests and cultures of the people they perform for, simple but flexible production techniques that can be adapted to all kinds of indoor and outdoor venues, and lengthy creative development processes ... [and] a new kind of actor, one who is not someone's servile employee but, instead, a self-conscious socially responsible co-owner of the means of creative production. (van Erven, 2001, p. 138)

The better known companies from that period tended to be professional companies touring with collectively devised, popular, political shows. However, they inspired and left behind the principles for community theatre groups in many areas, who 'concocted their own versions of the collective creation process to dramatize their local stories' (van Erven, 2001, p. 139). Such work was a physical expression of a Freirean pedagogy:

> As a form of deliberate and systematic action, all cultural action has its theory which determines its ends and thereby defines its methods. Cultural

action either serves domination (consciously or unconsciously) or it serves liberation. (Freire, 1989, p. 180)

Theatre festivals and workshops across the continent were one way of disseminating the modes of performance, and Freirean pedagogy was circulated through journals and workshops in educational circles far beyond South America.

However, while the roots of community-based work lay in politicised and oppositional activity, the rise of community arts in America, Britain and Australia was largely underpinned by government funding, through Arts Councils and other national funding agencies. Indeed, Gay Hawkins, in a survey of the community arts movement in Australia, argued that the term 'community arts':

> had no real currency in Australia until it was invoked in Commonwealth cultural policy in the early 1970s. As difficult as it may be for many community artists to accept, community arts are an official invention. (Hawkins, 1991, p. 45)

That the state should support work that was oppositional or politicised might seem surprising. However, the way in which government agencies perceived the role of community arts differed somewhat from the role that the more alternative, or counter-cultural, workers in community-based activity saw for themselves.

The 1974 Baldry Report (UK), which set out to investigate the work of community artists, did not regard them as essentially 'alternative' or 'oppositional':

> their primary concern is their impact on a community and their relationship with it: by assisting those with whom they make contact to become more aware of their situation and of their own creative powers, and by providing them with the facilities they need to make use of their abilities, they hope to widen and deepen the sensibilities of the community in which they work and so enrich its existence. To a varying degree they see this as a means of change, whether psychological, social or political, within the community. (Kelly, 1984, p. 16)

This improving, but limited, definition of community arts was to earn the sector government funding, since the idea of any change was firmly to be contained 'within the community' itself and not to impinge on larger political or social realities. In the UK large proportions of predominantly working-class communities had been dispersed from 'slums' to new estates of tower blocks during the 1950s, and the provision of improving cultural activity for community-building on these housing estates was perceived by some government agencies as a panacea for local unrest. A similar activity accompanied 'urban renewal' in American inner-cities during the 1960s and 1970s. To view the actions of local government most cynically, local communities were also constituencies. However, despite the state's best intentions there was much crossover between the personnel, groups and aesthetics of the 'alternative' groups of the 1960s and 1970s and the community-based practices of early community theatre groups.

In Australia, another kind of collaboration between oppositional principles and the Establishment was evident in the birth of community theatre – in the relationship between theatre companies and the universities. Two universities were crucial in the evolution of community theatre in Australia. First, the School of Drama in the Victorian College of the Arts in Melbourne, established in 1976. Although it was conceived as a drama school to challenge the dominance of the Sydney-based National Institute of Dramatic Arts (NIDA), Peter Oyston, who headed its programme, set out to train a more resourceful performer or theatre worker, and formed the students into small theatre companies. Part of the degree course was designed to train 'animateurs', 'primary creators who could make new theatre works of various kinds in various conditions ... and be in a position to find their own audiences' (Milne, 2004, p. 161). Companies which emerged from this programme included the Murray River Performing Group, WEST Theatre Company and Theatre-Works. A similar style of programme was established in the newly created Deakin University further south in Geelong, Victoria, in 1978. James McCaughey was both head of the drama programme and artistic director of a community-orientated theatre company, the Mill Community Theatre Company. Rose Myers, now director of Arena Theatre, was a graduate of the programme.

It was a very interesting model. The company would be working on a project, whether it was a community-based project that was something to do with Geelong's history (although they also did texts as well), and the students from the three years would be working on that same material with them at the same time. There was a big community workshop programme component of any development of work and a community theatre night-time project [Mill Night for adults, on Thursday nights]. ... There was a real surge in the community theatre movement right across the country and there were a lot of regionally-based companies. ... That's all died off.   (Myers)[2]

Companies who devised work for communities include WEST Theatre Company (Melbourne), Sidetrack (Sydney), Death Defying Theatre, now Urban Theatre Projects (Brisbane/Sydney), Doppio Teatro, now Parallelo (Adelaide), Zeal Theatre (Newcastle), Back to Back Theatre (Geelong), Street Arts Theatre (Melbourne), Junction (Torrensville) and Melbourne Workers' Theatre. These groups shared practices, collaborated and generated the sense of themselves as part of a coherent movement of community theatre through a series of national conferences held in the 1980s in Adelaide, Geelong and Marrickville, Sydney.

American theatre companies who use devising in making performances for specific communities, or who use devising as a tool for making performance with communities, are numerous. This chapter might consider the work of The ProVisional Theatre (LA), Soul and Latin Theatre (East Harlem), Living Stage (Washington), Cornerstone (LA), Roadside Theatre (Whitesburg), Dakota Theatre Caravan (South Dakota), Teatro de la Realidad (LA), Teatro de la Esperanza (San Francisco), Wagonburner Theatre Troupe (Native America), Carpetbag Theatre (Knoxville, Tennessee), or the United Mime Workers political mime (Champaign, Illinois). Jan Cohen-Cruz argued that community-based arts in America developed their current form in the mid-1970s when the national protest movements were waning. For her, community arts emerged 'with a heightened consciousness to think globally but act locally, activist art practitioners looked to local contexts in which their work could play a role'.[3] A key marker she noted was the founding in 1976 of a coalition of community theatres as Alternate ROOTS (Regional Organisation Of Theatres South). This coalition included the Free Southern Theatre (founded 1963), which had been a leading black theatre of the South during the Civil Rights Movement, but which redefined its commitment to a broader programme of supporting communities of place, tradition and spirit and became Junebug Productions.[4] In many ways the history of Junebug echoes the history of devising companies more broadly, as politically activist groups from the 1950s and 1960s began to transpose their devising practices into community-based and community-focused work during the late 1970s and 1980s.

Devising Practices and Community Theatre

A very diverse range of devising practices has been used within community arts over the last forty years. In order to map out such diversity we might consider four spectra along which a company's practice may lie: the level of involvement of theatre professionals; the level of participation of community members; the relative importance of process or product; and the political impetus of the work, from radical to supportive of the status quo.

Many of the earliest companies who devised within community arts, particularly in the UK and US, were professional acting groups, and lay at one end of the spectrum of professional involvement. Professional actors generated a performance from local stories or histories and performed it for a geographically-defined community within a theatre building. Peter Cheeseman's documentary dramas at the Victoria Theatre, Stoke-on-Trent (1962, UK), were early examples of this. Theatre-in-Education, which also evolved in the mid-1960s, was usually sponsored by regional theatres or educational authorities and was driven by the same principles, offering professionally devised performances for specific communities within an educational setting. Ann Jellicoe's significant work with community plays lies at a midpoint on this spectrum of professional involvement. Jellicoe's work was not devised but used plays written by professional playwrights from local history; however, the plays were produced and performed by community members rather than professional actors.[5] At the other end of the spectrum lies work generated from within the community itself without professional initiation, such as Helen Crummy's leadership of the Craigmillar Festival Society (Edinburgh), which became an inspirational model for many other deprived communities who wanted to produce economic and social change through arts activity.[6]

A counterpoint to the level of professional involvement is the extent to which communities participate in devising processes. This raises complex questions about the kind of devising strategies used within community arts and the value and function of that devising. Participation, in community terms, is different from either actor-centred devising (Chapter 2) or politically activist work (Chapter 4). It is far less prescriptive, and more diverse, than the action-defined audience participation of The Living Theatre's love-heap in *Paradise Now* or Pip Simmons Group's slave auction in *The George Jackson Black and White Minstrel Show*, CAST's Muggins plays or Albert Hunt's Russian Revolution project. Within community arts, devising participants might be offered a range of roles: as source and resource material, hence the popularity of the storytelling-based work of Junebug (US) or Roadside (US); as performers in pre-existing scripts evolved from community research, as in Ann Jellicoe's (UK) or Cornerstone's work (US); as co-devisors, as in SALT's short-lived experiment (US) or Icy Tea's experience (Inala Community Theatre, Australia); or as participants in a therapeutic process, as in the Living Stage's recent work with teen mothers (US), or Geese Theatre's workshops with offenders (US/UK).

A third axis of community work concerns the relative importance of the performance product and process, and the relationship between the two. At one extreme might lie highly-technical, professionally devised performance for communities, such as Arena Theatre's (Australia) recent Anthropop trilogy and *Eat Your Young*, discussed below, which toured festivals and large-scale community events. At the other end of this spectrum would lie some of the work of the Prof. Dogg Troupe of Inter-Action (UK), which sought only to facilitate creative play and improvisation among participants, without any interest in a resultant production. Over the last forty years the pressures on community workers at both ends of this spectrum have grown. For community theatre companies who devise performances for community audiences, the pressure from funders to provide a professional quality performance sometimes militates against interactive or open performance structures, appropriate to the context. At the other end of the spectrum, lies the idea that the *process* of participation in the making of the work, not the product itself, has a positive impact on participants to bring about change: social, political or, most often these days, personal. Hence a plethora of work with specific client groups which offers participation in devising and improvisation as a form of personal intervention, seeking to change personal behaviour, as in much recent Boalean work based on Moreno's psychodrama. Funders of this kind of interventionist community art increasingly wish to see concrete evidence of ameliorative changes in participants. It can be difficult to assess sometimes whether this change leads the community or individual to resist the status quo or to conform more effectively to mainstream demands.

The fourth spectrum is the level of political input into the devising process. Over the years, many of the explicitly political devising groups considered in Chapter 4 have turned to or incorporated community-based work within their portfolio, one example amongst many being 7:84 (Scotland). Although devising has often been presented as an inherently oppositional activity, because it directly involves untrained participants in artistic endeavours, it does not follow that either the devising process or the devised product in a community context is *always* politically explicit. Many theatre workers, while seeing themselves as left-wing, do not expound a direct, explicit, party political stance in their work. Rose Myers, director of Arena Theatre, Melbourne, articulated the difference as she saw it:

> If you talk to Melbourne Worker's Theatre (a politically left, socialist group) in the end as individuals they probably are [socialist]. But it's the grey areas that are more fascinating to us. Say we've got a fascist premier or rightwing government. Their company take might be 'The government is oppressing us'; our take is, 'What's attracting people at this point in time to vote for that government?' What does it say to us about the human condition?[7]

However, this is not to imply that the content of Arena's shows is apolitical. *Eat Your Young* explored the long-term incarceration of young offenders:

> What does it say about our humanity when we decide to segregate young people in this way and our main interest in them is how we can have an economically rational model? The politics of the art makers has to come into the equation because they are engaged in the work so heavily. But for me the starting point among the team has to be what we are interested in exploring, rather than statements we want to make.   (Myers)

Arena Theatre tends to devise performance *for* a community of young people, rather than devising *with* young people. Likewise, Sara Brady's critique of Cornerstone Theatre and Touchstone Theatre's collaboration, *Steelbound* (USA), a performance scripted from interviews and performed by former workers of the Bethlehem Steel foundry in the steel plant, argued that personal testimony and documentary theatre may not produce radical theatre – the production did not tackle the steel company's greed or racial discrimination (Brady, 2000). Jan Cohen-Cruz concurred that had Touchstone Theatre's involvement stopped there the project would not have appeared radical, but the group went on to produce 'a collective creation, *Never Done*, focusing on women and people of colour in Bethlehem in the 'forties, and taking on discrimination' (Cohen-Cruz, 2000, p. 378). Though the collectively created work was the more explicitly political in its comment in this instance, it is by no means universally true that devising *with* a community necessarily produces more politically explicit material.

Often community artists feel that collaboration with a community group must accommodate the diversity and internal conflicts of that community, which may militate against a clear political comment.

Alternatively, some community artists have felt that the purpose of working with a community is to celebrate and reaffirm its significance or history, in which case critical counter-narratives or difficult topics may be repressed or ignored. In 1984, WEST Community Theatre, Melbourne, undertook a project with Vietnamese refugees. Work with this community group was in itself a political act, given the right-wing media's scare-mongering attitude to the influx of refugees at the time. However, the facilitators discovered that 'skills training and a substantial amount of group devising' led to the evolution of *The Vietnamese*, a dramatisation of the journey and resettlement of this community, which blamed the exodus of the refugees squarely on the 'communist' invasion. Any analysis of the complexity of the Vietnamese situation, and the American inflammation of the conflict, which had been the source of such protest fifteen years earlier, was absent (Watt, 1992, p. 12).

Having marked out some of the central issues in the use of devising in community contexts, the rest of this chapter develops a close look at the processes of a variety of representative theatre companies. First, we look at the rise of Theatre-in-Education, which identified a very specific community audience and began to experiment with a variety of devising strategies within the formal constraints of educational institutions. We then go on to look at the two leading, but very different, strands of devising work with communities: that done *for* communities by professional groups, and that done *with* communities, by members of the communities themselves.

Devising and the Genesis of Theatre-in-Education

The rise of Theatre-in-Education (TIE) in the 1960s was not surprising as, in part, the rhetoric asserting the positive value of the expressive arts that underpinned the community arts movement was closely linked to changes in pedagogic practice that had developed in the schools of post-war Britain and America. Not only had the 1944 Education Act in the UK introduced compulsory and free education for all, it had sharpened the significance of educational theory. In the pre-war years, drama had fought for a place in the curriculum, suggesting itself either as cultural improvement, or as a mode of 'child-centred' progressive learning through which to teach other subjects. Theories of child development changed over the mid-century and the role of 'play' in the creative development of an individual became a key concept, as we explored in Chapter 2. There had been an explosion of interest in behaviourism, child development and personality studies, made accessible by writers like Abraham Maslow (*Motivation and Personality*, 1954), Carl Rogers (*On Becoming a Person*, 1961) or Paul Goodman (*Growing Up Absurd*, 1960).[8] It was out of this concern for 'play' and its value as pedagogy that the Theatre-in-Education (UK and Australia) or educational theatre (US) groups emerged. The echoes of this approach are clear in the aims of the first British Theatre-in-Education group, from the Belgrade Theatre in Coventry (1965), which were:

> to explore the values of drama in the development of the child's personality, to experiment in teaching methods using drama and theatre techniques, and to stimulate an interest in theatre in adult life.   (Coult, 1980, p. 78)[9]

The relatively conservative nature of this language – a return to the idea of building an audience of the future and an exposure to improving cultural activity – belies the aspirations of many community theatre workers and TIE groups. They actually shared much with alternative theatre, notably a challenge to mainstream conservative values, a concentration on the *process* of production rather than just the product, and a desire to connect with the audience that translated into the language of empowerment and participation. Paradoxically, at their inception in the UK, the Theatre-in-Education groups were established by 'the state education system and the predominantly middle-class repertory theatre' (Coult, 1980, p. 76), everything that was anathema to the claimed ethos of the alternative theatres.

The Belgrade Theatre in Coventry was a first in several ways, not least in that it was the first new theatre built after the Second World War, in 1958. From the start, the theatre had attempted to forge links with the surrounding community, including taking a performance out to schools and running youth theatre clubs. In 1964 Gordon Vallins, appointed to reinvigorate the educational programme, developed a vision of diverse community liaison for the theatre. In the event, the scheme was scaled down to a team of four actor/teachers who dubbed themselves a Theatre-in-Education (TIE) team. Rather than a play, the team produced a programme 'of activities, usually devised and researched by the company ... presented in school by the company and involving the children directly in an experience of the situations and problems that the topic throws up' (Jackson, 1993, p. 4). Since the object of the TIE work was to experiment with teaching methods and to connect with theories of developmental play, pre-existing play-texts were not suitable. As David Pammenter noted:

> the TIE movement during its short history has had to rely almost entirely on its practitioners for its material. Its whole history has been one of self-devised work either with or without writers ... [although] the devising process has differed much from company to company.   (Pammenter, 1993, p. 53)

Maggie Steed, an actress with Belgrade TIE, remembered the passionate involvement of the actor/teachers in this devising work:

> We had to work out what the aim of the piece was, what sort of narrative the piece would need, and what were the conflicts that would best serve its aim. We'd go off and write our own scenes or improvise. We were completely thrown in the deep end. It was difficult but exciting. ... Our performing style – if there was a style at Coventry – was very full bloodied, and we sang and did all sorts of different things. Naturalism was a dirty word.   (Chambers and Steed, 2004, pp. 193–4)

One early programme, *Pow Wow* (1973), gives a flavour of the results. One class-group of children had to first

> identify and develop a relationship with a racist, acquisitive cowboy who runs his own Wild West show and later with an Indian who tells a different story about the demise of the Indian tribes in the face of the white man and his technology. At one point the children have to decide whether or not to free the Indian from his cage.   (Pammenter, 1993, p. 65)

Most of the topics chosen involved moral and social choices and demanded some political and economic education, as in Belgrade TIE's shows *The Car Makers* (1971) or *The Price of Coal* (1977), or Bolton TIE's *Poverty Knocks* (1973).[10]

Other TIE groups were quickly established between 1968 and 1970 at regional theatres, often peopled by alumni from the Coventry experiment: in Bolton, Leeds, Glasgow, Greenwich and Edinburgh; Nottingham and Peterborough followed in 1973, and Lancaster in 1975 (Jackson, 1993, p. 18). Crucially, these companies were funded by the Local Education Authority (indeed the Inner London Education Authority set up its own TIE company, Cockpit, unconnected to a theatre), and also had access to Arts Council funding (particularly after the establishment of a separate, fund-distributing Committee for Young People's Theatre 1966, inspired by the Belgrade example), in order that schools should not have to pay for the service. The extent to which these companies straddled both mainstream and alternative camps was evidenced by the heated debates that characterised the conferences the groups held. In 1975 there were so many TIE groups that the Standing Conference of Young People's Theatre (SCYPT) was formed, where:

> Marxist analyses of social processes, and the educational philosophies of Ivan Illich, John Holt and Paulo Freire generated not only heated debate about the need for 'alternative' approaches within the state [education] system but also a vital atmosphere of experiment with form, with ways of engaging children actively in their own learning.   (Jackson, 1993, p. 24)

Maggie Steed, who later went to work with the socialist theatre company Belt and Braces, recalled 'a lot of argument, a lot of blood spilt, a lot about the wrong ways to do things, and the right ways to do things, but it was very lively' (Chambers and Steed, 2004, p. 195). Such political arguments extended not only to content and the process of making work through devising, perceived as more egalitarian, but also to the organisation of the companies themselves, many of which were configured as collectives.

In Australia, John O'Toole and Penny Bundy argued that while British imports of Theatre-in-Education arrived in the 1970s and were a part of the officially funded programmes of several States' educational provision, there was an ongoing suspicion of the cultural colonialism that they also implied. Companies such as Derek Nicholson's Pageant Theatre (NSW), and Melbourne Theatre Company, were touring schools with theatre programmes around 1970–2; but, as Barbara Manning of Salamanca Theatre in Tasmania (1976) identified, more participatory work like her own grew out of visits to TIE companies in the UK (Fotheringham, 1992, p. 42). Some critics suggested that when funding for participatory Theatre-in-Education was widely cut in the 1980s few in the theatre or education communities mourned its passing. Whereas most early British TIE shows were devised, many Australian TIE shows were written, and small-scale participatory programmes had been very difficult to implement (O'Toole and Bundy, 1993, p. 138). Today in America, the UK and Australia the kind of participatory, small-scale Theatre-in-Education work has become something of a rarity, following the demise of subsidy and the resulting economic burden placed on schools. However, for Anthony Haddon of community theatre Blah, Blah, Blah

(1985, Leeds), new possibilities of participatory drama in schools have been made possible by recent, admittedly limited, funding for Education Achievement Zones in the UK.[11]

Devising *for* Communities

Emerging in the early 1960s out of the same desire to resist establishment practices that had driven the aesthetic revolutions of alternative theatre, and inspired by a socialist enthusiasm for reformulating opposition from the 'grassroots' up, the search for a 'community' of resistance was powerful. Joan Littlewood's commitment to the locality of Stratford East extended beyond making theatre herself, to the proposal of a Fun Palace as a community resource where the *community* would create beyond the confines of theatre, becoming involved in the 'therapy of theatre' (Littlewood, 1995, p. 706). The Fun Palace was never funded, perhaps not surprisingly, and Littlewood continued her work with the disillusioned youth of the area in other ways. However, paradoxically, some of the most significant community theatre initiatives emerged not from the alternative theatre companies of the 1960s' counter-cultures, but from the mainstream regional theatres.

When Peter Cheeseman established the Victoria Theatre, Stoke-on-Trent, in October 1962, not only was it the first 'theatre-in-the-round' but it also initiated a new style of community-centred work. Cheeseman evolved a mode of documentary drama drawn from local stories and history, where the work was entirely controlled, created and performed by the actors and the director. Initially evolved in 1964 when the resident dramatist, Alan Ayckbourn, was unavailable, it was described by Cheeseman thus:

> the plays are constructed from primary source material gathered during a preliminary research period and then rehearsed collectively by researchers, consisting of the resident dramatist, [Cheeseman] and the company in committee. They are then created on the floor at rehearsal.   (Cheeseman, 1971a, p. 79)[12]

Cheesman described a more radical impetus than the pragmatic absence of a playwright in his search

> to begin to bridge the cultural gap which separates the artist from the majority of the community and which I believe to be a gap created by style

> not subject matter ... [the company developed] a popular language, a
> style of our own which would make theatre livelier and more attractive than
> the current play format.   (Cheeseman, 1971b, p. 86)

The documentaries that emerged from this process were episodic,
with a diffuse structure usually linked by songs and music. The
costumes and set were simple, to accommodate the multiple locations
and the many roles each actor needed to play. In *The Jolly Potters*
(1964), about working conditions and 1842 Chartist riots, 'the
method employed ... involved the whole company in an immense
amount of research; the end product was a play in which almost every
word spoken was taken directly from historical records' (Bradby
and McCormick, 1978, p. 143). Other local historical topics were
tackled, notably in *The Knotty* (1966), about the birth and dis-
appearance of local railways and their absorption into the London,
Midland and Scottish Railway Company. The historical topic chosen
was never without relevance to the contemporary moment for the
local community:

> when [*The Knotty*] was produced the town of Stoke was being threatened
> with absorption into a larger administrative area, which would have
> lessened its independence and destroyed part of its character. This
> documentary, by establishing a parallel between the history of the railways
> and the current situation, led to a protest against the government proposals
> which as a result, were not implemented.   (Bradby and McCormick, 1978)

Not dissimilar to the Living Newspaper in style, but not so radical in
content, such documentary theatre was addressed *to* the community,
alongside the more traditional offerings of the repertory theatre, and
it was a style of working that was to become popular with other
regional theatres around the country.

However, Cheeseman's documentaries did not involve audience
participation. The only place where the Victoria Theatre did develop
audience participation was in the children's work, based on plays by
Brian Way. Even here Jim Lagden pointed out that the workshops
failed to reach more than middle-class children, who were required
to 'acquiesce in the making of what are already scripted decisions'.
A more exciting alternative, Lagden noted, was that initiated by a
group of local graduates from Keele University who were

> attempting to develop entertainment structures from Grotowski exercises.
> Used with groups of working-class children as a way to launch them into

genuine improvisation with no element of pre-conceived script, this has produced an exciting response in free invention and decision-making. (Lagden, 1971, p. 85)

The participatory performances involving children developed by Theatre-In-Education, which was emerging at about the same time as Cheeseman's documentaries, were far more radical in their view of audience involvement and were to be influential in the development of more participatory modes of devising, discussed below.

Devising performances from local research and issues to be performed by professionals in community venues also characterised the work of the Murray River Performing Group (Australia, 1979). A small group of four performers and three behind-the-scenes workers devised their shows collaboratively, or commissioned a writer to work with them. The first production was *A Big Hand for the Limbs*, which toured extensively in the region to publicly-accessible spaces like parks, community halls and pubs. The group had a changing membership and adopted a variety of styles:

Our community is our inspiration and provides the source of much of our work ... if you're writing a play that draws on the underlying cares and aspirations of people and that involves their kids, there is a tremendous responsibility to get it right and do it well.   (Milne, 2004, p. 211)

As an off-shoot of this group, a children's community circus developed, the Flying Fruit Fly Circus, which continued an Australian interest in physically devised performance discussed in Chapter 6. For both the children's circus and the Murray River Performing Group, devising was a means of generating relevant material more freely, and providing social and political commentary for the local community.

This kind of work was also pursued by one of the longest-lasting community theatre/youth theatre companies in Australia, Arena. In 1966, inspired by British Theatre-in-Education groups, an amateur group called the Toorak Players toured Melbourne primary schools with two shows. A commitment to Australian material meant that the company performed specifically written plays alongside devised performance. Arena briefly evolved into two companies in the boom period of the mid-1970s. The current artistic director, Rose Myers, arrived in 1994, with a commitment to using the full multi-media resources of theatre in the company's devising process, to produce 'new contemporary work that is a genuine force in the contemporary world ... defined by its engagement with interdisciplinary work or in contemporary pop-culture, rather than what age range is aimed for'.[13] The devising processes that Myers uses at Arena have developed over time, and differ depending on whether the company is producing the small-scale classroom-size project, such as *Oblong*, a recent piece for 3–8-year-olds about collectables, marketing and friendship, or their larger, more spectacular festival work. The process for the large-scale interdisciplinary work remains collaborative and based in devised cooperation:

> We do the research phase, probably myself and a writer, and then take the work into a development phase, where we have all the palette of artists that are going to work on the project; be that the filmmaker, the composer, a designer, the writer, myself and the actors. We'll workshop that material and we'll aim to come out of that development process with the structure of the work. It's usually at that point that the text becomes a solid document – this process is supposed to be a springboard, the writer's role isn't just to be a documenter ... but might take the workshop to new places that are a little bit more refined.   (Myers)

Eat Your Young was an examination of the privatisation of social services for children, and the way in which young people were treated in custody. The panopticon of contemporary surveillance was signalled by two huge circular screens with which the young people of the story interacted, an effect that added to the futuristic setting of the piece, although its concerns were contemporary. The generation of material for the performance came from research the company undertook, and was then workshopped for two to three weeks to develop the material. While the context of performance-making is different from the 'poor' theatre of the 1960s or the physical theatre troupes of the 1990s, the central work of the actors in devising is similar in many ways:

> Our process to have four actors on the floor for an eight-hour day, it's almost too much. ... If you do a week often by the end they're flagging. But some great work comes out of it too, when people are tired. I like to see what happens when people play a scene way beyond its natural end because good things come out of that too – at times. I'd rather break devising into two half weeks, with a good slab of time to process what happened on the floor.   (Myers)

The concentrated stretches in the studio, the moments of editing and reflection, the 'recognition' of good moments share much with the actor-centred companies discussed in Chapter 2. However, in the context of the 2000s, the actors who devise the work are unlikely to perform it, as the production process for the large-scale projects can take up to two years. The company uses a core of skilled devisers, but often casts actors from more traditional backgrounds to tour the work.

Since the late 1980s the company has attempted to integrate young people into the devising in different ways. Arena tests its work against different audiences throughout the process of the project, in ways that resemble some of the projects which devise *with* their communities:

> *Eat Your Young* had a two-day development with some artists throwing ideas around, some possible multimedia, and then a presentation to a drama teachers' conference saying 'This is where we are up to.' We showed them some draft sketches on stage and had a debate. Then we did a three-week workshop with writer, multimedia maker, and actors that culminated in a showing for 600 people in the Olympic Bowl, where we would show 25 minutes of work and then throw it open to the audience saying 'Where could this go?' and we improvised that back. We had a website ongoing from there, where sound, script and image would be put on, with five central questions for people to email responses to.   (Myers)

The large-scale work that Arena tours is not easily taken to rural communities without enormous subsidy. Myers is keenly aware of the complexity of making spectacular and engaging theatre that captures the attention of a visually and technologically sophisticated youth audience without excluding the rural communities that lie beyond the remit of festivals or city-based tours:

> We are looking at ways we can open up the process to make it more affordable. The regional areas of Australia can be quite depressing and that divide is so problematic. You will hear of how different areas vote, and how the regional areas have been badly affected by drought and they feel like a separate state that has been abandoned.   (Myers)

The awareness of a regional divide in part conditions the choices of material for the group. The latest large-scale show, *Play Dirty/Skid 180*, involves rapid image feedback, live music, physical theatre and live freestyle motorcross stunts, in an exploration of the disenchantment and disenfranchisment of young men, and the seductions of extremely risky behaviour. 'We like people who aren't theatre-goers, it's much more adrenalin charged, a much more excited dynamic exchange' (Myers).

Devising *with* Communities

If devising is not a professional activity by trained actors, leading towards production, what does participation in devising represent? Broadly speaking there are three main strands to the use of devising *with* communities. Some groups use devising primarily as a tool for encouraging community involvement. Here the aim of the exercise is far less the performance product than the desire to forge a sense of community, or to challenge a community through participation. A second strand of devising with communities is more interested in the content of the performance – the desire to empower community participants to speak publicly about those issues or concerns that are not being addressed by existing government agencies or public discourse. Finally, and far more widespread in contemporary practice, are groups who use devising with participants as a primarily therapeutic activity, usually in order to bring about personal change.

To consider the first of these propositions, for some early groups, involvement in devising activity was less about building performance and more about building community. Ed Berman's Inter-Action Theatre was one of the most radical experiments of community arts and action, and it continues to the present time. Founded in 1968 as a cooperative, the group's explicit agenda was 'to involve people in the improvement of their own communities, making them better places to raise their children and join with other adults to provide leisure and recreational facilities', which was in tune with the broad canvas of the growing community arts movement (Itzin, 1979, p. 197).[14] The multiple activities that the group undertook in Kentish Town, London, included a city farm; a community media van, the Fun Art Bus (a double-decker bus with cinema and theatre); an alternative education project working with truants (September 1974); a community resource centre, the Almost Free Theatre venue; Creative Play projects doing three-dimensional art with children in detention, in schools or on estates; and the Prof. Dogg's Troupe, a street and children's theatre ensemble. Underlying all of the group's work was a common principle:

> the use of different artists within a community to stimulate the participation of people in that particular art-form: usually – and mainly, in the minds of the practitioners – for some form of social improvement.   (Khan, 1980, p. 64)

The Prof. Dogg Troupe used open-ended play or Game-Plays, a combination of scripted elements and participatory improvisation.

The troupe would arrive on a housing estate as moonmen and invite the children to play with them. The performance would evolve through improvisation and play with the children, and the moonmen might come to represent immigrant communities or simply the idea of meeting new people. Likewise in the project led by sculptress Liz Leyh, *Make a Circus,* a few members of the troupe, dressed as clowns or ringmasters, walked through an estate 'beating drums, wheeling cartfuls of old clothes, paper and assorted junk, and armed with megaphones', inviting children to join them. Gathering the children into a circle in a nearby playground, they gave a circus performance. 'Afterwards the children were encouraged to perform their own circus – this could involve such improvised props and menagerie as a distinctly human-looking lion jumping through a hoop comprising two twelve-year olds' (Asquith, 1980, p. 92). Tony Coult saw the Game-Plays that Berman and Inter-Action used as the broader application of techniques pioneered by Theatre-In-Education troupes. There are also clear echoes of the game/exercise underpinnings of actor-based devising from the many alternative theatre troupes of the time, as we saw in Chapter 2.

The importance of presence in a community was key to Inter-Action's work as it developed. Talking in 1980, Berman admitted that 'in the early days there were lots of one-off visits to other sites. There was only about a 20% follow-up. Now the proportion has shifted radically. We have learnt that theatre is just a first step, and not art for art's sake' (Khan, 1980, p. 65). Berman's statement encapsulates much of the principle of the community theatre work emerging from the alternative troupes – a desire not to bring culturally improving experience to a non-theatre audience, but to empower communities themselves to social improvements. Berman articulated this aspiration in relation to the production of community art:

> The Old Masters had ateliers. ... What is new is that no prior training is required to be part of a community arts or social arts atelier. Under the guidance of an artist working in a community local people become a community atelier. They are local adults and children; they don't think of themselves as being artists or apprentices. The problem is they probably don't think of themselves as being 'creative' either. The very fact of having helped to make a single worthwhile item in their own environment can ignite the realisation that they too can be creative and constructive. Also some intensely interested but formerly untrained members of a project might carry on from this on-the-job training to lead projects themselves in future. (Berman, 1980, p. viii)

An example of this process was neatly given by the Dogg Troupe's work when, after a performance in the East End, they suggested that the audience initiate local activities themselves, and helped them develop a disused building into a community centre for mothers and a video unit for young people, where summer festivals and playschemes ran. The project took three years.

Likewise, The Combination, based in the Albany Theatre, Deptford, in London's East End, set out to 'build young popular theatre for an audience without higher education and the whole bourgeois cultural heritage ... participation is really in the meeting of minds in the right environment' (Khan, 1980, p. 64). The group had started as small fringe theatre in Brighton, but in 1970 the company had devised *The NAB Show* about social security and claimant advice, which they toured nationally supported by the Claimants' Union, and the company 'stayed behind after each performance to help organize or strengthen local branches of the Union', in the mode of agit-prop (Craig, 1980a, p. 23). Indeed, in content and spirit the work on this performance shared much with the rising tide of politically-active shows about housing benefit and social security from groups discussed in Chapter 4. The show was improvised from research by unemployed people, and playwright Steve Gooch worked the improvisation into a contemporary version of Aristophanes' *The Wasps*. Paul Curno, director of the Albany in Deptford, which was already a community and social centre, though not an arts centre, applied for one of the first community arts project grants from The Gulbenkian Foundation, and The Combination were employed as community arts workers. In 1972 they settled in Deptford and 'became involved with the local community and its grass-roots political and social organizations'.[15] An explicit political agenda underpinned their involvement in generating a range of cultural resources and opportunities for their locality. Jenny Harris has discussed the way in which the Combination's work had to change, as the community they were serving changed. When the group first arrived in Deptford the community was predominantly white, working-class, who had been resident together for many years. 'Within about three years, 80% of that community had changed. Nearly all of the old housing had been knocked down and tower blocks were built', people who had lived there moved out and the incoming group was around 25 per cent from ethnic minorities, 'so there was no community, no real adhesive community, which was very difficult' (Harris, 1985–6, p. 236). Community building included countering the rise of the extreme right-wing National Front Party in the area in the early 1970s through their Rock Against Racism festival and other multi-cultural activities. Their strategy led to an arson attack on the theatre by right-wing activists. The Combination, under Jenny Harris, still works at the New Albany, Deptford.

A rather different group who have survived to continue their practice of community animation from 1969 until today is Welfare State International. Initially John Fox and a group of his students devised a series of touring shows, emerging from the avant-garde experiments at Bradford College of Art where he taught, but they failed to connect with audiences in the way Fox was seeking: 'we got all the trendies coming out to see how well we performed, not to listen to what we were saying' (Coult and Kershaw, 1983, p. 5). The group turned instead to the rougher, folk stories they had been beginning to evolve, which followed the travails and *Travels of Lancelot Quail* (1972), an everyman figure, who shared something with CAST's Muggins character, but was more of a folk clown. In 1972, Welfare State were invited to a residency in Burnley, which allowed them a closer relationship to a community. Their aim was to undertake

> skill-teaching, and research into the arts and the community. As well as consciously regenerating the popular theatre tradition, Fox had always wanted to work on the assumption that the company should teach people the skills necessary to make their own celebrations, skills fast disappearing in a mechanised and de-skilled society. (Coult and Kershaw, 1983, p. 8)

Although Welfare State have toured shows and split their attention between intimate domestic rituals and large-scale community work, the heart of their practice has remained community-based. Since 1976, when a large component of the performers in the group split away to form the collective IOU, Welfare State has continued with John Fox and Boris Howarth (who had worked with Margaretta d'Arcy and John Arden on their early community work in Kirbymoorside and elsewhere) as the core, with regular freelance makers and performers who are involved for specific projects. In 1979 the company established its base at Ulverston, Cumbria, and undertook a well documented three-year residency in Barrow-in-Furness.[16] Community members were involved with the making of performances, with tasks ranging from acting in role to the construction of artefacts like lanterns for processions. Welfare State continue this mode of work today, although they have eschewed their large-scale spectacular community projects of the past, to concentrate on the small-scale folk and popular arts alongside 'nascent ritual (using theatre) as part of a way of living rather than a repeated dramatic production, where theatre is an end in itself' (ibid., p. 29).[17] The activities that groups like Inter-Action or Welfare State International invite their participants to be involved in are at a considerable remove from the work of actor-centred or contemporary physical devising by professional practitioners. Yet, while these companies' work with communities does not always produce recognisable productions with 'acting' at the heart of them, community participants do indeed devise a range of events, using a broad palette of acquired creative skills.

Turing to the second strand of devising work *with* communities, an Australian company committed to the facilitation of community *empowerment* through devising were Street Arts Community Theatre Company (1982, Brisbane). This politically activist group set up a long-term project in Inala, an isolated 1950s Housing Commission area on the outskirts of Brisbane, which drew on the Scottish Craigmillar example in designing arts activity as the impetus for regeneration.[18] Pauline Peel, one of the facilitators of the group, saw Street Arts work as different to politically explicit community work, which implied that:

> what we should be doing was going to Inala and giving them a Marxist analysis of what their situation was. ... We just argued that you're better to get them talking about their situation and finding ways of directing them so that they make their own conclusions.   (Watt, 1995, p. 18)

Street Arts had three principles: never go where you are not invited; never do one project when you can do three; always ensure you leave something behind. Street Arts began work in Inala in 1983 in a distinctively Australian way, with a series of circus workshops in the local primary school and evening workshops for adults. Out of these contacts a devised performance from the community members emerged, *Inala in Cabaret*, which was 'less than a total artistic success, its legitimation lay in the larger strategy of the venture' (Watt, 1995, p. 24). The company interlaced Theatre-in-Education shows, and small-scale workshops, with regular, large community productions. The following year the company facilitated a big, outdoor show, *Once Upon Inala*, which incorporated 150 local people, some of whom contributed to the more traditional writing of the project with Nick Hughes. After working on this show, Peel became more acutely aware that 'a community is made up of a whole lot of target groups – and then you start to determine where you need to do affirmative action' (ibid.). One of the target groups the company identified on the estate was the large proportion of single mothers, and in 1985 they worked on 'a smaller project with twenty local women called *Kockroach Kabaret*' (ibid., p. 24).[19] The skills for making performance for *Kockroach Kabaret* were to be used by the participants for their own ends in many projects after Street Arts had stopped working in the area, through the establishment of an independent, community-participant theatre company, Icy Tea (Inala Community Theatre).[20]

Other groups working with communities used devising as means of giving voice to the voiceless, expressing those concerns not usually aired publicly. An early community-based group in America used the services of an animateur, Maryat Lee. Lee had worked with a community in Harlem in 1951 in order to produce a piece of theatre about drugs, *Dope!*, which had a long performance life and, coupled with her course at the New School, was in many ways the beginning of community theatre in the US.[21] In 1968 a young people's group from a local school wanted to generate a play about drugs for other students, and this led them to contact Maryat Lee. The short-lived Soul and Latin Theatre (SALT) in East Harlem worked on three short plays (*After the Fashion Show, Day by Day*, and *The Classroom*), which dramatised their experience and a desire to change attitudes towards homosexuality, drugs and poor schools. The scripts 'worked out in rehearsal from scenarios by Miss Lee, are as true to the vocabulary and rhythms of street talk as a tape recorder'. The reviewer in the *New York Times* gives a very clear sense of the strong connection, shared dialogue and interaction between young black and Puerto Rican performers and the audience of their peers, who 'would have reduced the cast of *Dionysus in '69* to tears' (Sullivan, 1998, p. 101). The reference to Schechner's Performance Group, with its attempt to engage a predominantly college audience in theatrical interaction, is telling. Community-based theatre as exemplified by SALT's production had no separating divide between 'artist/performer' and audience, and it addressed itself to vividly shared concerns with its audience so directly that it opened a space for the audience to respond immediately. The review of the performance reports that an audience member shouted 'I had a teacher like that once!' in recognition and encouragement to the performers.

David Glazebrook ran a similar project in Melbourne. In 1979 Australia was in the grip of recession and youth unemployment rose dramatically. As an extension of the values of participatory drama in schools, teachers and social workers were employed to run drama workshops to encourage young people on the dole to 'develop some self-esteem, confidence and personal development, if not actually equip themselves for "proper jobs"' (Milne, 2004, p. 229). Glazebrook involved a group of young unemployed people in devising a performance to go into schools, in order to inform younger children about work and unemployment. The group was called the Avenue Players, and the performance was a series of sketches drawn from their experience of 'dole queues and of the hostility they often met when they got to the front of them, endless job-searching and frustration, peer-group and family pressures' (ibid.). The project successfully ran for two years, temporarily employing over sixty people. This is a prime example of ameliorative social services activity, which was funded by the Community Youth Support Scheme rather than receiving any arts funding. The project was designed to be both informative for audiences, but also personally effective for participants. The performance was intended to encourage young people to take up youth scheme places, rather than to question or challenge the economic and political environment that produced the level of unemployment.

Finally, we might look at companies who pursue devising practice as social and personal intervention. Geese Theatre Company, founded in 1980 by John Bergman in the USA and in the UK by Clark Baim in 1987, works with offenders and young people at risk in the Criminal Justice system. They have a two-pronged approach, running workshops and residencies as well as performances given by professional performers. Two of the most popular performances in their repertoire, *The Plague Game* (about maintaining relationships with family while in prison) and *Lifting the Weight* (about making the transition from custody to the outside world), are devised as open structures where characters seek interaction with the audience and play out alternative suggestions and endings as instructed by the audience. Other performances, particularly *Violent Illusion*, which looks at physical and sexual abuse, are followed by or involve workshops, where offenders are led in an exploration of role-play and the devising of short scenes or scenarios. The company acknowledges as influences The Living Theatre, Odin Teatret, Richard Schechner, and the improvisation practices of Viola Spolin and Keith Johnstone. This links their work very closely to the actor-based work we explored in Chapter 2, perhaps unsurprisingly, as it is predicated on the psychologically therapeutic nature of performance, with the mask as a physical metaphor for the public, external shell that can be lifted to reveal inner, 'true' feelings.[22]

A comparative group in the US is the Living Stage Theatre, which was founded in 1966 by Robert Alexander as the outreach wing of Arena Stage, Washington D.C., to work with 'underserved' communities. Four to six actors run workshops with groups of participant-actors for over a year.

> With the actors they create characters and improvise scenes exploring a wide range of issues that are of particular importance to the participating group. These scenes are never rehearsed and developed into a public performance for an outside audience, but instead are used to understand, analyze, and explore solutions to a specific problem that members of the group face in their daily lives.   (Haedicke, 2001, p. 270)

Based on Freirean philosophies of participation and activation of communities, Living Stage undertake long processes of workshops with small groups. Two three-year-long programmes with teen-aged mothers in 1991 and 1994 involved expressive play for the teenagers themselves, as part of a mechanism of passing that play on to their children. The workshops included improvisation, role-play and forum theatre, which they both made and participated in. Susan Haedicke's account gives a flavour of the long workshop processes, which evolve complex scenarios and contexts for improvisation that develop imaginative, empathetic and problem-solving skills in the participants. This is community theatre at its most therapeutic, unconcerned with public performance, working to effect personal change in participants, principally that they might become more successful within existing structures and institutions.

Conclusion

Devising was a central element to the emergence of community arts. The idea that a process of making performance for non-professionals should be a therapeutic or empowering possibility has devising at its core. It was very often through the rhetoric and practice of devising strategies that community arts programmes came into existence. The conflict in rhetorical and ideological stance between community theatre as improving cultural exposure and community theatre as empowering radical action, permeated much of the writing on and about community theatre in the 1970s and 1980s. In the 1980s and early 1990s, it was this claim to radical action that was to spell the end for much of the funding for community arts.

Devising with communities raises many ethical considerations. Games and exercises from actor-training contexts are adapted to new situations with participants who will never wish to pursue professional training. Improvisation games, verbatim interviews, and role-play are utilised not to develop skills in improvisation, performance or character work *per se*, but in order to create feelings and models of collaboration, to build self-esteem by demonstrating respect for opinions and experience, and to experiment with alternative ways of thinking or behaving. The ulterior motive to the process of devising is usually less a concern for aesthetics and more a concern with effect. The idea that devising can produce beneficial effects in these contexts is predicated on a humanism that champions the social over the individual, hence the use of group activity, communal making or discussion, and collaborative endeavour towards performance. Government agencies have sometimes been nonplussed by this concern with the social, and have construed it as a radical political stance. However, such a humanism also usually assumes a trans-cultural understanding of human behaviour, need and desire. Does utilising the same devising tools in radically different contexts always produce a sense of shared community? Does the ideology of this humanism assume that participatory devising processes will empower, train or change individuals for the better, in a vision of social progress, whatever the political content or context of the work? This chapter has been concerned to examine the emergence of devising within the field of community arts. Broader considerations of the ethical and theoretical questions around the use of devising in current contexts are beginning to appear, as in Helen Nicholson's study of *Applied Drama* (2005) for this series.

6 Contemporary Devising and Physical Performance

Since the late 1970s and early 1980s in the UK and Australia there has been a dramatic increase in the number of theatre companies who have termed themselves 'physical theatre'. Their work in varying measure melds dance, mime, visual arts, circus and drama together to generate what has become stylistically one of the most recognisable forms of contemporary devised work. This second wave of physical performance shared something with its earlier progenitor in the collective actor-centred performances of the 1960s and 1970s, but it emerged at a very different moment in time. This chapter examines the way in which the changed circumstances of theatrical and cultural industries have led to differences in the devising practices of contemporary physical theatre, and in particular to the question of the cultural identity of the bodies devising on stage.

Economics and Patronage

In the early 1980s in the UK the Conservative government, ideologically averse to the idea of subsidy, urged the subsidised arts sector to embrace the forces of the market. More than ever before, the Arts Council, under the chairmanship of Sir William Rees-Mogg, a Conservative appointment, was progressively involved in a redistribution of funds across the theatre sector and in a reduction of funding in real terms, in order to encourage companies to look for sponsorship elsewhere, particularly from business. Ironically, in an environment of reduced subsidy very small-scale touring groups were able to survive without funding, and Ralph Yarrow has argued that funding for small-scale touring remained good in the late 1970s and early 1980s (Chamberlain and Yarrow, 2002, p. 13). Indeed, the small-scale theatre company could be regarded as a model Thatcherite business, 'the entrepreneurial action of small professional groups' as William Rees-Mogg articulated in his paper *The Political Economy of Art* (Rees-Mogg, 1985, p. 8). Baz Kershaw has emphasised the extent to which business rhetoric was applied to the theatre and arts companies, who applied for 'investment' rather than subsidy, looked for 'customers' rather than audiences and were encouraged in the efficient management of their 'brand', as we explored in Chapter 4. This rhetoric, coupled with a shift in the mechanisms of grant application, had repercussions for the way small devising companies perceived themselves and organised themselves. Notably, although devising is still regarded as a collaborative creative tool, such creative work is perceived as separate from the pragmatic organisation of the company. Few of these physical devising companies ran on collective lines or chose to work without an established hierarchy. Most saw and see themselves as part of a now professional, alternative sector of the cultural marketplace. This is not to make a value judgement on the relative merits of different ways of working, but to illustrate a very different context within which the contemporary devising of physical theatre occurs in the UK.

The Australian context shared some of the same pressures in the late 1980s, when the subsidised State theatre companies were suffering a decline in comparison with commercial managements, who were offering a diet of Lloyd Webber and Cameron Mackintosh musicals (Milne, 2004, p. 244). Because of Australia's size, the cost of touring performances was prohibitive for small-scale companies and, unlike the European experience, small-scale touring to numerous regional studio theatres was an impossible route by which to establish a company. In the last twenty years, physical theatre work has been funded by a mixture of means: federal funding through various Australia Council initiatives; regional State subsidy; and more recently a very different style of entrepreneurial festival or venue management (Fotheringham, 1998). Festivals have played a key role in the development of this sector of work since the early 1990s, and since the late 1990s some venues have also been keen to develop innovative work and to support small-scale physical theatre groups. However, funding from festivals and venues is only project-by-project, and therefore offers particular challenges to groups wishing to maintain a stable ensemble or through-the-year training alongside performance development. This has contributed to a shift in the organisational structures and the operating mechanisms of physical theatre companies.

There has been little comparable increase in devised physical theatre in America, although since the mid-1990s companies with a focus on physical performance have begun to become a force in American theatre. There are a few long-established companies such as Dell'Arte in Blue Lake, California (1974), whose founders worked with Lecoq, and Touchstone Theatre, Bethlehem, Pennsylvania (1981), whose early work, in the 1970s, was improvisational street performance centred on mime and physical theatre. Umo Theatre (1987), based in Washington State, is unusual in that the company works as a collective, sharing artistic direction for shows. They devise using clowning (especially buffoon and red nose) and puppetry developed from Lecoq training. In the autumn of 1985, New York played host to a visiting Butoh company and Pina Bausch's *Tanztheater*, and these visits proved inspirational and instrumental in the development of postmodern dance and dance theatre. Since the 1990s Anne Bogart's Saratoga International Theater Institute (SITI) company (1992) in Saratoga Springs has developed from a training institute to a year-round training and producing company, where Bogart melds her improvisational techniques with Tadashi Suzuki's training. More recently, Pig Iron Theatre Company, Philadelphia (1995), which calls itself a 'dance-clown-theatre' ensemble, has developed a range of interdisciplinary work that might more readily sit under the rubric of postmodern performance. In part, the absence of this strand of work in the United States, until very recently, has been a result of cultural differences explored below, notably, different mechanisms for performer training and a difficult economic environment for small-scale touring companies.

Apart from the explicit arts funding context of the UK and Australia, a second context for the development of the wave of devised physical performance was a response to the dominance of television and film, with their overriding emphasis on naturalism. While television may have been a lucrative employer it offered only limited options for actors, certainly in terms of the range of acting style. Simon McBurney of Theatre de Complicite spoke for many physical theatre companies when he asserted that 'for theatre to be reclaimed it must celebrate its difference as an art form from television' (McBurney, 1994, p. 23). Not only did many companies articulate their desire to find different modes of working, but there was an economic imperative to do so. A growing pool of actors was emerging from the expanding sector of training conservatoires and university drama and dance departments in the 1980s and 1990s. At the same moment, there was a decline in regional producing theatres in the UK and Australia, the financial squeeze meant fewer productions were mounted, and an increasingly competitive marketplace was produced. The resurgence of interest in physical training has a paradoxical dynamic: on the one hand it marks out performers from the pool as professionally skilled and capable over and above their fellows, thus as commercially advantaged for television or mainstream theatre; on the other, actors who choose to engage in ongoing physical training often initially conceive of themselves as standing against the commercial theatrical marketplace and particularly the demands of naturalism, and thus television, in favour of a more 'live' experience.

The growth and diversity of 'training' for actors, dancers, mime or circus performers has multiplied exponentially since the late 1970s, and has been central to the production of this second wave of physical performance troupes. There has been a marked rise in the provision of dance training and in the provision of circus training. Recent studies of Jacques Lecoq's school in Paris, and the satellite work of colleagues Philippe Gaulier and Monika Pagneux, have made a persuasive case for Lecoq training as a central element and the inspiration behind many of the physical theatre companies in the UK and to a lesser extent America and Australia since the 1980s (Chamberlain and Yarrow, 2002). Lecoq's school had been operating continuously since its foundation in 1956 and individual performers had emerged to work with a range of theatre companies; for example, Celia Gore-Booth was influential in the evolution of Shared Experience's *Arabian Nights*, and Footsbarn and Théâtre du Soleil had members who brought their expertise from the Paris School. However, in the early 1980s the influence of Lecoq's work became far more visible in the UK and Australia because successful *companies* were established who developed his methods, including Moving Picture Mime Show (1977), Trestle Theatre (1981), Theatre de Complicite (1983) and the Drama Action Centre (1980) in Sydney. Lecoq was invited to make two significant visits to London in 1982 to the two-week British Summer School of Mime, and in 1988 to give a five-day workshop and perform *Tout Bouge* at the Queen Elizabeth Hall, London (Murray, 2003, p. 23). The visibility of physical theatre in the UK was increased when several companies, most notably Theatre de Complicite, were adopted by mainstream venues and institutions. Part of the contribution of Lecoq's training is that it draws on the French tradition of the popularisation of traditional mime, as Simon Murray argued, and emphasises play, improvisation and composition as key skills of the performer (Murray, 2003).

Alongside this development of key physical training schools within the European tradition, there has also been much more interest since the 1980s in intercultural theatrical exchange. Rather than simply developing intercultural performances or studying productions from diverse cultures, Western practitioners have been far more captivated by the training demands of traditional theatre forms such as kalaripayattu, Kathakali, Noh, Kabuki, and more recent adaptations of these forms in the post-war dance form Butoh, and Tadashi Suzuki's training. Groups interested in this kind of work often hold onto an idea of continual training as part of, and precursor to, the devising process, as Simon Woods of Zen Zen Zo Physical Theatre articulated:

> In some ways the training journey is more interesting than the production. Watching a group of people who go through this incredible process of transformation, physically, spiritually, mentally, intellectually over a period of time together in the training room is a truly profound thing. The performance then is like opening a door to say 'This is where we're at; this is what we're thinking about,' and then the door closes again and we go back into the training room. We believe this is quite different to the way a lot of theatre is created and even conceptualised in Australia at this point in time. (Bradley and Woods, 2003)[1]

Of course, not all physical theatre companies devise work. For some groups, the physical work is an interpretation of a pre-existing new or classic text, such as much of the work of Stephen Berkoff or the current work of Shared Experience (UK). For those lying closer to the dance spectrum the generation of work is closer to choreography, as with the blend of Suzuki training and contemporary dance in the aesthetic of Jacqui Carroll's Brisbane-based Frank Productions, who rework classic texts (Pippen, 1997). One of the most significant influences on this dance theatre hybrid work is German *Tanztheater*, pioneered by Pina Bausch, whose disruptive, disturbing anti-ballet has developed since she took over as director of the Wuppertal Dance Theatre in 1973. The aesthetics of her performances, which perhaps initially drew on her experience of expressionist choreography, American formalism and the emergence of alternative theatre in the

1960s, are drawn from the real. Movement is action-based, and dancers are required to stagger over rubble, dance in water, struggle with everyday objects such as revolving doors or kitchen appliances. Fragmented movement phrases, repetition to the point of exhaustion and disconnected text all resist clear narratives, but feel familiar. Dancers are expected both to display extremes of emotion, and to theatrically comment on that emotional work as parody. Rather than Bausch's working methods, it was her aesthetic that was to prove very influential on many of the physical theatre companies from the early 1980s onwards.

In those physical theatre companies that do devise, the work ranges widely in nature and character depending upon the particular disciplinary mix that produces their unique hybrid form. Broadly speaking there are four main strands to the current work in physical theatre or performance: that which lies closest to dance, as in the work of companies like the Clod Ensemble or DV8; that which draws its influence from popular arts such as clowning, street entertainment, some aspects of mime and circus, as in many of the Lecoq-inspired companies or groups like Legs on the Wall, Sydney; that which draws inspiration from traditional theatre, or traditional mime, and focuses predominantly on narrative and storytelling, as in the work of Theatre Alibi (1982) or Trestle Theatre (1981); and that which develops a crossover between live art and physical performance, as in the work of Entr'Acte (1979). Of course such categories are porous and Entr'Acte provides a good example of the movement that physical theatre companies might make over time. Entr'Acte was first founded as the Sydney Corporeal Mime Theatre, centred on Decroux-influenced performances that were devised 'incorporating multiple artforms including spoken dialogue, poetry, music, photography and video', and offering the audience multiple points of focus resisting narrative (Milne, 2004, p. 365). In many ways the early work of Entr'acte might more properly be considered within a postmodern performance paradigm. Interestingly the company's policy moved dramatically in 1995 to incorporate and work with narrative in *Eclipse* (charting the death of a young woman from an unnamed disease), because the company were experiencing a shift in the theatrical environment, which they summarised as:

artists' multiple commitments to other companies; consequent loss of longevity in company training; effectively a shorter time frame for creation; a shift in audience expectations; diminishing financial security; advances in digital technology; and a major recognition by the federal government of the value of original theatre and performance in representing Australia overseas.   ('Eclipse', 1999, p. 189)

The studies of physical theatre companies and their work that follow reveal the complexity of these hybrid forms. Such complexity is not simply aesthetic, but is also conditioned by the material environment, including government funding priorities, changes in company personnel and venue, and audience expectations. Since the 1980s, with the coining and development of the 'cultural industries' and 'cultural marketplace', individual devising companies have by turns thrived and faltered, but the sector of devised physical theatre has undergone a period of phenomenal growth.

Circus, Dance and Sport: Physical Theatre in Australia

It is not surprising that physical theatre in Australia has become one of its most significant sectors of performance work over the last twenty years. Australia has a long history of spectacular popular theatre, most obviously in traditional touring circus, which celebrated 150 years in 1997 (Tait, 1998, p. 216). The popular pastimes and entertainments of circus, music hall and vaudeville have, like sport, served the working-class, pragmatic desires of white Australians. Following the emergence of the writer-led, distinctively Australian drama, the 'New Wave' of the 1970s, for both funding bodies and practitioners 'the term "Australian" – which in the 1950s and 1960s acted as a simple mark of origin – returned as a positive category of order' (Meyrick, 2003, p. 51). This valorisation of a distinctively 'Australian' culture also drew on the popular and the body-based as part of a resistance to an imperial definition of Australia as a colony. Richard Cave's study of the commercially successful show *Tap Dogs* unpacks some of the elements of physical culture in Australia. *Tap Dogs* (1995) involved a group of ex-steel-workers, all young, white, working-class, muscular men performing aggressive, athletic, thumping tap routines on a series of steel structures and ramps, generating a loud percussive score. Wayne Harrison, the promoter of the show, described audience responses both within and beyond Australia:

They found it culturally exact in terms of what Australianness in a male context is all about: that, yes, it could be incredibly creative, but at the same time there was a kind of paradox there, that it was not appearing to or striving to be creative in the first instance. And that seemed to translate as an Australianness, it seemed actually to encapsulate the essence of an Australian maleness and then an Australianness beyond that. That it was cultural but non-cultural at the same time.   (Cave, 2003, p. 163)

Margaret Williams charted the ways in which other bodies have begun to develop and claim their place in 'Australian' culture. She has marked the cultural move towards acknowledging 'a body rich in its diversity; a body increasingly accommodating indigenous Australians, the influences of immigrants, the female voice and gay and lesbian Australia' (Hamilton, 2003, p. 181). Today this body-based devising draws more fully on Asian and Pacific Rim cultures and practices, most fully exemplified by the popularity of Butoh and the use of Suzuki training.

Circus performance and dance have been a vibrant element of this body-based cultural development, and from the late-1970s companies have included Soapbox Circus, Melbourne (1978), which evolved into Circus Oz (1978), Flying Fruit Fly Circus, Albury-Wodonga (1979), Rock 'n' Roll Circus, Brisbane (1987), Circus Bizircus, Freemantle, WA (1990), Footscray Women's Circus annual show in Melbourne (1992), Club Swing, Melbourne (1993), and Vulcana Women's Circus, Brisbane (1994). Circus Oz came out of a political desire to make performance for people where they were and on a level that was most accessible. Legs on the Wall, one of Australia's best known physical theatre companies, emerged initially in reaction to Circus Oz, and their desire to take the nascent inter-relation of circus and story/theatre further. Debra Iris Batton of Legs on the Wall characterised the relationship of physical performance to Australian cultural identity in that decision:

The company's impulse to begin was in reaction to Circus Oz (rather than a style of theatre training such as Lecoq), so there is a distinctive home-grown quality to the work. In responding to a group of Australians who reinvented circus for themselves, circus with a particularly Australian focus and a sense of socio-political activism, Legs have reacted to an Australian art form, rather than creating a form that is derivative of inherited European traditions of theatre. Legs wanted to find their own way forward, to make it up themselves. A bit like the great tradition of the early settlers – jerry rigging – using what you've got to make what you need.   (Batton, 2003)[2]

Lynne Bradley and Simon Woods of Brisbane-based Zen Zen Zo Physical Theatre began their search for a theatre language that moved beyond naturalism. Although their work does not draw on circus and popular traditions, they echo something of this placement of their devised work in a distinctively Australian context:

> In our search for rich theatres of the body, our first port of call was Asia. ... Now I think what we do is an amalgam of something that is purely indigenous and our own, and something that is influenced by Asian theatre styles. ... The move away from Euro-centric theatre dovetails with the development of Australian history and identity and where our recent influences as a nation have come from. Art parallels politics in that sense. (Bradley and Woods)

To some extent the work of physical theatre companies in Australia has combined a rejection of the British tradition, particularly that tradition as characterised by classical, language-based performance, with a conceptualisation of a distinctive and diverse Australian culture.

Legs on the Wall was founded in 1984 by three social science students who 'were interested in street theatre and circus as a form for dealing with social issues. And they really liked Circus Oz but felt it could go further in terms of theatre, it could do something that really does deal with social issues' (Batton, 2003). This shares much with the generation of Circus Oz itself (1978), which evolved in part from the Australian Performing Group, Soapbox Circus and the Adelaide-based New Circus, with an innovative agenda to produce politically activist circus. The initial group evolved into two male and two female performers and made a commitment to gender equality in employment and opportunity that the company still pursues. The company is also committed to 'a collective process, there was no artistic director and it was very much driven by the performers in the company' (Batton). An early Legs show, *Bruce cuts off his hand*, used clowning to explore the politics of workplace accidents, playing in the industrial Newcastle area. Brian Keogh, a founder member, described the early work as a cabaret style 'covering genres from the comic/absurd in *Big Trouble* (a detective story about fish) to the Gothic in *Hurt* (four people in an asylum with a slightly crazed piano player)' (Keogh, 1999, p. 170). An early ecological street performance involved figures completely clad in newspaper abseiling down the side of shopping centres, threatening the public, disguised as demonic, walking, cardboard boxes, who apparently swallowed, and packed, an unsuspecting audience member. Over the years, as the personnel of Legs on the Wall and the cultural environment has changed, so political activism has come to play a less prominent role, although performers still 'have to have an attitude to what's going on in the world around them' (Batton). The core of the work remains 'integrating text, acrobatic skill and aerial imagery in a no-holds-barred approach to storytelling'.[3] And their social and political commentary is still evident in the subject matter of the performances they create: migration and diaspora in *Homeland* (2000), the politics of sport in *Runners Up* (2000), and, in two forthcoming works with writers, sexuality in *Tranny Boy* and a meditation on war in *A Cloak of Feathers*.

Performers controlled the early process, bringing in directors and writers when necessary. Although the company no longer has a permanent ensemble because of funding constraints, the attempt to remain performer-centred means Debra Iris Batton is currently artistic coordinator, but not artistic director, and inhabits a range of roles including performer, choreographer, director or movement dramaturg by turn. Batton's background is an exemplary illustration of the hybrid forms within which Legs works; her first training in dance, which took her eventually to community dance and physical theatre projects in the Northern Territories, was followed by a spell with Circus Oz:

> I am of course very aware of the Circus Oz influence. Following 15 years of elite gymnastics, I studied Dance at university, and was fascinated with choreography, particularly when the source for movement could be anything. I was interested in the Judson Dance collective and inspired by making work that was about movement invention rather than learned steps. Dance Works (Melbourne) were an important influence at that time. A small ensemble committed to collaboration, not only in the work itself but also in the credits, which would be something like, Choreographed by/with the dancers. (Batton)

This emphasis on the creative ensemble has remained central to Legs on the Wall, whether its performers come from circus, dance or theatre backgrounds, 'we actively seek to have an ensemble that comes from different places and that's part of the dynamic of the creative process ... we kind of enjoy the clash' (Batton). The work does have a clear link to circus in its spectacular acrobatics and harness work at height, and, in the early shows, a vibrant acknowledgement of the audience, but it also uses language, produces narrative and guides the spectator on an emotional journey. The company has worked with Tess De Quincey on her Butoh-inspired

Body Weather project, and with vocal teachers, and has also run masterclasses in improvisation and other kinds of training for their regular performers, to resource their devising skills. This integration of hybrid physical disciplines and skills is characteristic of many contemporary physical devising companies, as we shall see.

The importance of the physical discipline, technique and training is that, during a physical devising process, it is from this training and technique that creative work emerges:

> there might be training in something aerial that we haven't trained in before and while we're watching it people begin to see stories or make connections with what they're doing. ... Just working acrobatics leads to an idea, you're just working with a form, absolutely with a form, and sometimes I liken that much more to visual art.   (Batton)

Similarly the creation of images, narratives or emotionally charged moments of a performance can develop from the physical structures that the form requires:

> we will bring riggers in at an early stage of Research & Development to invent new systems, just to try out for the sake of it, to see what language is there. I think that's a bit of a circus mentality. You know, 'I reckon there's this machine and if you built it I could do something on it.' So you build it and you do something on it.   (Batton)

The evolution of the work from form to production takes a long three-stage process, and these stages can be spread over up to three years, which presents some difficulties in the immediacy of the performance as Batton wryly noted:

> Being a company in the small to medium sector one of our key strengths is being able to be responsive, but if it takes us three years to make something from the first R&D stage we say 'Why did we want to do this again?' (laughs).   (Batton)

The first phase of the devising process is Research and Development, where themes and the technical possibilities of a range of aerial, harness and acrobatic forms are explored. This is followed, after an interval, by a three-week creative development stage, where the bulk of the material is generated and explored. Like many devising companies working today, the company has found that having some reflective time between the initial research and the creative development phase has proved vital. The process of setting up improvisations in the creative development does not draw on Stanislavskian ideas of character and motivation, but centres on formal tasks and interactions between performers. For example, in the making of *All of Me*, the thematic centre was relationships which moved from normal to abnormal psychology, and the research was based on personal stories and experiences of the performers; but the tasks the performers explored were 'to think of new and bizarre ways of travelling over the top of one another, we threw and jumped onto each other a lot from very high places' (Keogh, 1999, p. 171). There is an eschewing of 'acting' or emotional performance:

> We encourage our performers to just do the task. The emotion comes out in the work in a much more pure and interesting form than when they try to impose emotion.   (Batton)

Nigel Jamieson, as the outside eye, could see narrative structures and interactions emerging from the work, and Mary Morris brought radically varied drafts and elements of script and poetry to the third phase, the rehearsal process, to add to the performers' contributions.

All of Me (1993), which still runs in the company's repertoire, marked a key turning point in the company's stylistic. It follows the story of the birth, life and eventual suicide of a young girl, within a family that breaks down. The text of the show comprises just three or four short poems charting the breakdown of the relationship between mother and father, and father and daughter. The structure of the piece centres around two ladders downstage right and upstage left of the performance space, which illustrate the emotional journey of the characters, as they race up them to play, struggle up as if for air, or make their slow descent into exhaustion and depression. This show had far more emotional and narrative content than previous shows, and a different, less immediate and knowing relationship with its audience:

> And that was quite a change for the company. Prior to that I don't think the company called itself physical theatre, I think it was called New Circus or contemporary circus or circus theatre, it nearly always had circus in its name. And after that it became physical theatre and no longer used circus as a title.   (Batton)

The work that Legs on the Wall does is still clearly linked to circus in its technical feats and its devising process, but the company has evolved a broader range of narrative, emotional, imagistic and elegiac qualities that draw on dance and theatre aesthetics. *Homeland* (2000), developed for the Olympic Festival, was performed outdoors on the side of a multi-storey building on Sydney Harbour. Directed by Nigel Jamieson, the performance projected a series of slides onto the building against an emotive, live soundscape from the Martentsa Choir of eastern European traditional songs. A couple wearing 1940s dress danced from the top of the building and were joined by a couple in modern dress, climbing up from the base. While the piece imaged only white, heterosexual couples, the female performers worked equally daringly and muscularly with their male colleagues. The straightforward imagery was of reconciliation between people from different starting points, and across time. The images of a mother cradling her son, or lovers turning cartwheels of delight hand-in-hand, echoed something of the surreal imagery of a Chagall painting. The membership of the company here determined the limited message of the devised piece – the reconciliation of European-heritage settlers in Australia. Such work as this both is and is not dance, circus or theatre. It is a tribute to the cultural force and popularity of this style of circus hybrid work that Legs on the Wall, like Circus Oz, has been funded by the *Theatre* Board of the Australia Council for some years, although not to a level that permits a permanent ensemble.

Stalker Theatre has been concerned with many of the same issues in devising work and its trajectory has been similar to that of Legs on the Wall. It was formed by David Clarkson in New Zealand in 1985, and transferred to Sydney in 1989 with Rachel Swain and Emily McCormack. The company usually performs outdoors and fuses work on stilts of various heights with new dance, acrobatics and the architecture of sites and structures that the performers can use. For David Clarkson, the earliest work used 'the stilts as a sculptural and visual medium' and has evolved to include more mediation of, and meditation on, the human form. The transition of Stalker's work echoes the broader moves of Australian cultural and political identity, shifting from playful street theatre in the 1980s towards images and fractured narratives which engage with the myths and desires of intercultural and indigenous experiences. The political aspects of the work have been implicit from the start. Clarkson's first stilt company in New Zealand, Splinter, emerged using an explicitly political street form:

> The first show we did was a political theatre piece – it was an anti-nuclear show. It had very archetypal characters like famine, war, Western woman,

Capital. I played the Everyman figure on the floor. That got the form up as far as I was concerned. It was stilts, it was outdoor, it was archetypal, it was political. I loved the idea of it not being in an enclosed space. There couldn't be an ownership over the work as there can be in other work.   (Clarkson)[4]

Clarkson's concern with the social and political resonances of archetypes, human interaction and human relations with the environment has underpinned much of the later work of the company. It also resulted in the development of the separate Marrugeku company, which involved the collaboration of performers from Stalker Theatre company, led by Rachel Swain, contemporary indigenous dancers and musicians from Western Australia, and artists from the Kunwinjku tribe of Western Arnhem Land. Both companies have been keenly aware of the way their work is taken to represent Australian identity. From the early 1990s Stalker Theatre predominantly toured Europe, South America and Japan, where it was among the very few Australian companies then on the international circuit. For Clarkson, their rigorous touring schedule also added to the cultural mix of the company's work: 'just seeing groups like Dogtroep, like La Fura Dels Baus, Derevo, Ballets C de la B, just knowing that certain types of work were possible. We all cross-fertilised each other in many ways. And we bring that work and inspiration back here' (Clarkson). The meetings at European festivals led to collaborations with Catalan visual artist Joan Baixus and Japanese designer Kansai Yammomoto. Clarkson is now experimenting with some of Enrique Pardo's techniques, while Swain's latest work for Stalker, *Incognita*, is a collaboration with Koen Augustijnen of Les Ballets C de la B of Belgium.

The core company members shared a training in Lecoq-based work either at or through the Drama Action Centre in Sydney (1980). The devising and collaborative skills of working with improvisation, mask and mime were melded with the strictures and possibilities of stilt work. Their first show, *Fast Ground*, a street piece where strange, covered figures gradually shed their skins to become more playful creatures, was work they evolved themselves and this led them to seek out a director to provide an outside eye to the creative process. Nigel Kellaway's work on *Toy Cart* (1989) offered the company a new range of stylistic choices but used a choreographic mode of work that was somewhat at odds with the creative devising process of the company's background. After *Angels Ex Machina* (1993), Clarkson or Swain took a more directorial role: 'we realised at that stage that *we* were the ones who were most professional in our form, and the form we had developed. It made sense for us to direct' (Clarkson). However, there are difficulties associated with the shift in power dynamics within a company when one member of an ensemble moves into a directorial position; in effect, this led to a splintering of different work under the title of Stalker. Over time, as the permanent ensemble has dissolved and a directorial role has emerged, the working methods of the company too have changed. Clarkson described the evolution of a current show in their repertoire, *Four Riders*:

> I guess ... I'm the dominant force. Each actor does an amount of research ... several of them have got degrees in drama and a great deal of research will come back. So, you've got this sea of information and ideas which you then pull together. Then the show just starts to resonate. You start to get cross-references and the layers build. I might set a movement exercise, I might say 'Walk in a particular way and focus in a particular way' and to see them doing it suggests this whole mood which could link to another section. ... I tried to make the creative process as owned by as many of the cast as possible. But because Stalker is now 17 years old, when people come and join us they can't hope to have the depth and breadth of experience that I or Rachel or Sophie has. There is then a disparity of knowledge which very easily translates to a disparity of power.   (Clarkson)

Like Legs on the Wall and Zen Zen Zo, discussed below, Stalker now has a pool of known performers to whom it returns for new shows. Shows tend to remain in the company's repertoire for several years and evolve, requiring new performers to be rehearsed in for a range of tours. The rigours of international touring, which is how the company supports itself, do not appeal to every actor.

The concentration on imagery related to the landscape and space of Australia was central to *Blood Vessel* (1989) (about the 'discovery' of Australia), and is an ongoing theme, particularly so in the work of the Marrugeku company's *Mimi* (1996). The process of working on *Mimi* was markedly different from the previous productions because of the interaction with the stories and performing artists of the Kunwinjku people of Western Arnhem Land. The Mimi are mischievous spirits, depicted as very tall and thin with dreadlocks like plumage, who live in the rocks of the area. The reinterpretation of the stories of the Mimi was a delicate process, which first required the permission of the elders of the community. It involved the whole company of traditional dancers and singers, and of Stalker performers, in the creation of a musical and physical score, which did not 'retell' the story, but developed images in a context. The movement, the accompaniment of the didgeridoo, electric guitar and voices, and the lighting, which threw dark shadows and brought out the rich reds of the landscape, generated a dream-like quality in the performance. The performance toured various communities of Arnhem Land, festivals in Perth, Brisbane and Sydney, and abroad, including the world Expo in Hanover in 2000 where it 'represented' Australia. 'Where it worked best was either touring these communities or in Sydney. The landscape and scale of it all speaks to an Australian audience, it's always going to be something exotic and foreign in Europe' (Clarkson).

This concern with the shifting nature of Australian identity underlay the decision to devise for Zen Zen Zo Physical Theatre. Zen Zen Zo was founded in 1992 in Brisbane by Lynne Bradley and Simon Woods, who gathered a small ensemble of performers looking for alternatives to naturalism. They became interested in Asian performance forms, particularly the avant-garde dance form Butoh, and Tadashi Suzuki's method of actor training. The directors spent time in South-East Asia, in India, and five years in Kyoto, Japan, studying Japanese dance-theatre, where they were joined by company members between 1993 and 1995.

> Lynne: Because we were initially working across two cultures, we felt that it was crucial to understand them both at great depth. We spent a lot of time studying in Japan – studying with the originators of the forms we now teach and utilise. Only then did we begin adapting and changing and creating something new.
>
> Simon: I think that there is a really important distinction between outright *imitation* of a form – which has many limitations – and *adaptation*. When certain techniques, ideas and philosophies are adapted and personalised, that is, mixed with one's own unique sensibility and worldview, then there is the potential to launch a practitioner into another realm artistically. (Bradley and Woods)

Since returning to Brisbane in 1996 the company have focused on the 'creation of new work in the area of physical theatre', alongside a rolling programme of workshops and training in Butoh, Suzuki Method and yoga. The performance work has been either radical adaptations, or newly devised pieces, or Butoh dance works (Bradley and Woods, 2003, p. 3). The group has never operated as a collective, but for the first few years of its life it was a relatively stable ensemble, led by the two directors. That stability permitted the evolution of a mode of working for the directors from a highly formalised Butoh or Suzuki training mode to a more collaborative devising mode:

> Lynne: The first couple of shows that we did when we came back we pretty much had it planned before we walked into the rehearsal room. So we would tell the actors 'Move here, do this,' everything was choreographed. It was very successful. But gradually, particularly as we were working with the same group of people again and again and they had developed the same bag of skills as us and reached a high level, they wanted to be more influential and we wanted to hand over. But in the way we had been taught to create we didn't know how to do that. (Bradley and Woods)

As part of an active search for a more egalitarian creative mode the directors explored clowning and then developed the Viewpoints method evolved by Anne Bogart at the American SITI theatre company (1992), which Bogart and Tadashi Suzuki founded. Bogart's method, which she considers 'distinctly American', is a form for generating short, improvisational movement sequences, based on choreographer Mary Overlie's work in the 1970s, and charts a link back to the 1960s Judson Church Dance Theatre and the evolution of postmodern dance (Whitworth, 2003, p. 25).[5] Zen Zen Zo have found it 'an excellent tool for unlocking the creativity of our company members, as well as empowering them to do the majority of the creating in our productions. Simon and I have acted more as "facilitators" or "editors" than auteur-style directors over the past few years as a result' (Bradley and Woods). The existing alignment between Bogart's work and the Suzuki Method has meant that this mode of creation sits comfortably with the cross-cultural training of the company.

The modes the company uses for devising share much with other contemporary Australian groups: a three-phase process of one or two weeks for creative development, two to three weeks of further development, and a four- to five-week rehearsal period. Because the company is unfunded for ongoing work, these phases tend to be spread out part-time over a year. The first stage of creative development happens in retreat:

> Lynne: We usually go up to Montville which is up in the mountains. We have a fantastic little hideaway there, and we take the whole company for a week or two and we just do composition for 24/48 hours straight in this amazing landscape, jamming round the ideas that we are interested in. Because it's coming out of the non-rational brain, and nothing in real life is

> interrupting us, and because we are living together, eating together, training together, working together, this incredible material is created. It's during that creative development that we usually find what we call the anchor or the kernel of a new work. (Bradley and Woods)[6]

Themes and ideas for productions are usually initiated by the directors, who compile research material as a resource for the company. Early devised works were written by the company, but, like many companies discussed throughout this book, they have found it more effective to work with a writer, either in the studio or piecing together and developing a working script from the first stimuli.

The use of the writer in the second phase of development, while obviously connected to the development of narrative, is part of their main concern to provide structure for the work, 'a journey for the audience'. This is echoed in the structuring of the wordless Butoh dance works they have created, *The Way of Mud* (1993), *Unleashed* (1996) and *Steel Flesh* (1998), which chart an intense, unnervingly close relationship with an audience and move through a variety of moods, tempos and dynamics:

> Lynne: I've introduced comedy, and why not? Because Butoh is about exposing the inner self and saying this is what it means to be human. In Australia part of that is a very comical, gutsy, raw self. It's not all about gloom and doom in Australia in the 21st century and I can't pretend that it is. So in excavating what it is for the Australians, I've invested comedy into it. Maybe someone wouldn't call it Butoh anymore, but for me it's very strongly there. (Bradley and Woods)

As an example, in *Unleashed*, after a very intense sequence examining the repressed body, the company unfurled into 'Butoh babies' whose curious, innocent delight in their own bodies and each others' punctured the mood and unsettled the audience, so that the following sequence of manic cruelty against the body was more strongly felt.

The integration of a variety of Japanese, Indian and American theatre forms and trainings into Australian culture for an Australian audience has led the company to reflect on the politics and aesthetics of devising. As Simon Woods pointed out, in cultural exchange there can be a tendency to enshrine or romanticise practices from elsewhere. Suzuki training and the performances the Suzuki Company of Toga (SCOT) have changed dramatically since the late 1960s and early 1970s. The need to adapt and evolve exercises from these traditions is key to integrating them into a new, different, Australian cultural practice:

> Every time we think through what an exercise means we ask: What are the
> fundamental principles, where has it come from and what are we trying to
> achieve? What are the particular points of relevance for us? We do an
> immediate cross-check and ask ourselves, 'Does this exercise need to
> evolve or change for it to be more relevant to us?' And the answer is usually,
> 'Yes'. (Bradley and Woods)

For example, Zen Zen Zo have adapted the vocal training borrowed
from Suzuki. In Suzuki's training, actors are pushed to make
enormous demands on the voice, and the method can seem repetitious
and monotonous. Yet 'when Suzuki is in rehearsal, he probably works
90 per cent of the time on what the actors are saying ... on nuances
and delicacies and subtleties within the text. But if you don't speak
Japanese you don't get that, you just get the volume' (Bradley and
Woods). Within the Australian theatrical culture there is no comparative tradition of chanted text as in Kabuki and Noh, instead
emphasis is placed on spontaneity. While Woods agreed that Suzuki's
demand for vocal strength and breath training could bring creative
discovery for the actor, for an Australian audience he uses a diversity
of exercises to explore 'subtler, softer levels' (Bradley and Woods).

This negotiation between two cultures was central to the company's
decision to devise. On their initial return from Japan the media
represented them as a company doing Japanese theatre, producing
something alien and exotic,

> particularly in those days with the media's very limited knowledge of
> Asian performing arts, [with its] very orientalising typecasting. In response
> to that we had to really search to find our Australian identity. (Bradley
> and Woods)

By representing Asian cultural practice as 'other', the mainstream
Australian press occluded both the extent to which Australia is a
Pacific Rim economy and culture, as well as the experience of many
Australasian Australians, whose creative practice and lived experience
bridges such an apparent cultural divide. The politics and tensions
of this engagement between cultures are played out in many of Zen
Zen Zo's works, most recently *Wicked Bodies* (2004). While not
as explicitly political as some of the work of the Sydney Front for
example, for Bradley there was a clear, implicit political agenda in the
devising work:

> *Wicked Bodies* is a piece based on five physical theatre performers from
> different backgrounds. There are two Chinese Australians, one Sri-Lankan

Australian, one Anglo-Saxon Australian, one French-Canadian Australian. Each of them has a different physical theatre skill and a different cultural story to bring to the mix. I was really interested in looking at how their different stories could be told through physical theatre and their bodies, and what that would say about current Australian identity.   (Bradley and Woods)

For each of the companies discussed here, the role of the body within physical devising is conceived differently from the way it was in those companies of the 1960s and 1970s. There is a greater emphasis on the diversity of bodies within the work and on the diversity of cultural influences displayed by the bodies of performers in the light of culturally distinct physical training. Rather than the abstract, neutral idea of the body as the authenticating ground of creative work, as much of the rhetoric of earlier actor-based companies implied, in contemporary physical devising the body has become a site of conflicting identities. And rather than a transcendental body which offers insight into the universal human condition, the bodies of contemporary devised physical performance are thought of as revealing the cultural complexity of bodies subject to different training regimes.

Physical Theatre, Devising and British Identity

Since the early 1980s there has been a swathe of UK theatre companies who have employed the term 'physical theatre' to describe their work. In a review of the Independent Theatre Council's thirtieth anniversary, Madeline Hutchins suggested that one reason for the rise of small-scale companies was that forming your own company was one way to the all-important Equity union membership, which made an actor employable by television and mainstream theatres (Hutchins, 2004, p. 4). Graham Devlin recorded that 'in 1975/76 the Arts Council massively increased the funds available to the now rather grandly styled "independent sector" and the companies were able to become far more professional' (Devlin, 2004, p. 3). However, the cuts of the early 1980s did bring to a halt some of the more politically radical and challenging of the small-scale touring companies, and physical theatre companies were predominantly surviving on project grants, rather than through-the-year revenue funding. In the late 1980s and early 1990s the Arts Council began to bring more touring companies onto their revenue books after the recommendations of the Arts Council Cork Report of 1986, which urged the Council to support 'what in the eighties was called "new" mime and may now be described as "physically based performance work"' (Brown, Brannen and Brown, 2000, pp. 382–4). In 1989/90 these groups included Theatre de Complicite and Trestle. Between 1991 and 1997 physical theatre companies did disproportionately well in gaining touring franchises: Black Mime Theatre, Kaboodle, David Glass Mime Theatre, and The Right Size all gained funding.

The phrase 'physical theatre' encompasses an enormous quantity of hybrid work. Early in the 1980s physical theatre tended to refer to two kinds of influence: groups who were interested in extending the expressive possibilities of dance; and groups who used clowning or popular theatre, often after time as students at Lecoq's school in Paris, where the *autocours* required small companies of students to improvise and devise short performances weekly. Since the 1990s many companies who devise physically have also been concerned with the crossover between live art, installation, performance art, site-specific work and physical performance. In the twenty-first century the tag 'physical theatre' has begun to sound dated to some of the groups working physically, who tend to apply the term 'physical performance' or 'visual performance' to their work, or use multiple definitions produced by the influence of postmodernism, the possibilities of technology and the seductions of site. A telling example of this transition might be evidenced in the work of Theatre de Complicite. Their early small-cast shows such as *Put It On Your Head* (1983), which examined English seaside behaviour, or *A Minute Too Late* (1984; revived 2005), which looked at the rituals and rawness of death and grief, were a celebration of the visual and physical inventiveness of the actors on the actors' scale, who made props and environments with their bodies. Apart from simple lighting and occasional recorded sound there was little technology in evidence. In contrast, in 1999 Simon McBurney explored site-specific work in a collaboration with John Berger. *The Vertical Line* was created for the disused Strand Station, where installation merged into live performance. In *Mnemonic* (1999) and *The Elephant Vanishes* (2003) the company and McBurney wholeheartedly absorbed into their devising the design possibilities, facilitated by technology, of mediated images and bodies encountering physical bodies on stage.

The rise of this professional sector of the British cultural scene is evidenced by the enthusiastic desire of the Arts Council of England to continue to fund devised physical theatre, and of the British Council to market this kind of work abroad as part of the 'best of British' culture. The range of physical, dance, circus and mime theatre companies who devise work might be illustrated by a simple listing of some of the most long-lived: Moving Picture Mime Show (1977), Tara Arts (1976), Kaboodle (1978), Kneehigh (1980), Trestle (1981), Theatre Alibi (1982), The Kosh (1982), Unfortunati (1982), Theatre de Complicite (1983), Mime Theatre Project (1984), I Gelati (1984), Ra-Ra Zoo (1985), Man Act (1985), DV8 (1986), Volcano (1987), Ralf, Ralf (mid-1980s, reformed in 2004), Right Size Theatre Company (1988), David Glass Ensemble (1989), Foursight Theatre (1989), Tamasha Theatre (1989), Ophaboom (1991), Walk the Plank (1991), Told by an Idiot (1992), Frantic Assembly (1992), Brouhaha (1993), Bouge de la (1993), Spike Theatre (1993, formalised in 1997), HoiPolloi (1994), Clod Ensemble (1995), Peepolykus (1996), Improbable (1996), Theatre O (1997), Quiconque (1999), Twisted I (2003), ESP: Experiments in Spontaneous Performance (2003). The extent to which physical theatre and devising have been absorbed into mainstream British culture as a generative force is illustrated by the school examination system for young adults at 18. The main examination boards at 'A' Level in Drama and Theatre Studies and the BTEC Diplomas in Theatre and in Performing Arts contain core elements which require students to devise, and some offer optional modules in Physical Theatre, Circus Skills and Drama Improvisation. The advice to teachers about representative companies students might examine predominantly refers to physical theatre companies, including Complicite, Kneehigh, Told by an Idiot, Trestle, Volcano and 'any genuine commedia dell'arte work'.[7]

Theatre de Complicite was founded in 1982 by Simon McBurney, Annabel Arden, Marcello Magni and Fiona Gordon. The company has expanded and evolved over the last twenty years to encompass a range of solo works, works with musicians, large-scale spectacular adaptations of stories, and classic scripts. Today McBurney characterises their work as 'a series of extraordinary and intricate collisions', in the generation of devised work or with scripts, stories or music.[8] Like many of the companies working today, Complicite does not work as a stable ensemble; indeed the very idea of an ensemble itself has undergone transformation. Very few companies are able financially to maintain an ensemble of any size, and most have a core of only two or three, usually the performer-directors who drive the company's work. However, physical theatre's performance style requires a 'sense of ensemble', with its complex physical interaction between actors, strengthened by a shared understanding of physical and visual composition. The question becomes how to build a 'sense of ensemble' in a group which does not survive for more than one show. McBurney has talked of the importance of shared activities that do not seem to be directly connected with 'acting', but are improvisatory or playful in other ways: actors might 'play children's games, or paint all morning, or work with clay ... work with buckets of water, or create instruments out of pots and pans' (McBurney, 1999, p. 76). Additionally, by the early 1990s part of the solution to this problem was the increasing availability of a wide pool of performers who had been trained, through drama schools or university, in dance, circus, mime and physical theatre itself and who had experience of work with several physical theatre companies. For example, Liam Steel, a performer with DV8 and Frantic Assembly, worked with McBurney on *The Noise of Time* (2002). For some groups, preexisting training through contemporary dance or Lecoq-related work, as in the case of many of Complicite's performers, can stand in for a 'sense of ensemble'. Performers have experience of a shared 'physical language' prior to work on a performance, and already know the range of work that they might engage in. The metaphor of 'physical language' here takes on a dual function, referring to both the building of an ensemble and the creation of units of image or text, the 'vocabulary' with which to communicate to an audience.

When working on *The Street of Crocodiles* in the National Theatre studio, Complicite allowed a rare glimpse of rehearsal to be filmed for *The Late Show* (BBC). Simon Murray noted the way in which physical exercises between performers fed directly into the creation of images for the stage picture. Pushing and pulling in pairs and groups, experimenting with different rhythms and pace produced, as Lecoq's training emphasised, the generation of emotion and mood from movement. McBurney insisted that the creation of the group images in *The Street of Crocodiles* was not a form of choreography: 'through innumerable improvisations the actors physically learned to shift together, like a flock of starlings. They learned to dip and wheel and found fantastic pleasure in it. This required enormous physical discipline and they worked extremely hard every day; it is this discipline of body and voice that is fundamental to my work' (McBurney 1999, p. 74). The body-based investigations of the studio are transposed directly into images on stage. The patterns of lifts, balances and supports that are exercises in the studio become images of human interaction, as in a scene in *The Street of Crocodiles* when Schulz, curled up like a child, is passed slowly and lovingly along a seated row of his family members, to symbolise his death. Slow processions across the stage and the carrying of actors form recurrent motifs in the work. Because the exercises or improvisations in the devising process are not concerned to explore sexual politics, or indeed politics in a broader sense, but emerge from a humanist individualism, the physical interaction that transfers from workshop into stage picture tends to reproduce predominantly heterosexual relationships, and traditional images of men carrying women – only very rarely do women performers carry male performers, and if they do so it is usually within an image suggesting oppression or struggle.

Complicite have continually attempted to resist the ossification of their work and devising processes, insisting there is no formula. Certainly their work has shifted both in its process and in the 'content' of the performance. Early shows were conceived and designed to be unfinished before the first night, since 'the ethic was one of continuous work rather than designed product' (McBurney, 1994, p. 16). Some of this practice has remained with the company, and performances shift and are reworked considerably, particularly during extended international tours. Originally Complicite's performance centred on physical comedy, in tune with the rise of the stand-up comedy circuit in the early 1980s, although the company were searching for a more thought-provoking theatrical language, 'the raw physical sensation of different emotions' (ibid., p. 16). McBurney had talked of the looser structure of devising rehearsals in the early days of Complicite's work:

We played together ... we'd kind of sit around banging tables and chairs for hours on end and then gradually somebody would come up with a character, just kind of out of desperation. And then somebody would play with somebody else and gradually these fragments would emerge. (McBurney, 1994, p. 17)

The pragmatic needs of working with larger casts has led McBurney to take a more obviously directorial role, and contributed to alterations in Complicite's 'style' of devising. A through-line that the company emphasise is the 'constant fooling around; the immense amount of chaos; pleasure as well as a kind of turbulent forward momentum'.[9] However, the dynamic of working as actor-director in a group of four within a small devising team, as in the first version of *A Minute Too Late* (1984) or *More Bigger Snacks Now* (1985), is very different from the more formal role of actor-director with a large cast. As Charlotte Medcalf, performer in *The Noise of Time* (2002), agreed, 'there's always collective feelings about things but in the end it's always going to be Simon's call' (Knapper, 2004, p. 68). The transition is exemplified by McBurney's different position within the generation of a unit or image, an exercise drawn from Lecoq's *autocours*. In the creation of early shows McBurney was always 'inside' the exercise of improvisation with objects and fellow performers to create an image. More recently he has described how 'sometimes I leave the actors to prepare something which we then look at; it can be tremendously liberating for actors to work without the director' (McBurney, 1999, p. 75). This repeated element of actors generating solutions for a moment of stage imagery draws on Lecoq; but here the devising work has become something closer to the compositional elements of Anne Bogart's Viewpoints, where a director interposes and edits what the actors have produced.

One of the elements of Complicite's work, and part of the reason it could be so readily welcomed into mainstream venues, is its accessibility and commitment to narrative. This is quite an achievement given the difficult texts that the group often start from, such as the sensuously descriptive and imagistic stories of Bruno Schulz, which found a through-line in *The Street of Crocodiles* in the narrative of Schulz's life, or the surreal subtexts of the disjunctive stories of Haruki Murakami which form the basis for *The Elephant Vanishes* (2003). Narrative is not, of course, plot. Characteristically, Complicite's work centres on recognisable characters, but often the stories of those characters are followed through extreme lengths of time, usually a whole lifetime and sometimes beyond. While the structure of sets the company uses strongly implies place – for example, the dark, rough wood-tiled backdrop suggestive of a peasant house in *The Three Lives of Lucie Cabrol* (1994) – their repeated transformation of objects creates a sense of epic time. The body-based games and exercises in rehearsal with physical objects, as well as with other actors, produce images which resist a simple mimetic relationship. In *Lucie Cabrol* a plank did not just represent a house. It stood in for any slope, step, or bed, and through the actors' manipulation became a transformed component in a series of emotionally charged images, ranging from the almost insurmountably steep slope of the mountain to an expression of sexual release:

> under the pressure of the final weeks we suddenly seized the planks we were holding to represent the barn [Jean and Lucie] were in, and started to fling them around the rehearsal room. The wall came apart and planks flew across the stage and we found the dynamic of love making transposed into the explosion of the space and the movement of the objects.[10]

Such discoveries are the result not of choreographic design, but of improvisation with objects and fellow actors in studio space. The body in physical theatre becomes a repository of narrative, not through the compressed naturalistic embodiment of a character's internal narrative summoned by 'emotional memory' and 'motivation', but through the fluidity of role from character, to stage-hand, to narrator, to object, each movement crystallising a distinct and disjunctive moment in the time, and thus the narrative, of the story.

The mode of physical devising that Complicite undertakes, with its sources in a European mime tradition, is not without significant political resonance. Complicite's work from the mid-1980s to 2003 has been centred on the early to mid-twentieth-century European experience. They have universalised this experience in epic storytelling forms and images using predominantly white, European performers, hence bodies, on stage. For example, in *Mnemonic* (2000), a narrator explicitly set up the performance as about the common ancestry of audience, performer and all humanity: 'a thousand years ago that line [of ancestry] would be longer than all people who have ever been born' (Theatre de Complicite, 1999, p. 7). This idea was played out in one of many physical embodiments, in an image where the place of the ice-man, preserved as an exhibit in a case, was taken by each of the performers in turn. For Helen Freshwater this 'emphasis on the body as a collective mnemonic, the lowest common denominator' was a resistance to the forgetting, or denying, of European Jewish history which the play explored (Freshwater, 2001, p. 218). However, the image and the performance, in seeking to universalise these performers' bodies as standing in for all humanity, also performed a very significant political act of forgetting all the different bodies whose encultured forms were not represented by the company.

A physical theatre company that is centrally concerned with negotiating these appearances and disappearances of the encultured body is Tara Arts (1977), the longest running British-Asian theatre company in the UK. Its artistic director Jatinder Verma has been a spokesman for a recognition of the creative wealth of Asian Arts in the UK for many years. For Verma the long-term contribution of Black and Asian artists has tended to be obscured by repeated acts of forgetting in the mainstream culture of the UK:

When it comes to Asian or Black Arts, there is no History, only 'moments of significance'. So we lurch from moment to moment of visibility, separated by a void of invisibility.   (Verma, 2003)

Verma has defined the mode of theatre he works in as 'a form of textual theatre which is strictly linked with the body and music' (Verma, 1999, p. 128). The aesthetic of the company has changed over time, moving through a variety of incarnations. Currently Tara Arts works with a predominantly storytelling mode, which functions both to establish an easy relationship with the audience at the centre of each performance and to mark the acts of translation, or transposition, which characterise their productions. A central strand to the company's work involves the adaptation of – or devising based upon – Indian plays and stories in order to bring this cultural aesthetic to both Asian and non-Asian audiences. Alongside this, since the late 1980s Tara has undertaken a series of radical adaptations of classic western plays such as *Tartuffe* (1990), a collaboration with the Royal National Theatre, *Oedipus* (1991), or *Le Bourgeois Gentilhomme* (1994). These transpositions of scripts and myths into a different cultural realm are often structured using a theatrical metanarrative or storytelling form. So, for example, *Cyrano* (1995) was transposed to 1930s Raj India, with Cyrano reconfigured as a prompt in a theatre, in love with a leading actress of a rival company.

Tara's work has been much involved with text, but devising played a role in their early processes, and continues to do so in the educational programmes. This influence came from Anuradha Kapur, an expert in folk drama, a director and teacher based in New Dehli. Kapur's first fully devised play, *This Story is Not for Telling* (1985):

> began life as a series of encounters with various techniques drawn from Indian 'folk' and street theatre: chorus, text-to-accompanying rhythm (both vocal and physical – i.e. footwork), the half-curtain, pointing (where the actor's text incorporates detailed directions – e.g. I look to the left. I raise my chin. My right arm rises. I speak. etc.). These exercises were then brought to bear on an eclectic range of texts: short stories from Borges, Brecht, Manto, Indian folk tales, etc. Texts being chosen for their ability to reflect the theme we were exploring, Communalism.   (Verma)[11]

In the mid-1980s, building on the work of Anuradha Kapur, Tara became interested in the medieval Gujarati form of folk drama, Bhavai, an equivalent form to *commedia*, with a basic plotline or *vesh*:

> This is embellished by a group of specialist performers: there is the fool, there is the equivalent of Arleccino (*Rangla*), all the kinds of stock characters are there, and they respond in whatever locality they happen to be in. There is movement and there is music, and there is this extraordinary 'text'. (Ley, 1997, p. 354)

The improvisational freedom of the form allowed ancient stories to be updated and transposed to address contemporary issues. So *Tejo Vanio* (1986) was a sixteenth-century farce transformed into a satire on immigration laws, and *Bhavni Bhavai* (1988) was an adaptation from a Bhavai play about the condition of the 'Untouchables'. Other productions have used different styles of devising, sometimes using free improvisation around scenarios from a story, which are then adapted into a script; at other times, as in their epic *Journey to the West* (2002), devising moods and situations from research interviews with members of the community, followed by devising from a rehearsal draft of the script.

A constant element for workshops and performance for Verma has been the presence of music and rhythm. He summarised the elements of a workshop process:

> My work always begins with the 'Surya' (Sun Prayer) exercise, which we've developed from various Yoga systems. After a basic grounding in footwork (drawing on various Indian dance techniques), which develops an expressive language of the body, we lead actors to gradually coordinate movement off free response to music; then to develop the coordinated mood of situations; then to develop situations themselves, with minimal voice. We use several games and exercises to sharpen the sense of listening-and-responding.[12]

Sometimes this improvisational work with music and rhythm finds its way directly into performance, as in a moment in an adaptation of Molière's *Le Bourgeois Gentilhomme* (1994), where musician and actor–singer improvised a new pace and movement sequence in harmony. Both pure and expressive forms of Asian dance have been important to the company's aesthetic, brought by dancer/choreographer Shobana Jeyasingh's work, not as a form of cultural preservation but translated into expressive movement by modern performers: 'the gestural language, the mimetic, expressive language in terms of the story – has to come from the way in which [the actors] use their bodies to express themselves now' (Ley, 1997, p. 357). Because not all the performers who work with Tara have a background in, or experience of, the multiple and varied forms of traditional Indian dance, Verma runs workshops in aesthetic forms before rehearsals begin.

The explorations and complexities that Tara Arts encounter in synthesising different cultural forms, using performers' bodies, which in themselves straddle different cultural trainings and experience, are cogent reminders that bodies are not straightforwardly expressive or readable. This was also an idea expressed in DV8's work, as Lloyd Newson, founder and director, argued:

> I think any aesthetic is political but unfortunately a lot of people don't take that on board. People refer to DV8 dealing with sexual politics – the Royal Ballet deals with sexual politics, it's just conservative rather than radical. (Newson, 1994, p. 45)

DV8 Physical Theatre was founded by Lloyd Newson in 1986 with fellow performers Nigel Charnock and Wendy Houstoun. Newson and other members of the company were dance trained (Newson had performed with Extemporary Dance Theatre company, 1981–5), but were one of the first groups to call themselves Physical Theatre, rather than a dance company. For Newson now, 'it's a term I hesitate to use because of its current overuse and abuse to describe almost anything that isn't dance or traditional theatre. My physical work requires trained dancers' (Newson, 1999, p. 109). The devising processes that DV8 used were dependent, particularly in the early work, on the specificity of the bodies and individuals who formed the company. Newson explained:

> There's only one person who does the role and the piece is built around them – around their improvisations, their personalities, the way they look, how they speak. ... The style of the company will vary depending on the amalgamation of those performers. None of us move in the same way: I want to acknowledge the differences and what they mean, not eradicate them. (Newson, 1994, p. 51; 1999, p. 110)

This is echoed in the devising processes, where personal experience, story, self-revelation is key to material and exercise. *My Body, Your Body* (1987), which looked at abusive relationships, used tape-recorded interviews with friends of the company as a stimulus.

The kind of performance DV8 developed was a mixture of contemporary dance, task-based activity, social dance, language and text. The absence of a guiding 'style' was central to the devising practice:

> I'm always looking for different ways to see and train the body. In the past we've incorporated yoga into the training and such skills as rope work, Irish dancing and aerobic workouts as well as the usual ballet, contemporary and contact improvisation techniques. (Newson, 1999, p. 111)

Over time, the way DV8 have worked in the devising process has changed. After 1990 and the success of the first tranche of DV8's work, Newson felt there was a risk of repetition unless he began to structure the company's work more carefully. Thereafter they have worked from scenarios he has composed in collaboration with other company members. For Newson, he 'still used improvisation but was able to divide [his] ideas more clearly. The improvisations became more structured and precise' (Newson, 1999, p. 109). Improvisations tend to begin with the physical and extend into the psychological and emotional:

> I might want to work on the physicality of 'greeting' ... perhaps from shaking hands to patting. I explore what happens to the changes in rhythm. What happens if the action remains the same but the speed or quality changes? What are acceptable and unacceptable places to touch when greeting and why? (Newson, 1999, p. 110).

During the 1990s the company returned again to collective devising, rather than choreography. Sometimes the structures for the performance were closely controlled scenarios led by Newson, often with a central, if fragmented, narrative. At other times, notably in the company's piece for the Sydney Olympics (2000), titled diversely *Can We Afford This* (in Australia) or *The Cost of Living* (in the UK and Hong Kong), they returned to a looser structure which bore the hallmarks of a different devising process, one centred on a theme – in this case of social prejudice about the body beautiful – but which featured multiple short devised episodes and images from seventeen very distinct dancers. In this, DV8 returned to the throughline of their impetus for devising, the personality and unique individuality of the bodies of the dancer-performers making the work.

In some ways the desire to use the personal more fully in their work also underpinned the formation of Improbable in 1996. In many ways Improbable epitomises the new formation of the professional devising company. The 'company' is a way of allowing the triumvirate of artistic directors/performers to pursue their work, together and independently, with the performers and creative team brought in for each show as needed.[13] Live improvisation on stage forms a key part of most of Improbable's work.[14]

> In doing improvisation on stage, the mechanisms are the same as in the rehearsal. For example, we start with newspapers, we do that in rehearsal, we teach that in workshops. Really we never rehearse, we only make theatre. Rehearsals are making theatre all the time. (Simpson)[15]

Recent improvised performances have included *The Animo Project* (2004) and *Lifegame* (1998–2004), developed from an experiment begun by Keith Johnstone, where an interviewee recounted memories and the performers transformed them into the images, music and objects of a theatrical story. Although not all the performances are so dependent on improvisation, many shows contain unplanned work: 'allowing the audience to have an integral part in the creation of a show'.[16] Their use of improvisation here draws on stand-up and comedy 'improv.':

> Improvisation is a part of the making or the performing of all shows. We only do basic improvisation in rehearsal. A game like one word at a time, you know, two people working with each other and talking one word at a time. That's the only impro we know. We use a version of Gaulier's The Game, *Le Jeu*. Phelim does all the workshops [with Gaulier and Lecoq] and teaches me. I'm too lazy to go. We don't do warmups, and we're fantastically unphysical. (Simpson)

What also comes with this style of work, when translated to deal with more serious content, is a sense of all the 'other' stories that the show might tell. Rather than the nostalgic coherence of Complicite's style of storytelling, each performance undercuts a simple storytelling aesthetic as the performers are profoundly unreliable, at times visibly uncertain, narrators. In *The Hanging Man* (2003), the cast lined up on stage as storytellers, guiding us into the narrative of a cathedral architect. But later in the performance, having explicitly confessed that 'we don't know this story', the performers moved into a mode of audience address where they were neither storytellers nor characters, and disrupted the narrative with personal associations, verbal games and exercises. In this, the performance shared elements with many of the companies discussed in Chapter 7.

An element that Improbable shares with other physical storytelling groups is a readiness to transform objects into whatever the story needs, and to imbue objects as puppets with mood, character or symbolic resonance. In *70 Hill Lane* (1996), which was based on a series of interlocking narratives about a poltergeist from Phelim McDermott's childhood, the house was marked out on stage using steel poles with sellotape stretched between them. The sellotape became variously an architectural feature, rays of light holding objects as if in mid-air, and a sound-effect of a threatening presence, before being scrunched up and animated as the poltergeist and – in a final image – a luminous moon. The discovery of these various images was made in just four weeks of rehearsal as the performance was built from improvisation with objects in the studio, which required the close integration of the design collaborators from early in rehearsal.[17] This spirit extends to the company's work with sets:

> The show is made from the kit. With *Hanging Man* we had a completed set and no idea how we were going to use it. It was really made in the technical rehearsal. We arrive and go 'What haven't we used yet' in the technical rehearsal, and the set becomes the story of the show. 'We haven't used that seat that goes up in the air on the pole yet, let's use it in this scene'. We have the story, and sometimes the actors have learned their lines, and sometimes we just have the story of that scene. (Simpson)

The actors, the set or the story are a pretext for performance, but almost never a script of any kind. Improbable has created performances for a wide range of venues in this way, from very small-scale puppet theatres to mainhouse repertory houses. Part of their adaptability to venues comes from the simplicity of the popular mechanisms of storytelling and the openness to an audience of each production, as well as the fact that their work is predominantly apolitical. Their devising mode is not one driven by a shared political or personal polemic or agenda, but has a conservative, even old-fashioned feel to it because of the function and structures of storytelling itself.[18]

Conclusion

It is impossible to separate recent developments and work in devised physical theatre from the economic conditions of its production. Physical devising processes usually need a commitment of time extending far longer than traditional theatrical rehearsal periods. Tim McMullan has described the long process of Complicite's work:

> We'd done various workshops in the year and a half leading up to actually starting rehearsing where we'd fooled around with a few ideas, putting stories in parallel just to see what would happen ... about 90 per cent of what we did got junked. (Freshwater, 2001, p. 215)

DV8's Lloyd Newson has considered co-production with the Royal Ballet but confessed:

> They can't provide me with the rehearsal time I would need to do a piece, despite showing interest. ... You can't just get the product without changing the system. (Newson, 1994, p. 50)

Conversely, Improbable made some of their shows, particularly those with large amounts of live improvisation in performance, within a standard five-week rehearsal period. The current situation in Australian and British funding makes the maintenance of a full-time ensemble, for these long periods, impossible for most companies.

Despite the demands it places on companies, devised physical performance has become increasingly international in its appeal and its touring circuit. Stalker, whose primary funding until recently came from international festival touring, have remarked upon a change in the international market. 'When we first started touring to Europe there were very, very few Australian companies, now there are a lot. That's changed the whole nature of the market as well' (Clarkson). International touring has produced a regular exchange of personnel across continents. Large-scale festivals in Europe, America, Australia and beyond have continued to facilitate the exposure of companies to a diverse range of different physical and spectacular performance, which in turn has influenced national companies' work. However, the demands of international touring managements have also conditioned or contributed to the shaping of the content of performances.

It is apparent that the idea of physical performance has shifted from the earlier companies of the 1960s, although there are many similarities in terms of the human scale of the work, the generation of images from physical improvisation, and the use of storytelling mechanisms as a structure for performance. Then, the body tended to be viewed as an authenticating expressive tool of itself. Today, the rhetoric that surrounds the devising of physical theatre companies is that the gestural and spatial interaction of bodies provides a different language from that of words, for the audience to decipher. So prior, or ongoing, training becomes a key component for any physical theatre devising company, since this is the acquisition of the 'common language' that performers will share, and which will form the foundation of the physical 'vocabulary' with which they will communicate story or meaning to the audience. This change also marks the professionalisation of devised physical performance. It is no longer a revelatory 'encounter' with a performer's working body that affects and communicates with an audience, but rather, the spectacle of the professionally skilled surfaces of the performers' bodies that are offered for interpretation.

7 Contemporary Devising and Postmodern Performance

Our focus in this chapter is on instances of contemporary devising that bear some relationship to the 'visual performance' scene of the 1980s and earlier. In some senses we struggle with our own terminology here, for by the 1990s and beyond, the performances addressed are no longer categorised as 'visual performance'. Instead they are typically referred to more simply as 'performance' – a term intended to signify their difference from what might be considered more traditional, text-based 'theatre'. The single word 'performance' might also signal a distance from the art practices that informed the work explored in Chapter 3, given that so many of its makers have come from university drama, theatre or performance departments. However, it is interesting to note that a recent show by Forced Entertainment continued to draw attention to an informing 'art history'; the publicity for *Bloody Mess* (2004) described it as 'an uncompromising political Pop Art'.

Where discourses arising from the artistic and cultural context of the 1960s and early 1970s, and the earlier avant-garde movements that shaped these, informed much of the work explored in Chapter 3, the performances discussed in this chapter are similarly related to dominant critical discourses of the time. The 1970s and early 1980s saw the emergence of various post-war, post-Marxist European critics (variously described as post-structuralist, postmodernist or postcolonialist), whose theories were, by the mid-1980s, circulating beyond the academy and informing not only critical responses to or engagements with performance practice, but also performance practices themselves. Theorists who rose to prominence and garnered significant influence during this period included, for example, Jacques Derrida,

Michel Foucault, Jean Baudrillard, Charles Jencks, Jean-François Lyotard, Edward Said, Gayatri Chakravorty Spivak, Hélène Cixous and Julia Kristeva.[1] By the 1990s various dominant critical theories or perspectives were firmly located within popular culture, and generally grouped (somewhat imprecisely) under the term 'postmodern'. In spite of important differences between theorists and positions, one might argue that the application of this term suggested a shared distrust towards universal explanations (typically 'foundational' in their status) and accompanying certainties of knowledge.

Performance practitioners would deny the intention of explicitly aiming to produce 'postmodern performances', recognising it as a term of (often lazy) retrospective critical description rather than of practice. Nevertheless, most practitioners (many of them university graduates) are fluent in the discourses and concerns of contemporary critical theory. If one understands postmodernism less as an aesthetic model than as a critical position that challenges the status of (or belief in) 'grand narratives' and of appeals to 'universal truths', then the occupation of this critical position necessarily prompts a particular relationship to devised productions.[2]

Devising Practices

The postmodern, for critic Linda Hutcheon, is bound up with 'questioning ... what reality can mean and how we can come to know it' (Hutcheon, 1989, p. 34). Evident in most contemporary devised performances is an acknowledgement of, conscious concern with, or deliberate interruption in, habituated meaning. Many performances make transparent the constructed narrative status of our (and its) interpretations/re-presentations of the world, implying or making explicit the processes and potential results of our meaning-making activities. Often performances enact interruptions to our typical ascription of meanings, or challenges to already existing 'authoritative texts'. They also most typically avoid offering a single or fixed meaning. As Nick Kaye proposed,

> The postmodern in art and performance ... occurs as a making visible of contingencies or instabilities, as a fostering of differences and disagreements, as transgressions of that upon which the promise of the work itself depends and so a disruption of the move toward containment and stability. (Kaye, 1994, p. 23)

It is our argument that collaborative devising processes match contemporary critical concerns, making it the ideal means to explore and embody those concerns in practice. In Chapter 4, we surmised that the perceived failure, by practitioners, of group devised 'plays' perhaps lay in the fact that the desired form was the conventional play-text. In contrast, a layered, fragmented, and non-linear 'text', one specifically courting various perspectives and viewpoints, perhaps lends itself more readily to the group devising process. Or, to put this the other way round, a group devising process is more likely to engender a performance that has multiple perspectives, that does not promote one, authoritative, 'version' or interpretation, and that may reflect the complexities of contemporary experience and the variety of narratives that constantly intersect with, inform, and in very real ways, construct our lives. We are not arguing, however, that a single author could not, definitively, produce such performances; just that a collaborative model makes this outcome more likely, if not inevitable, given the multiplicity of voices being added to the pot (assuming that all voices are heard).

The reflections of Tim Etchells, co-founder and director of the influential Sheffield-based company Forced Entertainment, founded in 1984, exemplified this understanding of the potential of devising as a mode of practice. If, as Etchells surmised, theatre typically aims for a single interpretation of a text, then perhaps Forced Entertainment had in mind something else; an image 'of theatre or performance as a space in which different visions, different sensibilities, different intentions could collide' (Etchells, 1999a, p. 55). John Ashford's understanding of experimental theatre as 'a compromised art ... a mucky, mutable, dirty, competitive, collaborative business' (Ashford, cited in Etchells, ibid.), struck a chord with Forced Entertainment:

> We always liked [Ashford's] quote recognising in it the great mess of our own process but also appreciating the fine word compromise – no clean single visions in our work, no minimalist control freak authorial line since by collaboration – impro, collage, the bringing together of diverse creativities – one gets an altogether messier world – of competing actions, approaches and intentions.   (Etchells, 1999a)

Bristol-based company The Special Guests, though formed almost twenty years after Forced Entertainment, adopt a similar 'messy' approach to devising, which would suggest that this mode of working is now, in the UK at least, widely shared:[3]

We begin making work by haphazardly playing around with text, improvisation, discarded diaries, song lyrics, second-hand shoes, ill-fitting suits and anything else we can lay our hands on. Sifting through a mass of half-formed ideas and flashes of inspiration a performance text is gradually mapped out. ... Text is made up, stolen, copied off the walls of public toilets and the sides of white vans.   (The Special Guests)[4]

Implicit in The Special Guests' statement, and common to devising processes, is the sense of 'randomness' about the 'texts' that are used. Thus Liz LeCompte, director of the hugely influential New York-based The Wooster Group, founded in 1975, insisted that when she chooses texts, 'they're random in a way. I feel I could use any text. ... I could pick anything in this room and make a piece that's just as complete as *L.S.D.*' (Savran, 1988, p. 50). The 'genesis' for their well-known *L.S.D.* (1984), seen by Forced Entertainment in 1985 at London's Riverside, was to be found in a moment experienced during the devising of an earlier production, *Nayatt School* (1978). During the making of *Nayatt School*, co-founder and performer Spalding Gray had brought in Arthur Miller's *The Crucible*, and had asked someone to read just one speech from it. One line from this – 'Your justice would freeze beer' – in the context of The Wooster Group's experience following *Route 1 & 9* (1981), and the withdrawal of funding, came back later to LeCompte, leading her to re-read *The Crucible*. For another project being planned at the same time, LeCompte had asked everyone to bring in a record album, and as a result heard *L.S.D.* by Timothy Leary. Working with these two different materials LeCompte 'suddenly realized that it was all part of the same piece' (LeCompte, in Savran, 1988, p. 177).

An account of the devising process used by another well established devising company, Chicago-based Goat Island, is similarly illustrative. The first material for *How Dear to Me the Hour When Daylight Dies* (1996) came from a pilgrimage made by the company to Croagh Patrick. Director Lin Hixson happened across a postcard near Belfast; the front of the card bore the picture of a man in swimming trunks kneeling before a shrine, with accompanying text which read 'a shivering homage' (Bottoms, 1998, p. 437). Using a familiar Goat Island process, Hixson employed this found object as a catalyst to encourage creative responses from the group, setting tasks such as 'create a solo tumbling homage dance' (ibid.), with the further instruction that each performer should 'assemble found texts or images to create a brief, personalized homage to someone or something of particular personal importance to him/her' (ibid., p. 438).

Obvious in such accounts of devising processes, as well as in devised products, is the sheer variety of materials used in the making of performances. Over the long process of devising *L.S.D.*, for example, the materials proliferated extensively. As Norman Frisch, dramaturg at the time, recollected, 'the material was pouring into the rehearsal room. The books, the drugs, the films, the transcripts, the props from the earlier shows, the record albums …' (Frisch and Weems, 1997, p. 491). Such juxtaposition of materials is a common dramaturgical structure shared by many contemporary companies. Another New York-based ensemble, Elevator Repair Service (1991), has consistently intermixed texts (and performance forms). *Room Tone* (2001), for example, drew on the works of Henry James and William James, also incorporating Balinese gamelan music. Goat Island's spoken text for *How Dear to Me the Hour When Daylight Dies* (1996) drew on seventeen different sources. Many more additional texts would have been used for the composition of the physically exhausting, repeated-movement sequences that are Goat Island's trademark (Bottoms, 1998, p. 431). The Wooster Group's *Frank Dell's Temptation of St Anthony* (1988) spliced together almost a dozen texts.

Juxtaposition is not a phenomenon of the 1980s and beyond. The 'history' of The Wooster Group is instructive of an ongoing 'conversation' around practice and a shared lineage. Richard Schechner, himself influenced by various companies and forms including Grotowski, The Living Theatre and Happenings, founded The Performance Group in 1967; Liz LeCompte and Spalding Gray saw their *Dionysus in 69* (1969) and joined the company in 1970, working first on The Performance Group's collaboration, *Commune* (1970), with Gray as a performer, and LeCompte as an assistant director. The form evident in *Commune* clearly shared features with The Wooster Group's own later work; *Commune* 'juxtaposed a wide range of materials: *Moby Dick*, folk songs, spirituals, Thoreau's *Walden*, the murder of Sharon Tate by the Manson "family," the Mai Lai massacre and autobiographical texts by the performers' (Savran, 1988, p. 3). As David Savran commented, LeCompte was influenced, during her six years' 'apprenticeship' as Schechner's assistant director, by 'his use of disparate texts and acting styles and his development of work through improvisations' (ibid.). Importantly, she was less persuaded by his 'highly symbolic and ritualistic' *mise en scène*, and his 'dangerously psychoanalytical' approach to performance (ibid.). LeCompte effectively appropriated some of the experiments undertaken by Schechner, but redirected these away from the influences of Grotowski, The

Living Theatre, Open Theatre, etc. It is also notable that LeCompte was inspired by the work of Robert Wilson; Wilson's *Deafman Glance* (1970) presented 'a visual language that was not necessarily psychologically real' (LeCompte, in Savran, 1988, p. 4). She recognised that Wilson's work utilised a 'musical' rather than a 'logical form', and a 'geometrical structure' (ibid.). The reach of influence is also evidenced by the fact that Spalding Gray had earlier been a participant in Robert Wilson's Byrd Hoffman School.

Just as various materials are embraced by most companies, so there are many different ways then to organise them. However, the majority of devising companies also share a desire to resist choosing or fixing any central idea prior to, and even after, making work; the performance evolves entirely from the process of its making, from the materials, movements, and structures that surface as each different component is brought into contact with each, enabling new associations and possibilities to freely emerge. Thus Liz LeCompte insisted that:

> When I go downstairs [to the studio] I don't have any thematic ideas – I don't even have a theme. I don't have anything except literal objects – some flowers, some images, some television sets, a chair, some costumes I like. In the last piece, something someone brought in by mistake. That's it. And then ideas come after the fact.   (LeCompte, in Kaye, 1996, p. 260)

Two closely related ways of working with disparate materials that emerge during devising processes are 'montage' and 'collage'. For David Graver, in collage the 'foundness of the objects points persistently back to the world from which they came', in turn causing a disruption in any assumed autonomy of the artwork (Graver, 1995, p. 31). David Savran similarly recognised The Wooster Group's collage principle, where

> LeCompte takes up a found object, a fragment, that comes onto the scene without fixed meaning, and places it against other fragments. ... A sense of the object's arbitrary nature is preserved ... by virtue of its *dislocation* within the text. ... [The object] remains discrete, its casual nature now evident as a causal disjunction ...   (Savran, 1988, pp. 51–2)

LeCompte herself has insisted that

> anything can co-exist together – without, you know, losing its own uniqueness – without being absorbed and regurgitated. They are separate,

and they can stay separate and at the same time inform each other – within the same work.   (LeCompte, in Kaye, 1996, p. 257)

While The Wooster Group apply a structure of 'collage', Stephen Bottoms has suggested that Goat Island utilise 'montage', where found materials become 'constituent components in a new structure' (Bottoms, 1998, p. 432). The material, lifted from its 'original' context, is put to use in a new way, for new purposes, and though the materials are diverse, they nevertheless appear to 'belong' (ibid.). As Graver similarly explained of the montage, 'the disparate fragments of reality are held together and made part of the work of art by the work's constructive principle' (Graver, 1995, p. 31).

In spite of the differences between 'collage' and 'montage' procedures, both companies share a distrust of a central, already defined, purposeful point in their work, avoiding any such organisational foundation. Where Bottoms perceived Goat Island's work as adopting a 'rhizomic structure',[5] in which the sources, through a process of accretion, build out towards the horizon rather than collapsing inwards, Savran made similar claims for the collage effect of The Wooster Group's work.

The textual network of which every Wooster Group piece is composed is never simply an elaboration of a single pretext, since none of the floating fragments, regardless of its size or prestige, ever becomes a fixed centre around which a piece is built.   (Savran, 1988, p. 52)

Bonnie Marranca perceived that the effect of The Wooster Group's collage activities was the production of *texture* in place of 'text' (Marranca, 2003, p. 2), an 'anthology' of 'pieces' or fragments (ibid., p. 4). Etchells has similarly reflected on the place and productive effect of the fragment in Forced Entertainment's work: 'Disconnected from its "original" place, lacking context, lacking "beginning" or "end", lacking place in an argument, lacking "reason" – the fragment is both statement and question' (Etchells, 2004, p. 281). This elusive quality of the fragment makes it an 'ideal compositional unit'.

For certain critics, collage is a process suited to our 'postmodern times'. Thus, Roger Copeland has insisted that:

collage appeals to an age that has come to distrust claims of closure, 'unity,' and fixed boundaries. ... Seemingly unrelated elements begin to 'resonate' off one another – across gaps of both space and time – resulting in protean, unstable, and wholly provisional relationships.   (Copeland, 2002, pp. 13–15)

Mirroring Russell Hoban's understanding of the shifting mode of perception required by developments in technology (see Chapter 3), Tim Etchells related Forced Entertainment's dramaturgical structure to the montage mode of television, where the 'fragment' is 'a unit of informational exchange' (Forced Entertainment, 1998, video):

> Now, with the remote in place, the TV is an endless montage of constructed fictions, constructed realities and occasional static, which is in itself endlessly re-montaged by every viewer, not only through channel hopping but also through the intersection, in their homes, of the TV image and their lives. (Etchells, 1994, p. 111)

Writing in 1988, before the advent of the internet, email, or even mobile phones, Etchells proposed that 'almost anyone can see that the new image glutted media landscape of Western Europe needs new theatrical forms to explore it' (Etchells, 1988). LeCompte similarly admitted that 'There's no question that my work has been influenced by MTV, and specifically before MTV by ads on TV – the cutting, editing, distancing, story-telling. ... Telling a sometimes disjointed story in a very rapid way is definitely a great influence' (Aronson, 2000, p. 195).

We should also remember, however, that the techniques of collage and montage have an avant-garde lineage. The members of Forced Entertainment are cognisant of their historical roots. As they stated, 'When we work with different things, I think we're hoping to find a way of making them go together that's unexpected' (Forced Entertainment, 1998, video). The echo of Lautréamont's famous phrase, 'the chance meeting of an umbrella and a sewing machine on a dissecting table' (Lippard, 1970, p. 6), is certainly audible in their understanding that by putting together 'two guns, a pantomime horse, and a pair of curtains', you might go 'somewhere you could never have predicted' (Forced Entertainment, 1998, video).

Evident in all of the devising processes discussed is the apparent operation of chance, the precedents of which are also to be located in both the avant-garde experiments of the early twentieth century such as those of the Surrealists and Duchamp, and the later, related performance events from the 1960s. Alexander Kelly, co-director of another Sheffield-based company, Third Angel, not only stressed that devising is a 'responsive way of working' but further observed that the process 'embraces serendipity: accident, chance, the unexpected and unpredictable' (Kelly, 2004, n.p.). Forced Entertainment are also explicit about the importance of 'accidents' in the devising process. For performer Robin Arthur, 'accidents are the occurrences that give rise to leaps of logic', whilst for Terry O'Connor, they are 'Like windows, they give you the opportunity to see something that you wouldn't have thought of by yourself' (Forced Entertainment, 1998, video). LeCompte similarly explained that, during an improvisation, someone will do something, and

> I take that chance occurrence and say, that is the *sine qua non*, that is the beginning, that is the text. I cannot stray from that text. ... It's an action-text that may have nothing to do with any thematic thing we're working on. I call it chance work, like throwing a handful of beans up in the air. And when they come down on the floor, I must use that pattern as one pole against which I work my dialectic. I cannot alter it unless, somehow, another structure, another bunch of beans that I throw up in the air, comes into conflict with the first. Then one bean must move, one way or the other. But only at that point.   (Savran, 1988, p. 51)

LeCompte combined chance and formal procedures in this example as a means to generate the work within limits. However, somewhat paradoxically many practitioners, whilst insisting on the play of chance and randomness, of 'foundness' and just 'using what comes up', simultaneously apply the term 'intuition', employing phrases such as 'waiting for things to happen' or 'knowing when something feels right' to explain processes of devising. Thus Etchells, reflecting on the 'accidents' of devising, stated that though 'nobody really intended it ... everybody knows when it happens that it's a really perfect thing for you to work with' (Forced Entertainment, 1998, video). Spalding Gray, commenting on the process of devising involved in The Wooster Group's first collaborative performance, *Sakonnet Point* (1975), recorded that 'there was no central theme', but from the experience of doing improvisations, 'we all knew that [if] ... you watch and pay attention, that something would take shape organically that would be expressive of that space, of the history of that space' (Savran, 1988, p. 177). Chance or randomness are combined with some unquantifiable, yet persistent, sense of 'appropriateness'. Though the work does not exist and is unknown in advance of its making, there is nevertheless an assumption that there is a work to be 'discovered' or 'recognised'. The pattern fits when it fits the pattern. Intuition, then, and perhaps also the supposedly random 'play' of 'chance', might simply be a performance of experience or of imitation. One feels that something is 'right' because it fits a model of the already known, already sought; the 'found' gesture is only, in fact, seen – or enacted – because it is already learnt, is anticipated, or is being looked for.

The feeling of 'rightness' is perhaps also encouraged by the fact that companies often intentionally 'recycle' materials, starting where a previous performance left off, or developing further an interest in a concept, a performance moment, or a theme not fully explored in an earlier piece. The 'sensibility' of one performance often continues into the other. As Norman Frisch noted of The Wooster Group, the company created performances 'out of the refuse, the material that was cut out of the previous productions and things that people, for one reason or another, are just not yet ready to let go of' (Frisch and Weems, 1997, p. 491). This was an observation with which another Wooster Group dramaturg, Marianne Weems, agreed:

> I think the new piece is always built on the shards of what's left over from the last one. The Group recycles images and icons and architectonic fragments, and that process contributes part of the epic sense of continuity in the work.   (Frisch and Weems, 1997)

Third Angel similarly perceived that some of their work is 'an ongoing series of explorations, so often one project leads into another'.[6] The opening section of the company's *Where From Here* (2000) was in fact devised for another collaborative project, but in that event did not get used (Kelly).[7]

This recycling of materials between shows is also a common feature, and spectators familiar with a company's work might be expected to read across their archive, or the 'palimpsest' performances, and in this sense no work is autonomous. Goat Island frame their practice as being a series of 'responses for each other back and forth ... over a long period of time' (Goat Island, 2000, p. 3). Though this refers to their general process of making a work, it also refers to the responses engendered between work, where various threads (of form and/or content) continue to be spun. Their recent work, *When Will the September Roses Bloom? Last Night Was Only a Comedy* (2005), made the device of repetition explicit by staging the performance over two nights, whilst acknowledging that some spectators would see only one performance. Eighty five per cent of the material on the second night was repeated from the first night's performance. In an illuminating reflection on the device of 'repetition', Matthew Goulish, responding to a producer who asked about a performance, 'What is the reason for all this repetition?' replied, 'What repetition?' (Goulish, 1996, p. 94). Where one person might see 'a single moment repeating', another person might see 'a non-repeating series of similar moments'. Each act or movement sequence is inevitably separated by time, and by all the other acts and movements which have intervened, so that there can be, in reality, no repetition. As Bottoms noted,

> To repeat something again and again in varying contexts ... is to create a kind of mini-history within the piece itself, one which in turn opens out a broader 'history' for the spectator, as she attaches personal significance to each 'unit' of the performance ... and then considers that unit's shifting resonance in each fresh context.   (Bottoms, 1998, p. 442)

Claims of 'repetition' (and also of 'copying' or 'borrowing') need to be approached carefully.

Devising a performance generates an enormous amount of material. Lacking the structure prompted or demanded by a linear narrative, performances might be determined by the application of formal systems, resonating with earlier performance events discussed in Chapter 3. For Goat Island's *How Dear to Me the Hour When Daylight Dies*, for example, the material was placed using the structural device of a 'palindromic configuration', which the group felt mirrored the structure of a pilgrimage: 'one makes a journey and then retraces the same steps in mirror image on the way home' (ibid., p. 439). The Wooster Group's early work employed structural patterns in relation to spatial configuration, combining this with the process of 'recycling' or the notion of the 'palimpsest' that we have already noted. As designer Jim Clayburgh revealed,

> The ground plan for *Rumstick Road* became the ground plan for *Nayatt School*, only reversed in the space and lowered. Then the house finally fell apart to a skeleton structure on legs at the end of *Point Judith* and moved from wood to tin. The *Route 1 and 9* house ... was the same one built at the end of *Point Judith*. It's a constant evolution of the same ground plan, with just a transfer to another space or the change of an angle. Even when I designed *L.S.D.*, the ground plans of all the other shows were on the stage as my reference for working it out.   (Marranca, 2003, p. 7)

For all companies the structuring process also simply demands the trying out of combinations in order to consider how different components work together, in terms of visual and rhythmic variations and textures, and what their combinations might variously signify. Material circumstances, such as the space available, financial restrictions, and matters relating to Health and Safety legislation, also act as 'limits'/'catalysts'. The impact of such material circumstances on decision-making processes should not be underestimated. As Third Angel admitted, 'sometimes ideas are changed or born from the restrictions that are placed on the project due to money, time or space'.[8] In Chapter 3 we similarly saw that many structuring decisions taken by the People Show were pragmatic, based, for example, on the necessity of someone being in a specific place on stage, at a specific time in the performance.

Having discussed some of the processes utilised by various contemporary performance companies, at this point it is vital to remind our readers that there is no one 'model' of devising, which can be simply or easily appropriated. Further, it is also important to recognise that companies themselves develop. The interests of practitioners and companies shift, as do their forms and processes, and collaborators – sometimes between one show and another, and sometimes over a longer period. As Lin Hixson noted, 'there are many different approaches to collaboration' (Jaremba, 1991, p. 46). Indeed, Hixson's personal trajectory reveals the extent to which an artist's practice develops, often in accordance with the nature of the collaboration. Her early experience with the Los Angeles-based company Hangers was one of 'doing', rather than 'talking' (see Jaremba, 1991). After Hangers, Hixson collaborated with performance artists, resulting in works that corresponded more to this 'individual' sensibility: 'Those pieces were like stringing beads. Elisha [Shapiro] would do his thing, we'd figure out a transition, another person would do their thing' (ibid.).

Many of the best known companies have been in existence for many years, and it is that time – experience combined with knowledge of their colleagues – that has enabled them to develop their own processes. Though Forced Entertainment had already had some practical experience of devising while at university, it is worth noting that the company nevertheless had to find, through further practice, their own way of working.[9] At first they utilised the collective model favoured by some of the political companies explored in Chapter 4, where the members 'rotated everything' (ibid.), although according to Etchells' recollections, their reasons for doing this were not ideologically founded. Though they might have devised performances at university, they did not yet know how to make performances with this specific grouping of people. 'We didn't know what people were good at, so we all kind of had a go at performing, we all had a go at directing, and we did three or four shows that way' (Etchells, 2004).[10] From this experience, they 'certainly figured out that not everybody liked to do everything, that not everybody was good at everything, or that certain people had passionate desires to pursue one thing or another'. Fairly early in their practice, 1985 or 1986, Etchells decided that he was not going to perform, but was instead going to stand outside and direct (ibid.).

Forced Entertainment have, since their inception, developed their modes of practice, moving from non-text performances, where there was little live spoken text, to Etchells writing a great deal of the performed text, to text which arises directly from improvisations which are video-recorded and learnt, or from the performance of live improvisations. All Forced Entertainment members are now fluent in what has, over the years, become a shared language. In this respect, though Forced Entertainment text is quite distinctive it would now be difficult to know whether Etchells wrote it or not. Goat Island are also exemplary in indicating the shifts that occur over time. In Stephen Bottoms' opinion, from *It's Shifting, Hank* (1993) onwards, the work became longer and more complex, perhaps because it also became more interdisciplinary, responding to the different training or areas of skill that each performer brought into the group. Bryan Saner, for example, is a dancer, sculptor and carpenter, while Mark Jeffery trained in installation and performance art.

The change of 'personnel' in companies undoubtedly affects the work, given that the devising process draws so extensively on the contributions of all participants. Frisch's reflections on The Wooster Group are instructive in this respect; he suggested that each and every one of their shows is, in fact, a record of who was participating, where they were in their own lives, and what went on both inside and outside the rehearsal room, during its making; this is what the work is 'about' (Frisch and Weems, 1997, p. 491). The Wooster Group's devising processes have also changed over time. Thus Frisch recorded that at the time of devising *L.S.D.*,

> each Wooster performance was quite unique, incorporating large amounts of improvised action and randomly timed events. So what we had was a rigid scenario for a performance, but never a set text. Or rather, it was a score – like some enormous jazz masterwork, recognizable as itself from night to night, but ultimately just a container for that night's jam. (Frisch and Weems, 1997, p. 484)

However, The Wooster Group's *Brace Up!* (1991), starting from one central text, a new adaptation of Chekhov's *The Three Sisters*, was quite a radical departure in terms of the devising process. Dramaturg at the time, Marianne Weems stated that '*Brace Up!* was not about people bringing in an enormous variety of different kinds of material. We started specifically from *Three Sisters* and that's where we stayed for a long time, about two years actually' (ibid, p. 497).

The endurance of companies over time undoubtedly has an effect on the work produced. As Norman Frisch insisted, 'After five or ten years of working with the same colleagues – that's when you really begin to be able to get down to something.' When Frisch suggested that 'it all flows from that shared ...', Weems illustratively finished the sentence with the word, 'sensibility' (ibid., 1997, p. 503).

Postmodern Concerns: Process into Product

Whilst the definition of 'postmodernism' remains appropriately con-tested, it is nevertheless apparent that a certain postmodern aesthetic code has become citable and, through repetition, is assumed to be synonymous with a postmodern practice. Adjectives such as contin-gent, unstable, undecidable, transgressive, disruptive, open, decentred, self-reflexive, knowing, parodic, ironic, intertextual, paradoxical, and fragmented, are just some of the most familiar ones used in relation to 'postmodern performance'. Jon Whitmore, for example, in the context of his text *Directing Postmodern Theater*, applied the term 'postmodernism' to performances that 'are primarily nonlinear, non-literary, non-realistic, nondiscursive, and nonclosure oriented' (Whit-more, 1994, p. 4).

That one might be able to describe a performance as 'self-reflexive' or 'fragmented' or 'transgressive' or 'contingent' or 'postmodern' even, seems to us to miss the point. Such descriptions concern themselves only with form, and not at all with the potential 'effect' of form, or in Nick Kaye's words, the 'event' of performance (see Kaye, 1994). And yet, as Carol Becker stated, 'art often envelopes form in content or content in form' (Becker, 2000, p. 94). Work we consider to be 'postmodern', then, does not employ form for form's sake. Instead, particular forms are chosen for intended effect (even if these cannot be guaranteed). Though one might identify certain common devices or features that recur in contemporary devised work, it is necessary to ask *why* companies do what they do. Importantly, much of the work that we cite here bears evidence of a political commit-ment towards challenging dominant ideologies or narratives, and is often rooted in contemporary concerns. Apparent from the various examples explored in this section is the overriding concern in con-temporary devised performances with both the status of theatre, and the status of 'reality', a concern played out in explorations of the relationship between them. Many performances explore the mechan-isms of theatre as a representational medium and, simultaneously, the representations that serve to construct our social worlds.

Contemporary performances, located in the cultural context of the late twentieth and early twenty-first century, take their place at a time when the 'grand-narratives' that previously enabled us to make sense of our world and to project its development (typically its humanist or Enlightenment 'narrative trajectory') have been discredited. The work of Forced Entertainment, for example, has consistently engaged with the processes of 'narrativity', aiming to confront the complexity of contemporary experience while at the same time showing our typical desire for narrative closure in the face of apparent chaos. For Etchells, their early performances were 'about the striving for something ... some kind of order or sense, or the ability of the protagonist to, just for a moment, hold the world and see it properly' (Etchells, 1997). At the same time, the work acknowledged the impossibility of this aim of revealing or fixing reality. Embedded in the company's publicity accompanying their work is the contemporary critical language that proposes this crisis in narrative. A concern of *Showtime* (1996), for example, was 'how do we make sense of the world, and is it actually possible to do so' (ibid.), while in *Some Confusions in the Law About Love* (1989) there was 'a pathos, an anxiety about the way reality feels weakened, a fear that representation has failed us' (Etchells, 1990).

Though companies refuse to propose or dictate one single meaning to any work, they do not reject the possibilities of multiple meanings, of the accumulation of signs. Thus Marianne Weems revealed that every day, during rehearsals with The Wooster Group, LeCompte would find a new 'meaning' for a piece, discovering 'tiny narratives' depending on what moment or event she was working on. This did not make all the other meanings redundant, nor did it revise them, 'because all these readings are eventually allowed to sit next to each other in a polyphonous way' (Frisch and Weems, 1997, p. 498). All meaning, then, was provisional and partial.

Given that The Wooster Group's work is filled with potentially infinite meaning, what it means will vary considerably between individuals, even between the performers. As with the People Show, discussed in Chapter 3, each company member might have his or her own 'ideas' of what the performance is about, or their role in that. Norman Frisch has stated that 'the nature of [a work] is rarely, if ever, agreed upon by the players involved' (ibid., p. 499). Goat Island members similarly, in an interview with Irene Tsatsos in 1991, revealed that they all interpreted certain sections of *Soldier, Child, Tortured Man* (1987) from very different perspectives (see Tsatsos, 1991, pp. 66–74).

In place of the singular metanarrative there is contingency, partial and plural perspectives, and an understanding of the rules that pertain to 'narrative construction', of *making* truths. For example, though Goat Island resist offering a centralising, and therefore stabilising, point to their performances, the accretion of various texts produces a richness that prompts infinite connections to be made from the materials, rather than no connections. Allusions are themselves dependent on the experiences that the spectators bring with them. In *Can't Take Johnny to the Funeral* (1991), performer Karen Christopher made a small circle in the air, with her finger. She was

> thinking of a woman I once knew who had to leave her children in the custody of the state. I am not doing an imitation of her or anything. The gesture comes from a gesture I made spontaneously once while describing the way my own mother listened to a particular 45 record over and over again.   (Christopher, 1996, pp. 8–9)

Christopher recollected that one woman, upon witnessing her gesture, 'saw a woman waiting for her man to come home from war', whilst another 'saw her 2-year-old winding up to wreak havoc'. For Christopher,

> these things were really seen by these women, and other people saw their own images too. Because of what led to this moment, what came after, each person's reference points, and my own intentions and those of Goat Island, the moment does not look the same to everyone. It is not as simple as a magician pulling a coin out of a person's ear, but it is no less a collaboration between the performer and the spectator. The moment occurs with the involvement of all parties.   (Christopher, 1996)

One 'event' of postmodern performance, then, may be to awaken spectators to their implication in meaning-making precisely by being 'fragmented' and 'nonclosure oriented' (Whitmore, 1994, p. 4), or narratively incoherent. Stan's Cafe's *Be Proud of Me* (2004), for example, though deliberately mimicking the narrative structures of the psychological thriller, in the end refused to fully deliver the expected conclusion and instead left us with hints of more than one possible story, fragments that we could use to construct our own conclusions. The 'open text', performs a contemporary spin on the notion of spectators' collaboration. David Savran has commented on the effect of The Wooster Group's texts, where the work

> urges the [spectator] to make the kind of choices usually considered the province of the writer/and or performer. As a result, each piece must be considered only partially composed when it is presented to the public, not because it is unfinished, but because it requires an audience to realize the multitude of possibilities on which it opens. As each spectator, according to his part, enters into a dialogue with the work, the act of interpretation becomes a performance, an intervention in the piece. (Savran, 1988, p. 55)

The spectators, then, are driven to make their own choices, and to be cognisant of that *activity*, or the politics and ethics of the choices they actually make, the meanings they attribute.[11]

Andrew Quick, surmising the potential effects of The Wooster Group's fragmented dramaturgical form and intertextual practice, proposed that their work 'shakes things around, puts everything in a spin, so to speak, but it always somehow corresponds to and articulates the complexity of life's experience rather than simply observing or telling the story of how systems break apart' (Quick, 2002, n.p.). 'Shaking stuff around' is one way to describe the practices *and* potential effects of many contemporary devising companies and their performances; a 'shaking' of various found, appropriated and invented materials leaves it – and us – shaken. In much contemporary devised performance, the appropriation, reworking or redeployment of sources results in the shaking loose of both familiar meaning and habituated meaning-making strategies. The refusal to proffer any straightforward, 'given' meaning is intended and political. In the self-consciously impassioned words of Etchells,

> This is not the place for respectable or soap-box certainties – only live issues will do. Investment wants us naked, with slips and weaknesses, with the not-yet and never-to-be certain, with all that's in process, in flux, with all that isn't finished, with all that's unclear and therefore *needs to be worked out*. Don't give me anything less than this. Don't give me a truth that's more fixed, i.e., more of a stupid lie. (Etchells, 1999a, p. 49)

One frequent technique used to reveal 'how representation legitimizes and privileges certain kinds of knowledge' (Hutcheon, 1989, p. 53) is the appropriation of other representations, and the *re-presentation* of them. The *re-* is important here; the aim is not to present 'the same' work, but, through working in a different context, to present something quite different, from the same material. For Linda Hutcheon, appropriation and parody are a means by which to contest assumptions about 'author/ity', 'originality', 'authenticity' and 'ownership', staging a direct attack on modernist notions of 'foundations' and 'essences'. Of course, it is to be remembered that any texts that are appropriated are, themselves, already representations. Appropriations, therefore, are representations of representations, and where such a doubling is enacted critically, the means of both representations will be laid bare; not in order to provide the authoritative representation, but to unveil representations' mechanisms. Though Hutcheon used as her example postmodern photographs, her analysis of these is helpful:

> Reappropriating existing representations that are effective precisely because they are loaded with pre-existing meaning and putting them into new and ironic contexts is a typical form of postmodern complicitous critique: while exploiting the power of familiar images, it also de-naturalizes them, makes visible the concealed mechanisms which work to make them seem transparent, and brings to the fore their politics, that is to say, the interests in which they operate and the power they wield.   (Hutcheon, 1989, p. 44)

The opening section of The Wooster Group's *Route 1 & 9* (1981), 'THE LESSON (Upstairs): In Which a Man Delivers a Lecture on the Structure and Meaning of *Our Town*', offered a clear example of this idea of 'complicitous critique', working with, at the same time as working against, its appropriated texts. Multiple television screens projected a video of the performer, Ron Vawter, re-presenting a broadcast lecture originally given by Clifton Fadiman, which purported to explain the meaning of Thornton Wilder's *Our Town* for the viewer. The Wooster Group's reconstruction of this documentary drew attention to the processes by which Fadiman's lecture accrued authority (see Savran, 1988; and Kaye, 1994).

Another useful example of self-reflexive challenges to 'author/ity' was Desperate Optimists' *Playboy of the Western World* (1998). Though the title of the performance was the same as J. M. Synge's well-known play, the company devised a piece around the play, rather than presenting the play itself. A complex, weaving narrative was constructed from the 'events' surrounding the premiere of the 'original', enabling an exploration of history, myth, interpretation, cultural identity and the 'act' of theatre and theatrical representation. The opening lines of the show nodded knowingly towards the contemporary concern with the status of narrative. Joe Lawlor, speaking into a microphone, addressed us reassuringly:

> Good evening. We have been thinking about a question for quite some time now and it goes as follows: 'What do we need to know?' And we've decided that in response to this question, what we really need to know are the facts. That's just about it. Plain, simple, ordinary, no messing about, cutting straight to the point ... facts. No ... literary ornamentation ... just the facts. So for what it's worth, that's exactly what we're going to give you this evening. Just the facts. No more, but no less. On January 25th 1907 in Dublin, Ireland, at the Abbey Theatre *the* single most important, radical revolutionary play was premiered ...

In the event, the impossibility of presenting 'facts' was revealed as the narrative variously fractured, faltered and weaved across episodes, time and continents. The narrative, such as it was, was also punctured by interruptions from video-recorded talking heads, who shared their memories, interpretations and opinions of Synge's play, each offering up a particular perspective and partial viewpoint. Malloy's admission that some of them had not actually seen the play issued a powerful warning concerning the 'authority' of interpretation. Malloy's follow-up statement, offered as reassurance – 'but they're Irish so they can have a good go at it' – comically questioned both assumptions about identity and the relationship between (national) identity and 'rightful', or 'authorised', knowledge.

In order to undermine its own 'authority' any so-called postmodern narrative must be self-reflexive, containing within its structures its own means of destabilisation. In much contemporary work, performance is presented *as* performance, as a representational medium and as part of the representational system. Performance is often used to unmask performance. Thus Uninvited Guests' *Guest House* (1999) showed the process of constructing their multi-media show, within the show itself. One device used in the performance was that the performers cast and directed each other:

> Performer: Can we see that stumble Jo? [*Jo stumbles.*] Ok, let's look at that again, but with a bit more of a look of frustration on your face and a sign or a noise of anger.

Of course, the audience did not know, watching this, whether it was a scripted, rehearsed (and therefore 'fictional') enactment of the process of construction, or whether this was an improvised moment, or in fact somewhere in-between; it is possible that it was a re-enactment of an actual rehearsal. In a sense, we were enabled to 'see' how the performance was created, although this is, in fact, a dizzying 'game' of representation. For Paul Clarke, director of the company, 'The process of developing the performance work was included in the "recursive system" of the performance product. In a sense, the "completed" performance work became a representation of a "work in progress"' (Clarke, Uninvited Guests).[12]

Undermining the 'authority' of any text, including their own, many contemporary devised works deliberately confuse the ontological status of the given; it is often difficult to determine fact or reality from fiction, actor from character, acting from not-acting. Actors often appear to shift between 'being themselves' and 'acting', with this shift perhaps revealing the act of acting, letting us witness the actors simply 'doing a job in front of another group of people' (Forced Entertainment, 1998b). Similarly, in many contemporary devised performances, extending the practice of 'doing' rather than 'acting' as experienced in the Happenings and later performance works throughout the 1960s and 1970s, performers purport to present only themselves. Such work is marked by a supposed absence of acting. In both of these instances, any 'revelation' of the 'real' is consciously and unavoidably unstable, given that the performers are 'being themselves' *on stage*. On stage, can there ever be a performer who is not acting? Is the so-called 'underneath' of the act simply another act?

An early work by Blast Theory, *Something American* (1996), consciously played with this undecidability between being and acting. On stage, an American cop shared anecdotes and fantasies with us. Text projected onto a screen informed us 'He is a cop'. This was then replaced with another message: 'He is pretending to be a cop', and finally: 'He is a performer in a cop's uniform'. Near the end of the performance, the 'cop' appeared to corroborate this by speaking directly to us, without an American accent: 'Hello, my name is David. I was born in London and I've been to America twice on holiday.' Was this, then, the real person? Was this performer really called David? Or was 'David' simply another 'character'? Our habitual means of engaging with 'performance' and 'theatre' are short-circuited in such instances, as we are not certain whether, in fact, this *is* a performance; or where the acting begins and ends.[13]

Tim Etchells, mirroring Jean Baudrillard's theory of simulacra, has proposed the fake as being 'more pertinent than the real', and suggested that since theatre is 'so inherently bound up in fakery' it is the ideal medium with which to explore contemporary observations and concerns relating to the status of 'truth' and its relationship with representation (Etchells, 1990). For Etchells, one result of media saturation is that our own experiences become combined with, and therefore to some extent inseparable from, mediated experiences. Within this context, 'most of our experience is second, third or fourth hand' (Etchells, 1990). In the mid-1980s, both LeCompte and Etchells cited the influence of mass-mediated forms, but since then analogue television has been joined with other forms of media technology and telecommunications, including digital film and television, DVDs, mobile phones, camera phones, video phones, the world wide web, video conferencing, and emails. A few figures are illustrative of the impact of 'new' technology on our daily lives. By the end of 2002, approximately 49.9 million people used mobile phones in the UK, a rise of 11 per cent in one year; 17.3 billion text messages were sent in the same year, an increase of 43 per cent in one year. In 2003, it was estimated that 48 per cent of households had access to the internet from their home; a substantial increase on the 19 per cent recorded in 1998 (*National Statistics UK*, 2004, p. 236). By late 2000, the total number of internet users worldwide was estimated at 407 million, about one in twenty of the population (Norris, 2001, p. 44).[14] Over the past decade, the number of television channels available to viewers in the UK has risen from 56 to 271, and in 2003, 270,000 hours of television were broadcast. The average amount of time per week spent watching television in 2004 in the UK was 26.1 hours per household (Ofcom).[15]

Given the expanding technological landscape, it is unsurprising that contemporary devising companies now engage with this next generation of media. As technology has developed, so contemporary performances may also now utilise newer media forms in both devising processes and devised productions, such as live use of the internet, live email communication, computer projections, etc. Inter-media forms have joined interdisciplinary practices. In the past few years, Blast Theory have become increasingly virtuoso in the use of new media. *Desert Rain* (1999), for example, appropriated the medium of virtual reality in order to make tangible for the spectator – or participant, in this instance – the blur between fiction and reality, connecting with some of the same issues around the notion of the simulacrum. (Jean Baudrillard's *The Gulf War Did Not Take Place* (1991) was the inspiration for the performance (Clarke, 2001, p. 44).) As with the interactive nature of most new media, this performance was entirely participatory, with each 'spectator' entering a 'virtual world', having a set amount of time to successfully complete the tasks, find their human target, and reach the end. The publicity for the performance claimed, 'In a world where Norman Schwarzkopf blurs into Arnold Schwarzenegger, Desert Rain looks for the feint line between the real and the fictional, the virtual and the imaginary' (Blast Theory).[16] The context for *Desert Rain*, of course, was the first Gulf War, so any engagement with the tension between fact and fiction was deliberately political. As Gabriella Giannachi has written, while the war might have been represented as 'virtual', there were real casualties (Giannachi, 2004, p. 120), a fact brought home to the participants by the small box of sand surreptitiously placed in their pocket, accompanied with a quotation from Colin Powell suggesting his lack of interest in the number of Iraqis killed during the war (ibid., p. 119). *Desert Rain* 'may be seen not only as a comment on the war itself, but also as an exposure of the crucial role that technology played within both the making and viewing of the conflict' (ibid., p. 116).

An American ensemble company, The Builders Association, founded in 1993 by director Marianne Weems, formerly dramaturg and assistant director with The Wooster Group, have recently used the interface between live and mediated experience in order to engage with contemporary concerns relating to globalisation, including the compression of time and space and the 'hybridisation' of identity, enabled by technology (global telecommunication and global travel). The term 'hybridisation', suited to 'postmodern' times, suggests an identity that is multiple, rather than fragmented, a location which is both/and, rather than either/or – both American and Asian, for example. Hybrid identities challenge the concept of any fixed, singular identity.

In *Alladeen* (2003), co-produced with the British company Motiroti, the company took the mythical tale 'Aladdin', but transposed this to the global information highway. Our contemporary world of computer-generated images and increasingly fragmented knowledge, enabled in part by the internet as a tool of infinite, accessible, and non-hierarchised information, was reflected in this multi-form performance. Computer-generated scenographic images of urban centres continuously changed, providing the backdrop for mobile phone cross-continent relationships; recorded video segments placed 'real' people (nevertheless mediated) within the flow of the generated image and the live – but acted – action.

Though multifocused and using multiple representational forms, *Alladeen*'s primary engagement was globalisation, figured in the identities of people living in London, New York and Bangalore. Individuals travelled through each of these places (virtually and bodily – 'Sam', the man from India, pretends to be someone else, calling from America). The representation of the impact of global capitalism as experienced by telephone operators in a call centre in Bangalore was ambivalent. Though operators were trained to pass as American by taking on an assumed name, an assumed accent, and acquiring a second-hand knowledge of their assumed country of origin, the performance incorporated video documentation of operators who were quite clear about the economic returns provided by this work. They were represented as having agency in, and awareness of, their choices, with their work positioned as a means to an end, one way to realise wishes. As we witnessed their training in 'being' American, the dominant narratives of that culture were laid bare for us; the right name was important, such as 'Sam', as was knowing the local sports' teams, the weather, the food, popular culture.

We do not have the space here to consider in depth the impact of new media on different modes of devising, which include the devising of internet performances where spectators from across the world share time and virtual, rather than physical, space. One already noticeable trend, however, is that, in much of the work, the performer is being replaced by a spectator–participant, who uses technology in order to be part of the performance event. Obvious allusions might be drawn here to the participatory Happenings of the 1960s, although whether more contemporary experiences are driven by a desire for democratic forms of participation remains to be seen. Nevertheless, the use of technology within devised performance inevitably prompts questions about the power of technology – who designs it, who owns it, for what purpose, what is it capable of, how might its uses be recontextualised and redeployed?

Practical Considerations

Whilst the focus of this chapter has been on the intersections between contemporary performance companies who utilise a devising mode and 'postmodernism', we also wish to consider other factors that are not directly linked to critical concepts but which nevertheless have an impact on the devising processes and outcomes of contemporary groups. Most companies cited in this chapter have one designated director, and unlike the experiments in collaboration discussed in Chapter 4, this role does not rotate.[17] The responsibility of the director, however, is determined by the working practices (and histories) of each company. The director of Birmingham based Stan's Cafe, James Yarker, for example, claimed a role as 'originator' of projects:

> As artistic director I tend to bring the core ideas to the table for each new project. These may well have been influenced by discussions with other company members, they may arise out of previous shows we have worked on or common lines of thought, but I tend to set the agenda first off.[18]

Though Yarker might initiate the devising process, he has admitted that once the agenda has been set, 'everyone else gets their hands on the idea and there is no real preciousness about who's coming up with what'.[19] Goat Island's Lin Hixson, as we have seen, is more of a catalyst or prompt, setting devising exercises for the group to respond to as a way of generating material; the decision about which material is retained and which discarded is taken collectively. Forced Entertainment also take decisions collectively, and Etchells' function as a director is that of 'filter'. The role of The Wooster Group's director, Liz LeCompte, in structuring the 'raw' materials, seems more central; though the generation of materials may be collaborative, the performance appears to be more singularly 'her' vision, her organisation.

The compositional 'nature' of the groups also differs between companies and might change over time. Third Angel, for example, is composed of Alexander Kelly and Rachael Walton, who co-founded it in 1995, and who remain its co-directors. Both also perform, as appropriate. However, the company have also invited artists to collaborate with them on various projects. Reckless Sleepers, originally founded in 1989 as an ensemble, now operates as an 'umbrella organisation' under the artistic directorship of Mole Wetherell. Forced Entertainment remain an ensemble composed of Tim Etchells, Richard Lowdon, Robin Arthur, Terry O'Connor, Claire Marshall and Cathy Naden. More recently they too have begun to invite other artists to collaborate with them on different projects. Thus, performing with *Bloody Mess* (2004) were John Rowley, Jerry Killick, Davis Freeman, Bruno Roubicek and Wendy Houstoun. In both the UK and the USA it is notable that 'personnel' are frequently shared between companies. Thus Jerry Killick has worked for both Third Angel and Forced Entertainment; performers with Elevator Repair Service have also performed with The Wooster Group, some of whom have performed with The Builders Association. Goat Island and Forced Entertainment have also recently begun to share performative lecture platforms. Just as Chapter 6 discussed the common language of physical performance, so we might locate a shared 'language' of contemporary devising behind such collaborations.

A feature shared with companies covered elsewhere in this book is that all of the companies discussed here commit to an extensive period of devising. The Wooster Group, Forced Entertainment and Goat Island, for example, typically take at least two years to make a piece of work, devising in a series of stages, which includes the initial generation of materials, improvisation around these, a period of further reflection, further improvisation and structuring, and then rehearsing. Usually, deliberately large time gaps are scheduled into the devising process, allowing the performers some distance from, and reflection upon, the materials. Third Angel, for example, now begin working on a piece for up to a year *before* the practical devising processes even start. Given the long time-scale, another feature undoubtedly shared by companies is the discarding of the majority of the material that is generated over such a long period of time. Companies also show works-in-progress.

Many of the companies explored in this chapter share an impressive creative versatility. All embrace the ideals of both the historical avant-garde and the mixed-media companies of the 1960s and 1970s, working across art forms. However, performing a slightly curious spin on the aims of their predecessors, in addition to this mix of media within performances, many companies use their versatility to also market themselves as being producers of different types of events. Not only do they make performances, but they also make separate installations, gallery exhibitions, films, and give performative lectures, etc. Chicago-based Lucky Pierre, a collective founded in 1996, are representative, having produced videos, performances, installations, radio and sound pieces. Third Angel and Forced Entertainment have similarly made installations, art exhibitions, durational performance pieces, and video works. Such multiple positioning enacts a refusal by companies to be placed in, and tied to, one category. What *are* Forced Entertainment?[20]

It is equally probable that the multiple positioning of companies such as Lucky Pierre, Forced Entertainment and Third Angel is a sign of economic vulnerability *and* entrepreneurial opportunity.

As Frederic Jameson commented, in the late twentieth century (and beyond), 'aesthetic production has become integrated into commodity production generally' (Jameson, 1995, p. 4). Forced Entertainment, for example, after a decade of making work, faced a withdrawal of funding by the Arts Council. As a result, they were acutely aware of their over-dependence and reliance on one funding source. Though the company had already begun to 'diversify' in terms of output, in 1997 Etchells wrote that the company 'want[ed] to be in dialogue with Combined Arts, and also Film & Video and also Channel 4 and really put our eggs in a whole number of baskets' (Etchells, 1997).

It is also notable that many companies now create different versions of the 'same' works, although being rendered in different mediums, the works are necessarily different. This is yet another instance of the destabilisation of the concept of the 'original'. The Builders Association's *Alladeen* consisted not only of the live performance, but also of a Web project and a music video, each of which existed in its own right, whilst also having connections between them, with material from each being used in the other. Pragmatically, for the producers the construction of multiple sites through different media provided different, wider opportunities for potential audience engagement.

Postmodern Style?

As we have stressed, 'postmodernism' is not reducible to an aesthetics. Whilst the sheer volume of contemporary devised work is to be celebrated, and its continuing practice encouraged, there is a danger that a dominant (and dominating), identifiable 'style' is emerging. As Geraldine Harris, of the department of Theatre Studies at Lancaster University, observed in 1999, 'like most lecturers in Theatre Studies over the last ten years, I have seen many shows, both student and professional ... "quoting" specific devices or sequences from shows created' by 'companies like Forced Entertainment and The Wooster Group', and 'often mixed with borrowings from Pina Bausch and/or DV8 sometimes by way of Impact Theatre Cooperative, Jan Fabre and Robert Wilson' (Harris, 1999a, pp. 11–12).[21] The devices that Harris then goes on to list included

> structures of repetition and interruption and of extreme theatrical self-reflexivity ... sequences in which the performers act as if becoming increasingly drunk or drugged, repeated on-stage costume changes ... systemic

choreography sequences based on natural movement and gesture which often involve the cast in a great deal of falling down (a Lancaster University favourite) and performed to the music of Ärvo Part, Michael Nyman or Wim Mertens, sequences of jumping, falling and being caught in the last possible moment, punishing and exhausting action sections in which the performers seem genuinely to become distressed or exhausted, autobiographical material drawn from the performers' lives, extreme slow-motion sequences, deliberately 'beautiful' sets, forties or fifties costumes, particularly print dresses and heavy overcoats, sequences based around suitcases, 'dance' lighting, as opposed to theatrical lighting, music used as a 'soundtrack', rather than as incidental, and so on.   (Harris, 1999a)

To Harris's extensive list we might add the use of a 'lecture' format; the structural organisation of text (as an A–Z, for example); the composition of endless lists repeating the same refrain; and the incorporation of 'postmodern' concepts in publicity material:

We explore themes such as personal identity, dressing up and disguise, cities, love lives (or lack of) and family ties. ... The performance is one that is designed to unsettle audience perceptions of a 'truth' associated with conventional theatre, and tries to find the real by recklessly employing the fake.   (The Special Guests)[22]

Though the performance companies explored in this chapter undoubtedly all engage with systems of knowing and are not simply repeating a certain style for the sake of it, contemporary devised performance, in terms of both form and content, is also now, often, 'predictable', and therefore in danger of presenting us with what we already know – even if that 'knowledge' is the 'uncertainty of knowledge'. We are now then, paradoxically, certain about uncertainty. Alternatively, repetition has taken its toll; as we think we know what we see, we read only the similarities that are presented, rather than any differences.

Harris rightly pointed out that within a postmodern paradigm a process of 'borrowing' or 'quoting' is in fact *part of* that paradigm, both an example of intertextuality and a challenge to the myth of 'originality' and the individual autonomous artist. Demystifying this process, however, Harris added that *any* performance, whether made using a devising method or through working from a text, is always in some senses 'intertextual', for one cannot escape 'already established traditions and pre-existing signifying conventions'; the creation of any piece of work will always involve some relationship with traditions and conventions, even if it is one of resistance. For Harris, then, devising, like the performance of a scripted play, involves 're-iteration and re-interpretation of pre-existing aesthetic traditions, discourses, images and signifying conventions which in themselves could be said to have the status of "texts" ' (Harris, 1999a, pp. 18–19). However, Harris's point is that the 'quotation' experienced in much of the devised student work that she witnesses 'appears simply as plagiarism', rather than re-interpretation, or re-contextualisation. Where students would expect to critically 'interrogate' a more conventional play-text, in order to understand its context and determine its various meanings, how these are suggested and where they might be disrupted, students' contemporary devised performance works rarely 'interrogate' the 'texts' of the various performances they copy and tend to ignore the performances' and their own contexts, aims and processes of constructions. The failure to take 'full and proper responsibility for their part in the process of making meanings' (ibid., p. 18) results in 'the reproduction of images and ideas that have the appearance of clichés, because the imprints of the histories that they carry have not been analysed and interrogated' (ibid., p. 19).[23]

Etchells has similarly worried that students who are taught this work, and who then proceed to make their own, have 'understood a set of formal codes, of stylistic options, but have not understood anything else' (Etchells). Pete Brooks's perception of the contemporary performance landscape, which he referred to as being the new orthodoxy, was one with which we have some sympathy: 'I find Forced Entertainment's work eloquent and moving but the sheer number of individuals cloning them fills me with despair' (Brooks, in Giannachi and Luckhurst, 1999, p. 4). Etchells, though acutely aware of the economic pressures of the touring circuit, regarded much contemporary devised performance as at best 'plausible', presenting all the right 'elements that should make up that "kind" of show. It looks serious, it's about something, you could put it in a brochure, it doesn't frighten people, it's not dangerous or incompetent. But neither is it necessary' (Etchells).

Conclusion

The mid-1980s and the last decade of the twentieth century were a period of 'narrative crisis', as our belief in overarching theories to explain our experiences and the worlds in which we lived, in particular the belief in 'progress', dissipated under the experience (or crisis) of world events. Widespread distrust of narratives was appropriately taken up by contemporary performance makers, who used the processes of collaborative devising to create works which were complex, multi-layered, multi-vocal and multi-visioned, resisting the imposition of any single perspective, answer, or 'truth'. Instead, such work insisted that our worlds were available to be rewritten, or reworked, and our own part in that, as spectators, was to be acknowledged as we actively struggled to find our way through the performance event.

A quarter of a century later, and this initially provocative, challenging, questioning work is firmly embedded in the syllabi of teaching institutions throughout the UK, as both process and product. The 'postmodern performance' coda is seemingly packaged into a series of off-the-peg 'styles', where one size fits all, irrespective of context, process or purpose. However, in reflecting on the beginnings of Forced Entertainment, Tim Etchells asked an extremely important question that we have not yet addressed: 'as a young maker of devised work, it's hard to get started. What are you going to do?' (Etchells). His reply was that, initially at least, you are going to look to those performances that you admire. One learns through watching as well as doing. This, from Forced Entertainment:

> Our lineage. In random edit form.
> A few fragments of Impact Theatre and Russell Hoban's *The Carrier Frequency*. A documentary on The Wooster Group with some sections of *L.S.D.*, another on Robert Wilson, another on Joseph Beuys. *Coyote*. Fast forward. Rewind. A piece by Bobby Baker. A piece by Station House Opera. Tables in the air. Pina Bausch. Can't find that tape. The Belgian choreographer Anne Teresa De Keersmaeker. Gary Stevens. Neil Bartlett. Spinning through the jumpcut influences, the likes, loves and dislikes of our 'world'. Tapes of poor quality and dubious origins. Tapes that said one thing but were really another. Third-generation copies. Incomplete tapes.
> (Etchells, 1999a, p. 20)

Writ large throughout the pages of this book is an acknowledgement of lineage, of productive cross-fertilisation. Thus, to take only one example, Goat Island's Lin Hixson has admitted not only the influence of Robert Wilson (Bottoms, 1998, p. 430), but has also practised/trained with, amongst others, Rachel Rosenthal and Rudy Perez and declared a fascination with the practice of Judson dancer, Yvonne Rainer, whose forms/processes shared something with Goat Island's (Hixson, 1995, pp. 22–3). In relation to the use of 'found gesture' and 'exhaustive repetitive action', Hixson also acknowledged the influence of Pina Bausch (Bottoms, 1998, p. 424). In fact, more accurately, Hixson admitted 'a debt'. Goat Island's practice is interesting in that it consciously pays 'homage' to others' work. For example, when devising *How Dear to Me the Hour When Daylight Dies*, Matthew Goulish combined two gestures that he had seen, on two consecutive nights, in different New York theatres, thereby making something different from either 'original' (Bottoms, 1998, p. 437). Adrian Heathfield has similarly noted the 'explicit copying of multiple but minute sequences' from Bausch's work in *It's an Earthquake in My Heart* (Heathfield, 2001, p. 18). Importantly, Heathfield recognised that 'as with all Goat Island's copying, there is a pronounced translation into a different context and language' (ibid.). This 'difference' is crucial and the idea of 'homage', combined with Heathfield's recognition of 'translation', has wider significance to the concept of 'copying' or imitation more generally. Simon Woods of the Australian group Zen Zen Zo (see Chapter 6) shared similar insights when discussing the difference between imitation and adaptation.

In a related concept, Goat Island also draw on the idea of 'response'. In their workshops, for example, they encourage participants to respond creatively to work shown, acknowledging that a work of art is made as a response to a work of art; 'a work of art that could not have existed without the work it is responding to' (Goat Island, 2000, p. 3). These responses are considered 'individual contributions to a conversation that stretches throughout the weeks of the workshop' (ibid.). We would propose that this idea of 'response' might also usefully refer to the much longer and wider conversation between contemporary devising practitioners occurring across time and space, evident in the 'lineage' recited by Etchells. Etchells has similarly claimed that, in one sense, Forced Entertainment were 'on the end of a huge Chinese whispers which started in Wuppertal and ended up in Sheffield with us' (Etchells, 1997). As a maker of contemporary devised performance, it would be impossible, and indeed unadvisable, to remain outside of the conversation of contemporary devised practice. Implicit to the idea of Chinese Whispers, however, is that what is spoken and what is heard is never quite the same, and that such differences arise from the differences between here and there; that is, differences of space and time. Etchells has readily admitted that Forced Entertainment initially copied Impact Theatre Cooperative. However, lacking the necessary skills to be totally successful in their imitation, the company were prompted to make their 'own set of discoveries about what we really wanted to do' (Etchells).[24] Copying led to difference. The Chinese Whisper did not, of course, end in Sheffield with Forced Entertainment; and as contemporary performance approaches the status of 'genre', it may well be time for a re-examination.

8 Conclusions

The Practice of Devising

It is easy to forget that fifty years ago devising as a process of creating work was almost unknown. Today, devising has become a commonplace and institutionalised practice. This book has charted the history of the development of devising across diverse fields of performance practice including physical performance, community drama, political theatre, visual performance and 'postmodern' performance. Given the prevalence and reach of devised works, what impact has devising had on the wider theatrical landscape?

One of the similarities that can be detected across different forms of devising is a shared dramaturgical 'style'. It has been our argument that devising, as a collaborative process of performance-making, potentially enables the production of a different kind of performance structure that in some senses reflects its collaborative creative process – typically compartmented or fragmented, with multiple layers and narratives. The devised work of The Living Theatre or of the Open Theatre, the political performances of Albert Hunt and his students or the early agit-prop work of Red Ladder, the visual feasts of Blood Group or Hesitate and Demonstrate and the spectacular physical feats of Legs on the Wall, or the 'failed performances' of Forced Entertainment, all employ fragmented and multi-layered structures, whilst still retaining some sense of 'narrative'. This repetition of fragmented dramaturgy has undoubtedly altered our comprehension of 'narrative', and of the possible shapes or trajectories by which narratives can or should be represented. The impact of this on the theatrical landscape should not be underestimated. Further, what might once have seemed bewildering or confusing is now largely accepted and even commonplace.[1]

It is of course possible that individual playwrights might success-fully produce a similar dramaturgical model, as witnessed, for example, in the work of avant-garde writers such as Samuel Beckett, Heiner Müller, Peter Handke or Suzan Lori-Parks and the texts that post-dramatic criticism has become interested in.[2] Arguably, the performance landscape that devising contributed to also informed this kind of playwriting. The preponderance of the fragmented nar-rative in devised performance alongside its relative scarcity in other performance fields does also suggest that the processes involved in devising are responsible for the generation of this type of work. During our research, the only instance where we encountered negative critique of the process of devising was when companies reflected on the unsuitability of the mode to the production of a 'coherent' play. Devising, in this context, did not appear to have engendered the required 'product'. In Chapter 4, for example, we saw that Gillian Hanna from the Women's Theatre Group described one collaborative attempt at devising a 'script' as 'a disastrous foray into the grave labelled devised writing' (Hanna, 1991, p. xlviii). By contrast, in the pursuit of multi-narrative, 'open' texts, collaborative devising seems a pre-eminently appropriate form. Those companies who devise their work but often retain a strong, linear narrative trajectory, such as Theatre Alibi (UK), in fact employ a writer, responsible for translating the work produced through improvisation, discussion, etc., into a story-based play.

The identification of a shared 'style' arising from the properties thought specific to devising also implies a shared process, and one feature identified across all companies explored in this book is that of 'collaborative practice'. Devising is unique in that its product is entirely dependent on the various contributions of the creators; each devised product is therefore also unique. Of course, a counter-argument to this would be that all live performances are unique, precisely *because* they are live, but also because all performances rely on the individuals who realise them. However, in the vast majority of cases, it remains the case that in the devising process nothing material pre-exists the collaboration of those involved in realising a perform-ance, and this feature does continue to set devising apart from other forms of theatre making. This practice of making performance has arguably re-conceptualised our understanding of the theatre industry, and specifically of the role of the performer within it, but by exten-sion also of other roles including those of the director and the writer, and the relations between them.

Whilst one common element to devising might be the use of collaboration to create work, there is of course no one model of collaboration. We would not therefore wish to further promote the idea that devising is necessarily any less or more democratic a form of creation than any other process since each company's manifesto, constitution, or working practice will determine the actual process of collaborative devising; moreover, this process is usually arrived at through experience. As Chapter 2 has made clear, even within the context of a radicalised culture, hierarchies were most frequently maintained. And the experiences of practitioners discussed in Chapter 4 revealed the huge difficulty of forging a non-hierarchical structure; further, too much was expected of the structure itself. Whilst political companies might ostensibly have been seen to be operating democratically, with all participants given equal opportunity to contribute fully, the structure in itself does not guarantee the delivery of equality. For example, within a culture in which women feel that their opinions carry less weight, they are less likely to voice those opinions. The fact that a structure exists which would allow them to voice their opinions does not make that voicing inevitable; nor does it mean that their voices would be heard or their opinions taken seriously; wider cultural and systemic change would be required to make it truly effective.

One of the most radical transformations that the mode of devising itself has effected in the theatre industry and in the conceptualisation of the theatrical field, is the championing of the *process* of making performance, in relation to that performance. In the 1950s and 1960s the emphasis on the qualities of the process of production and the concomitant demotion of the artistic product was caught up in the moment of political and social resistance outlined in Chapter 1. Appearing differently in different strands of work, such emphasis on process was rhetorically represented by makers as a resistance to the commodification of art, a validation of creative labour, and a rejection of the aesthetic standards of the Establishment. Notably, such ideology rarely figures in the language or practice of contemporary devising practitioners.

The relative importance of process and product has differed across fields and across time. In the actor-centred devising explored in Chapter 2, the pre-performance emphasis on the development of the actor had been part of a gradual evolution of existing acting and actor-training practices; the performance, in this area closely allied to the theatre industry, remained central to the majority of such groups' practice. Conversely, in certain aspects of community arts, the devising process became such an important validating aspect of the work, that community workers argued that it was not possible to apply aesthetic judgements to the performance product: its value lay in its making. In contemporary devising, now positioned within the professional 'alternative sector' of the theatre industry, the performance product has returned as a central validating element of a company's work: it is how they are assessed for funding and how they survive economically. Process remains significant, but more in the processual status of the performance rather than the practice of making. Devising companies operating within a postmodern paradigm, whose performances display an openness and a deliberate resistance to completion, and physically-based devising companies, whose performances display improvisational prowess, employ a self-reflexive theatricality that draws attention to the process of making within the performance itself. Such attention is not intended, however, to detract from the 'quality' of the product and as we have seen in Chapter 7, moments of self-reflexivity are often carefully rehearsed.

The Place of Devising

The question of the placement of devising processes and performance within the theatrical field is a fraught one. Companies have used a range of rhetorics about devising, casting it variously as alternative, avant-garde, radical, innovative or mainstream. As a mode of work within many small theatre, dance and art groups of the late 1950s and 1960s, devising became associated with the fringe, underground or alternative artistic and cultural movements. For many, the positioning of their devising outside the mainstream was a function of necessity, as Anna Halprin reflected:

> when an artist begins to work outside the officially recognized context of her discipline, the established artistic community will often ignore her. If this doesn't work (because the artist is either persistent or good or both) she may be called 'avant-garde', meaning that she is ahead of the times or so far behind that she seems to be ahead (which is what happens when things move in circles). The dance community in the 60s was too conservative to have an official avant-garde; the theatre world, however, was not. So my work began to be thought of as theatre.   (Halprin, 1989, p.54)

Likewise many companies, for example those discussed in Chapter 3, considered their devising practice as avant-garde or radical. However, both terms were hotly contested in the 1960s. For Ronnie Davis of San Francisco Mime Troupe there was a clear demarcation along political lines amongst early devising troupes that chose to call themselves radical. In a polemic article in 1975, he championed as truly radical those devising groups of the political left including El Teatro Campesino, Bread and Puppet Theatre and San Francisco Mime Troupe, and dismissed other groups as part of 'the right wing of radical independent theatre' that

> is more closely associated with the educational or entertainment establishment, is an extension or a deviation from the bourgeois theatre, and is closely aligned with the aesthetic avant-garde. It consists of the Becks and The Living Theatre, Joe Chaikin and the Open Theatre, and Richard Schechner's Performance Group.   (Davis, 1975c, p. 67)

Indeed, for the San Francisco Mime Troupe the epithet 'avant-garde' carried a reactionary political resonance.

> We thought of ourselves as outside agitators; outside the establishment, obviously, but also – in our role as artists – outside the movement, despite our sympathy for it.   (Sainer, 1997, p. 21)

The connection that Davis identified between devising and the entertainment establishment was one that was to grow during the 1970s, until by the 1980s the alternative movement had become a professional sector, readily funded and marketed by the establishment.

For contemporary devising companies working today, the rhetoric they use about the placement of their work is broadly similar, although the significance of the idea of the fringe or margins has greatly changed. Most companies still choose to place themselves rhetorically outside the mainstream, which they cast as restricted, tradition-bound, or conservative. For David Clarkson being outside the mainstream is a resistance to stasis:

> I don't think mainstream companies have to do this so much, but companies on the fringes you really have to reinvent yourself every few years.
> (Clarkson)[3]

For Lynne Bradley of Zen Zen Zo, the picture is much more complex as she attempts to invert the power relation between margin and centre:

> We like being on the margins of the mainstream because it's that traditional thing that the margin is where you can sit back and reflect on what is happening in society, and that marginal position is a very empowered one. In that sense we're definitely fringe. For a physical theatre company we cross over into mainstream places: we perform at the Optus playhouse, which is a mainstream space. We are very populist in our belief, 'for the people', we don't want to be obscure, that's why we have some good strong storytelling.   (Bradley and Woods)[4]

However, within the current theatrical industry, where a thriving alternative sector of small-scale devising work is maintained through revenue or project grant, the distance in fact between mainstream and alternative work has been greatly reduced. Despite the rhetoric of margins or fringe, these companies are part of a professionalised sector of the entertainment establishment.

A key component in the introduction of devising practices into mainstream culture, and the professionalisation of alternative devised theatre into a commercially viable sphere of work, has been the intervention of the universities and colleges (coupled with some input from the training conservatoires and, at one remove, from state educational institutions). As early as 1973 John Harrop acknowledged the pivotal role that university courses in the US had in maintaining the alternative theatre sector:

> Groups which have throughout the US, banded themselves together in lofts, barns, churches, crypts and the like to create experimental theatrical experiences are usually comprised of ex-university students whose theatrical interest and ability was catalysed and developed in theatre departments. But perhaps as many of these groups are founded in rebellion against theatre departments, as by students who keep together after graduation to continue work started in the university.   (Harrop, 1973, p. 77)

Sally Banes has outlined the key role that universities played in subsidising the rise of the avant-garde:

> [The] avant-garde has regularly formed its own alternative institutions, which in turn have been co-opted by the mainstream to become establishment schools and venues ...   (Banes, 2000, p. 217)

As we have noted, artists, devising companies and innovative dance practitioners have been regularly hosted at universities in the US and UK, where they have performed, and held residencies or teaching posts. Likewise in the UK a touring circuit of universities quickly established additional venues to the developing arts centres for alternative devising theatre companies to tour. Since the late 1980s and 1990s this crossover of artist and academy has increased, as the financial status of independent artists and companies has become precarious with cuts in National Endowment for the Arts funding in the US and Arts Council funding in the UK.

Historically, devising, considered an 'avant-garde' practice of performance making, needed a certain kind of enlightened patronage:

> one that endorses experimentation and artistic risk for its own sake (or for some other purpose or interest, such as the educational value of art making), one that tolerates or even encourages social and political resistance, and one that is willing to forgo artistic control over the final product. For numerous reasons the university fits this description.   (Banes, 2000, p. 219)

Universities have been key in the evolution of devising, not only because they have housed performances, but also because they have permitted residencies and taught devising on their courses. The foundation of Black Mountain College, North Carolina, in 1933 was a precursor to exploratory investigation that supported and facilitated John Cage's early work, amongst many other innovative theatre, dance and arts practitioners (ibid., 2000). Albert Hunt's work at Bradford College of Art in the 1960s was a spur to many of the leading performance art and visual performance companies of the time, as well as being influential in community arts teaching in Australia. More recently, in Australia the establishment of the Victoria College of Arts and Deakin University courses in community practice and practical theatre making, including devising, have been key. Graduates from these courses were responsible for the establishment of many leading Australian community arts companies, who used the devising methods adapted from their training.

Devising has also been taught practically on university Drama degree courses in the UK from the 1960s at universities like Exeter, Lancaster, Leeds, and in the days of Clive Barker at Birmingham and Warwick. Now devising is taught practically in the studio and in seminar studies of post-war theatre in academic institutions throughout the UK. Indeed, many members from various companies in the UK attended university Drama, Theatre and Performance departments, where they were introduced to the work of particular 'first generation' devising companies including, for example, the People Show, as well as American practitioners such as The Living Theatre and Allan Kaprow. The works of 'second generation' artists, such as Hesitate and Demonstrate, and Impact Theatre, were taught to and crossed over with the 'third generation', which included Forced Entertainment, Desperate Optimists and Dogs in Honey, who in turn influenced the 'fourth generation', such as Stan's Cafe, Third Angel, Uninvited Guests and Reckless Sleepers. This 'fourth generation' (along with the preceding three generations) are now 'models' taught to the next generation, who already are founding their own companies, including, for example, Deer Park; they, in their turn, will undoubtedly enter (or re-enter) the academy.[5] One potential impact of this, as addressed in Chapter 7, is the creation of a devising 'formula', based on the repetition of taught/appropriated models.

Even though drama schools and conservatoires have been thought of as predominantly guarantors of tradition, primarily training actors for existing commercial forms of performance, during the 1970s several of the newer drama schools in London evolved more radical programmes with devising as a training component. Notable among these was Rose Bruford Drama School, which established a Community Theatre Arts diploma in 1976, run by Stuart Bennett and Colin Hicks from Belgrade TIE, Coventry, and Perspectives Theatre, Peterborough, which explicitly set out to train 'people who can devise work, get it on the floor and communicate it to an audience' (Rea, 1981, p. 66). East 15 Drama School in London, which was initially developed in 1961 by actors who had worked with Joan Littlewood's Theatre Workshop, has recently introduced a new course in contemporary theatre, which employs devising throughout its three years. The Royal Scottish Academy of Music and Drama (RSAMD) similarly runs a BA in Contemporary Theatre Practice, where devising plays a key role. This is an echo of what the university sector has been doing for at least thirty years, because small-scale professional theatre companies on the fringe, in Theatre-in-Education or community work are more likely today to offer career opportunities for performers. Similar issues underlie the establishment in Australia of the National Institute of Circus Arts (NICA), linked to Swinburne University, which was founded in 2001 and offers a three-year BA in Circus Arts. Other conservatoires, such as Jacques Lecoq's school in Paris and the teaching of two of his collaborators, Philippe Gaulier and Monika Pagneux, have transformed the contemporary theatrical scene with their training of students in physical devising theatre, as discussed in Chapter 6.

Devising Today

In writing this history of devising, our aim has been to reflect upon the various forms of devising and their different aims, understanding that these are informed by, and generated from, the contexts in which they are located. The political and cultural context for the modes of devising explored in Chapters 2 to 5 was that of the 1960s and 1970s, and specifically the desire to challenge establishment practices and politics. Irrespective of the differences in process, this work was linked through its anti-establishment, pro-democratic rhetoric, primarily through the key term and practice of 'participation'. The different focuses of each mode differently transposed this rhetoric into the different performance fields. Thus, in Chapter 2, the subject of the work was very much the actor and the overriding aim was the liberation of the actor within theatrical production processes. In Chapter 3, the focus was less on the artist or actor, and more on the experience of the event – the 'eventness' of performance became the key to liberation. In Chapter 4, at least initially, the key concern was with theatrical structures – the necessity of finding a mode of performance-making that matched the political ideology of the radical left. Of course, the 'product', in terms of its content, had also to meet the political ideology of the time; here, process and product, in relation to overt politics, was explicit. The community work explored in Chapter 5 used the rhetoric of participation to focus on devising as a tool of empowerment for participants or to address non-specialist audiences.

Whilst the aims of the various modes of devising across fields were ostensibly related to the liberationist politics of the time, our more detailed discussions have revealed that in practice the actual processes did not always live up to these ideals. The majority of actor-focused companies, irrespective of their desire to empower the performer, were led by directors; the aim of involving the spectator in theatrical or performance events often, in reality, looked more like undemo-cratic instances of heavy-handed coercion than invitations to par-ticipation; in the political companies, the struggle to develop a totally democratic form was painful and never wholly successful as hidden hierarchies established themselves; while devising in a community context was and continues to be affected by anxieties around the politics of participation. Admitting this, it nevertheless remains the case that the experiments or developments across the various devising fields, whatever their actual outcomes, *were* linked to the political and cultural context of that time; and it is from here that we inherit various aspects of forms, processes and rhetorics of devising.

As the times have changed, so is it imperative that we position devising today within its own contexts. The informing discourse of the 1960s and 1970s cannot simply be appropriated and applied. In the twenty-first century, the ideologies underpinning the 1960s rhetoric of empowerment and participatory democracy have been subject to challenge, not least because the counter-cultural revolution appeared to have massively failed, along with other Leftist alternatives. Moreover, the challenge to dominant ideologies, figured in the crisis of 'grand narratives' (see Chapter 7), has brought the simplistic models of power, and of oppression and liberation, or oppressor and oppressed, under scrutiny, along with notions of resistance within the social realm. In a globalised world, the 'enemy' is not so easily identified.[6] Concepts of singular identity and cohesive community, of nation and nationality, and indeed of 'margin' and 'centre' have similarly been contested and problematised. Such challenges make it difficult, and arguably naive, to discuss devising in the terms previously ascribed to it.

The material context of the twenty-first century has also altered significantly over the past fifty years. Just as the 'products' of devising in the 1960s arose from, or were prompted by, those times, so the concerns and possibilities of contemporary devising practices are vastly different from those of our predecessors. Our times are marked by globalisation and advanced or multinational capitalism, reflected in the greater interdependency between countries (including between the rich and developing nations). As well as the global circulation of capital and goods (expanded recently by e-commerce), there is also a network of information exchange and flow of people. The way we access, receive and organise information – our mode of perception – combined with the sheer quantity of information now available, prompts different conceptions or configurations of, and interactions with, the world and, most importantly, with each other. In spite of overall increases in wealth, globalisation appears to have widened the gap between rich and poor. In 2004, reversing a trend of the past ten years, the number of people experiencing chronic hunger rose to nearly 852 million, an increase of 18 million since 2000, while 1.4 billion people (half the total workforce in the world) earned less than $2 a day.[7] Inequality, then, is one feature that has endured across the past fifty years. Certain concerns are also now identified as global, for example the AIDS pandemic, the rising number of refugees (up from

29 million in 1990, to 35 million by 2000),[8] the risks posed by climate change and developments in science, for example in biotechnology, which require international discussion in relation to ethical concerns and issues of control.

The few examples we have proposed here are intended to suggest the very different times in which contemporary devising takes place. Those who use devising processes today, within or across fields, are drawing from an expansive archive. Our intention throughout has been to represent the various contexts in which devised work has been made, and with what intentions, in order to highlight the importance of context to both process and product. Devising is a live practice located in time and space, and to that extent is inseparable from the contexts of its production. Variables include cultures, economics, geographies, and peoples, many of which we have articulated in the preceding chapters as we have explored the different fields of performance. The overriding purpose of this book has been to enable the makers of devised theatre to locate their own practice but also understand the relationship of this to the history of devising. Our aim has been to contribute towards informed devising practices, entreating practitioners, whether student, professional, or amateur, to make works for and of their times and places.

Notes

Notes to Chapter 1: Introduction

1. There are very few studies of devising itself and they tend to be practical manuals or workbooks for educational purposes, such as Oddey, *Devising Theatre: A Practical and Theoretical Handbook* (1994); Lamden, *Devising: A Handbook for Drama and Theatre Students* (2000); Bicât and Baldwin (eds), *Devised and Collaborative Theatre: A Practical Guide* (2002); or Kerrigan's *The Performer's Guide to the Collaborative Process* (2001).
2. The survey aimed to determine whether, how, and why devising was taught within curricula. Respondents have been recorded anonymously.
3. A list of books and articles which study companies in relation to their mode of production, rather than just an analysis of their productions, might include such studies as Williams (ed.), *Collaborative Theatre: The Théâtre du Soleil Sourcebook* (1999); Pasolli, *A Book on the Open Theatre* (1972); van Erven, *Community Theatre* (2001); Kaprow, *Some Recent Happenings* (1966b); Sainer, *The New Radical Theatre Notebook* (1997); Helmer and Malzacher (eds), *Not Even a Game Anymore: The Theatre of Forced Entertainment* (2004); *Theatre Papers, 1–5* (Totnes: Dartington School of Art, 1977–86).
4. In the interests of space and time, our limited survey here excludes most European devising practitioners. It would be a valuable addition to our understanding of devising if pan-European influences could be mapped. For the same reasons of space we have not considered the vibrant Canadian field of devising, which is beginning to be documented in journals and book-length studies. See a recent study of Theatre Passe Muraille and the introductory context in Bessai (1992).
5. Of course, this is not strictly true, as artists also typically work with sound and lighting designers, and sometimes with directors. The well-known performance artist Bobby Baker has also devised a group piece, *Take a Peek* (1995).

6. See Goldberg, *Performance Art: From Futurism to the Present* (1988); Goldberg, *Performance: Live Art since the 60s* (1998); Heathfield (ed.), *Live: Art and Performance* (2004); Sayre, *The Object of Performance: The American Avant-Garde since 1970* (1992); Vergine, *Body Art and Performance* (2000); Ferguson (ed.), *Out of Actions: Between Performance and the Object, 1949–1979* (1998).

7. See Barker, 'Foreword', in Bicât and Baldwin (2002); Goodman, *Contemporary Feminist Theatres* (1993), p. 103; Barker, *Theatre Games* (1977), p. 215; Barker, 'Foreword'; Oddey (1994), p. 23; A. Lyddiard in Lamden (2000), p. 42; J. Beck in Tytell, *The Living Theatre* (1995), p. 208; Lamden (2000), p. 1; Pasolli (1972); Halprin, *Theatre Papers* (1977), p. 7; Johnstone, *Impro* (1981).

8. Chris Baldwin writes: 'rather than being at the top of a hierarchical structure, the director is at the centre of the rehearsal fulcrum, ensuring that everyone is working together' (p. 13). Despite this attempt to soften the idea with the metaphor of a circle rather than a linear hierarchy, the principle remains the same.

9. C. Turner, *Reading Between the Lines: Writing for British Experimental Theatre and Performance* [forthcoming].

10. See Feldman, 'The Sound and Movement Exercise as Developed by the Open Theatre', in P. Hulton (ed.), *Theatre Papers*, 1, 1 (1977–8).

11. The idea of *habitus* is a complex one which Pierre Bourdieu outlines most fully in *The Logic of Practice* (1990). In essence, *habitus* refers to the relationship between individual perception and action and the organisation of wider social structures. Bourdieu has defined *habitus* as a generative structure of practical action, and as far as intuition goes, he emphasises 'the coincidence of the objective structures and internalized structures, which produce the illusion of immediate understanding' (p. 25).

12. In the minds of several companies *commedia dell'arte* represented almost a clown form, where the slapstick and physical interplay of the *lazzi*, or comic interludes, predominated. This understanding of the form is quite different from its sixteenth-century tradition, and from the work of Jacques Copeau, discussed here. See Rudlin (1994).

13. Useful introductions to European avant-garde movements include Harding (ed.), *Contours of the Theatrical Avant-Garde: Performance and Textuality* (2000); Redwood (ed.), *Theatre of the Avant-Garde* (1979); Apollonio (ed.), *Futurist Manifestos* (1973); Kirby, *Futurist Performance* (1971); Melzer, *Latest Rage The Big Drum: Dada and Surrealist Performance* (1980); Goldberg, *Performance Art: From Futurism to the Present* (1988).

14. *Sintesi* replaced narrative and plot, psychological character and logical structure with plays that 'compress into a few minutes, into a few words and gestures, innumerable situations, sensibilities, ideas, sensations, facts

and symbols' (Apollonio, 1973, p. 184). The alogical form bears similarity to the later Happenings.

15. Duchamp was perhaps the first artist to consciously employ 'chance' processes. In 1913, he created *3 Stoppages Etalon*, made by dropping one metre of thread onto a blank canvas, from a height of one metre. This configuration was then fixed with varnish. Duchamp repeated the process twice more, creating three canvases (Brecht, 1966, p. 4).

16. Its status as the 'first' automatic work is contested. Michel Sanouillet claims that prior to this, Tristan Tzara and Francis Picabia had in fact jointly written an automatic text, which Breton and Soupault would have seen in Picabia's journal *391* (Melzer, 1980, p. 169).

17. Interestingly, such knowledge or positioning seems often to have been retrospectively applied. It is curious to discover that in their own reflective writing of the time, companies such as The Living Theatre, the Open Theatre and the People Show, reflect very little on the supposedly non-hierarchical process of creation or lack of prior text. The critical writings that later comment on these companies highlight this aspect to a greater extent.

18. While this may not have always contained an intended 'critique', at the very least, Pop Art served to challenge the divide between high and low culture.

19. Tony Blair, speech on 19 July 2004, www.number10.gov.uk/output/Page6129.asp (accessed 5 September 2004).

20. For a detailed discussion of attempts to stage improvisation work and devised performance under British censorship, see Nicholson (2005).

21. See Littlewood (1995); Goorney (1981); Malina (1984 and 1972); Beck (1972).

22. All information is taken from the Arts Council Annual Reports.

23. Revenue funding provides ongoing support for the administration and work of a company through the year, and has usually operated on a three-year rolling cycle. This is as opposed to project funding, which companies must apply for on an *ad hoc* basis, and which does not cover the core costs of running a company.

24. There were earlier precursors of performance 'workshops': Anna Halprin's Dancers' Workshop in 1955 acknowledged its explicit debt to Bauhaus workshops; Erwin Piscator's Dramatic Workshop in the 1940s was where Lee Strasberg and Stella Adler taught and where Judith Malina of The Living Theatre studied; and Max Reinhardt had set up a theatrical workshop in Hollywood in 1934.

25. Pearson suggested that we might, in fact, actively solicit such oral testimony. In a paper delivered at a Forced Entertainment symposium (Lancaster, October 2004), he provocatively proposed that 'Maybe we concentrate too much on the analysis of contemporary performance from positions of spectatorship, on the authoritative documentation of

dramaturgy and its exposition, on constructing some kind of "official version", causing us to be rational and reasonable about work that was none of these things. And too little on histories written on and in the body, on oral testimonies that might discomfort the past: secret histories, stories of awkwardness, pain, trauma, scarring. The memories of those who did it, that might be elicited with the question "So how was it for you?", revelation of "the doing" as well as "the thing done"' (Pearson, n.p. 2004).

26. Frances Babbage gave a response to the academic symposium that accompanied Stan's Cafe's performance in *New Theatre Quarterly* (2000); see also, N. Rathbone in *New Theatre Quarterly* (2001), p. 90.

27. Stan's Cafe director James Yarker was taught by Pete Brooks, co-founder of Impact, while studying Theatre Studies at Lancaster University.

28. Interview with site artist and academic Cathy Turner, October 2004. Photographs of the two moments can be found in Helmer and Malzacher (eds) (2004), p. 76, and M. Shevtsova (2003), p. 10. The popping of balloons with a lighter was also the climactic moment of surrealist Apollinaire's *The Breasts of Tiresias* (1917).

29. Oddey (1994); Lamden (2000); Bicât and Baldwin (2002). There are also a range of books to inspire creative devising from the various strands of devising practice, including Tufnell and Crickmay (1990 and 2004); Martin (2004).

30. Histories which explore experimental theatre in various fields include Aronson, *American Avant-Garde Theatre* (2000); Milne, *Theatre Australia (Un)limited: Australian Theatre since the 1950s* (2004); Radic, *State of Play: The Revolution in the Australian Theatre since the 1960s* (1991); Kershaw, *The Politics of Performance: Radical Theatre as Cultural Intervention* (1992); Innes, *Avant-Garde Theatre, 1892–1992* (1993); many works by Banes, including *Greenwich Village 1963* (1993); Goodman, *Contemporary Feminist Theatres: To Each Her Own* (1993); Itzin, *Stages in the Revolution: Political Theatre in Britain since 1968* (1980).

Notes to Chapter 2: Devising and Acting

1. Incidentally, *The Hostage* was one of the first plays to take seriously the re-emergence of the IRA as a force.

2. Coren has noted that A. J. P. Taylor's history of the First World War, published in 1963, was dedicated to Joan Littlewood.

3. For Mike Leigh, actors generated characters through observation and Stanislavskian improvisation in isolation. The characters were then brought together and their improvised interactions in a specific scenario,

provided by Leigh, evolved into the final performance. Early Hull Truck performances used a shortened version of this kind of improvisation.

4. Charles Marowitz explored the possibilities of combining the Method with other modes, in *The Method as Madness* (1961).

5. The onset of the Second World War had brought an influx of exiles and displaced artists to America, such as Piscator and Brecht, practitioners who were more explicitly concerned with the social and political alertness of their performers. Judith Malina of The Living Theatre studied for a short time with Piscator in New York.

6. For further details of Halprin's work, see Banes and Baryshnikov (eds), (2003), Worth and Poynor (2004), and Halprin's various publication from the Dancers' Workshop.

7. Halprin discussed her work in *Moving Toward Life: Five Decades of Transformational Dance* (1995). The RSVP cycles were explicitly formulated in response to the experience of working with black and white performers in confrontation and reconciliation through task and movement, on *The Ceremony of US* (1969). RSVP cycles are carefully explained in both Anna Halprin, 'The San Francisco Dancers' Workshop', in A. Feinstein (ed.), *Theatre Papers*, 1, 6 (1977–8), and L. Halprin, *RSVP Cycles: Creative Processes in the Human Environment* (1969).

8. The Living Theatre had visited Europe twice before with *The Connection* and Gelber's second play, *The Apple* (1961), which had both been well received.

9. Robert Pasolli identified this exercise as one devised by Chaikin, called the Chord, which he considered an emblem of the collective experience of the Open Theatre (Pasolli, 1972, p. 33).

10. The reputation for 'free love' and drug use that the group had acquired made the authorities of the cities they visited extra-vigilant and the show was stopped in Vienna, when theatre students joined the plague scene on stage, and was banned in Trieste, when an actor appeared naked in one of the improvised tableaux sections.

11. Living Theatre, www.livingtheatre.org (accessed 5 January 2004).

12. Robert Brustein, who had been partly responsible for inviting the group back to America, felt that the religious imagery had turned the group inwards, reaching only an already knowing audience, turning the piece into a 'controlled happening' (Tytell, 1995, p. 249). See Kershaw (1999b).

13. The Living Theatre themselves described their evolution in the late 1970s and 1980s as a 'return to the theater, where they developed new participatory techniques that enable the audience to first rehearse with the company and then join them onstage as fellow performers'. Living Theatre, www.livingtheatre.org (accessed 5 January 2004).

14. In Chicago in 1955–7, Viola Spolin's son Paul Sills and the Compass Players pioneered a revue-style comedy group which presented *only* fully

improvised scenes and encounters as performance. The company evolved into Second City in 1959 and popularised a new kind of stand-up comedy. The wholly improvised sketch performance, firmly in the tradition of variety comedy, was quickly absorbed by television in Second City TV in the US, and into shows such as 'Whose Line is it Anyway?' in the UK.

15. Like many companies at the time, the evolution of a devising process was funded by a grant, in this case a 'six month actor/writer workshop subsidised by their first grant of $2000 from the Drama Board of the Arts Council' (Robertson, 2001, p. 47).

16. Nancy Meckler, interview with Cathy Turner, June 2001.

17. Other archetypal stories that The Freehold explored included *Alternatives* (1969), which looked at child development, *Genesis* (1972) and *Beowulf* (1973).

18. Nancy Meckler, interview with Cathy Turner, June 2001.

19. Psychology had become a powerful element of actor training, particularly the American 'Method' with its emphasis on emotional memory work, largely because of the need to service naturalism's demand for a legible interiority for characters.

20. Interest in Bhuddist thought influenced one of Timothy Leary's earliest books, *The Psychedelic Experience* (1964).

21. Although *Theatre and its Double* was not translated into Polish until 1967, Grotowski was aware of Artaud in the French.

22. In 1970 Grotowski announced a new direction for the company in the development of paratheatrical activities, which called for an active making of work by all concerned and took further the collective and improvisational activities without performance as a goal. The paratheatrical activity of the 1970s was explicitly linked to a therapeutic purpose, as the performers guided and encouraged participants in physical and vocal improvisation in groups, drawing on everyday activity and shared songs. In 1975–6, Grotowski announced a series of laboratory foci for professional therapists, and much of the work in the special projects was influenced by psychology and the sociology of artistic creativity in groups. Barba's Odin Teatret, founded in 1964 in Oslo, then Denmark, continued many of the investigations into theatre that Grotowski had begun, and continued to make theatre after Grotowski had moved into paratheatrical activity.

23. Part of the generative force of the group's work was the uniquely American version of transcendence through therapy: 'During rehearsals the performer searches his personal experiences and associations, selects those elements which reveal him and also make an autonomous narrative and action structure, strips away irrelevancies and cop-outs, hones what remains until everything is necessary and sufficient. ... Each performance he risks freshly not only his dignity and craft, but his life-in-process' (Schechner, 1971, p. 61).

24. For a detailed study of the ideology and practices of the Black Arts Movement see Smethurst (2005).
25. One of the most successful pieces the group toured was *Soljourney into Truth* (1977), a performance based on their experiences of Yoruba culture, using ritual and music, which they toured to Africa.
26. See Sainer (1997) for discussion and illustration of these groups.
27. One of the actors reported: 'I'd say 80% of the dialogue comes out of improvisations from the actors. Martha had some real specific and real general ideas when she came into it and was responsible for engineering work days full of improvisational stuff to get us to make those ideas concrete' (Flynn, 1984, p. 148).
28. At the Foot of the Mountain closed in 1991; its archives are held at the University of Minneapolis.
29. One example of feminist disenchantment with apparently radical experimental groups, although not expressly resulting in the formation of feminist devised groups, might be Megan Terry's decision to leave Open Theatre in 1969 to form a women's theatre company, Omaha Magic Theatre, or Roberta Sklar's break with Chaikin and her eventual founding of the Women's Experimental Theatre in 1976 (Brunner, 1980).
30. Although, pragmatically, establishment practice in copyright law, grant funding bodies' regulation and tax legislation made it difficult for collaborative ownership to be recognised.
31. The more radical nature of the San Francisco Mime Troupe is indicated by their 1965 tour, *The Minstrel Show or Civil Rights in a Cracker Barrel*, which they used in order to demonstrate that the minstrel form is epic and that 'social subjects can be bounced around and not reduced to "adjustment psychology"' (Sainer, 1997, p. 21). Similar material was tackled in a less clearly polemical way by Pip Simmons' Group's *The George Jackson Black and White Minstrel Show* (1973, UK).
32. Sainer includes *The King Play* (1968), a 'collective work developed by the Pageant Players', a piece of street theatre (p. 167). The company described themselves in a listing in *Theatre Quarterly*, I, 3 (1971), p. 81, as 'growing directly out of radical politics', and said that they once did only street work but now 'all pieces are developed in collective improvization'.
33. The company subtitle themselves a *société coopérative ouvrière de production*, a workers' production company, which reflects their political commitment and pragmatic organisation.
34. However, in all of the work of Théâtre du Soleil there is a social and political commentary, for example, the company's more recent version of Molière's play *Le Tartuffe* (1995) was a 'critique of fundamentalism in Algeria, Israel and elsewhere' (Williams, 1999, p. xii).
35. Mnouchkine places devised work in the trajectory of the company's history, and has argued that 'the whole period of creating work

collectively was, in fact, a preparation for our work on and with an author. I realise that now' (Williams, 1999, p. xvii).

36. Footsbarn lost its UK funding and was forced in 1980 to tour abroad. It reformulated itself as an international group although still with a commitment to rural communities, and is now based in France. Its repertoire evolved during the late 1970s and 1980s to include adaptations of classic texts, performed in what was now their 'house style' of fast, physical clowning and mythic visual imagery, coupled with live music. See www.footsbarn.com (consulted 12 March 2005).

37. Offshoots of the Australian Performing Group were Stasis, a group more interested in exploring the actors' potential in their adaptations of classic plays; Soapbox Circus, a touring community theatre and rock-music troupe; and later Circus Oz.

38. Press review by Lyn Gardner, 2000. Shared Experience, see www.sharedexperience.org.uk (accessed 3 March 2004).

39. While actors and directors often chose to figure themselves as alternative, experimental or distinct from the mainstream, many groups became nurtured by state patronage from booming economies and the burgeoning alternative entrepreneurship of the 'counter-cultures'.

40. The Australian group Tribe performed an hour-and-half-long version of this in their piece *Plague* (1970); see Robertson (2001, p. 19).

Notes to Chapter 3: Devising and Visual Performance

1. Kaprow's reflections on the term 'Happenings' are instructive. 'I used it in the title of the *18 Happenings in 6 Parts* because it was a neutral word that avoided reference to art. Then the press and some of the artists took up the word, and it became the name of a kind of work. Then, I tried, along with other artists like Bob Whitman and Claes Oldenburg, to get rid of the word. They didn't want to be associated with it, and I didn't blame them. We failed, and now everything under the sun is called a "Happening"' (cited in Kostelanetz, 1980, p. 111). As Jean-Jacques Lebel also insisted, 'There is no theory of the Happening; each participant has his own' (Lebel, 1967, p. 23). Other terms coined at this time, including Fluxus, Action Theatre and Theatre of Mixed Means, bear testimony to the extent of interdisciplinary practice.

2. For fuller explorations of Happenings, see Sandford (1995), Kostelanetz (1980), Goldberg (1988), Kaprow (1966a).

3. See Goldberg (1988) for summaries of both Kaprow's and Cage's events.

4. Suzuki had long been exploring the performer's relationship to her unconscious, to experience, and to self-realisation. He was himself influenced by the Surrealists. See Allain (2002).

5. See Chapter 1 for various examples. Further useful reading includes Redwood (ed.) (1979); Apollonio (ed.) (1973); Kirby (1971); Melzer (1980); Goldberg (1988).

6. For full details of *In Memory of Big Ed*, see Dewey (1963), Dewey (1977), Marowitz (1963), Kostelanetz (1980).

7. Reflecting the performance, Berghaus (1995) called the piece *Theatre*, while Henri (1974) called it *Street*.

8. As Williams has noted, the sacrificed 'butterfly' was, in fact, a piece of crumpled white paper.

9. The Destruction in Art Symposium (DIAS), hosted by the ICA and organised by the destruction artist Gustav Metzger, took place in the same year as the *US* presentation. John Latham is an English artist known for his assemblages of towers of books, 'skoob towers', which he packed with fireworks that he then ignited.

10. Hunt and his students would go on to form the more politically explicit Bradford College of Art Theatre Group.

11. It is notable that neither Hunt nor Nuttall included any female artists.

12. Emma Haughton, email communication, September 2004.

13. Geraldine Pilgrim, interview, December 2003. All quotations from this source will be referred to as (Pilgrim).

14. Kobialka has explained Kantor's unusual textual form: 'Because the function of his theatre was to produce its own autonomous space by questioning and destroying classical/traditional representation, Kantor had to find a language to be able to express this process' (Kobialka, 1993, p. xix).

15. Fiona Templeton, email communication, July 2004. Templeton met Howell when both were teaching at Hornsey School of Art.

16. Anthony Howell, www.anthonyhowell.org/perf1.htm (accessed 26 July 2004).

17. The Performance Art Platform was founded in Nottingham in 1981. Notably, many companies participated in the Platform, including Station House Opera, Forkbeard Fantasy, British Event Group, Robert Ayers and Company, Tara Babel, Dogs in Honey and Forced Entertainment. In 1985, the Platform was repeated in Brighton, at the Zap Club. The Performance Art Platform is now called the National Review of Live Art, an annual event staged in Glasgow. Many such festivals now exist in the UK, such as Sensitive Skin in Nottingham and In-Between-Time in Bristol, testimony to the support for such work.

18. See Marks and de Courtivron (eds) (1981).

19. Anna Furse, interview, January 2005.

20. Ibid.

21. Furse and Gilmour were joined by Stephanie Pugsley (who had worked with Gay Sweatshop) for this show.

22. Blood Group's final show, *Strokes of Genius*, again a duo with Furse and Gilmour, was performed in 1987.

23. See C. Turner, *Reading Between the Lines: Writing for British Experimental Theatre and Performance* [forthcoming].
24. This is not to suggest that other forms of performance have not retained a closer resemblance to Happenings, Fluxus, etc. Many Live Art practices certainly continue to mine that vein.
25. See C. Turner, *Reading Between the Lines: Writing for British Experimental Theatre and Performance* [forthcoming].
26. Writing in 1986, critic Steve Rogers regarded *The Carrier Frequency* as the 'one major contribution to theatrical progress in the 1980s' (Rogers, 1986b, p. 17). Impact flooded the stage for this performance. It is notable that Pina Bausch had also done this for *Arien* (1979). Other surfaces used by Bausch have included grass, dead leaves and a memorable field of carnations.
27. One can surely hear the spectral whisperings of Marinetti, Tzara and Breton here. A shared context for the various avant-garde movements of the early twentieth century was the technological developments of that time, closely associated with industrial expansion, urbanisation and mechanisation at the turn of the century. Responses to these varied, but an awareness of their impact on modern experience and on sensibility was widely acknowledged and influential. In the face of new modes of transport and communication, including motorcars, aeroplanes and the expansion of railways, alongside the 'foundation of modern office organization' – telephone, tape machine and typewriter (Bullock, 1976, p. 59) – perceptions of speed and time were inevitably altered.

Notes to Chapter 4: Devising and Political Theatre

1. The strike lasted for five years, ending in 1970 when the farm workers' Union received official recognition, and the majority of workers demands had been met. See Kourilsky (1972).
2. Judith Condon's review was published in the *Socialist Worker*, 21 November 1971.
3. Originally in 'New Grapes', *Newsweek*, 31 July 1967.
4. See, for example, Seyd (1975).
5. Many people had experienced different companies, and their practices. For example, Chris Bowler had worked with the Brighton Combination, the People Show, Belt and Braces; Gillian Hanna had worked with 7:84 and Belt and Braces.
6. For a useful study on 7:84, see DiCenzo (1996), and for the 'politics' of McGrath's role within the company, see in particular pp. 91–7.
7. Grove was a contributor to a discussion paper, published as 'New Perspectives on Theatre Today: Theatre Collectives: Alive and Kicking', *Platform*, 4 (1982).

8. The latter term also, of course, signals a distance from dominant under-standings of what a performance is. Some of the works explored in Chapter 7 do contain text, written by a company member, but the use of the text challenges notions of what a play might be.
9. Nabil Shaban, telephone interview with the author, January 2005.
10. Ibid.
11. Ibid.
12. More detailed information about the rehearsal practices of the group are collected in R. Ritchie (ed.), *The Joint Stock Book: The Making of a Theatre Collective* (1987).
13. Nabil Shaban, telephone interview, January 2005.
14. Originally quoted in *Santa Barbara News and Review*, 17 May 1974, p. 14.
15. The article was originally published anonymously.
16. The report was published in *Theatre is for All*, the Report of the Inquiry into Professional Theatre in England under the Chairmanship of Sir Kenneth Cork, Arts Council of Great Britain (1986).
17. Sphinx Theatre, www.sphinxtheatre.co.uk/index1.cfm (accessed 7 September 2004).
18. Nitro, www.nitro.co.uk/about.htm (accessed 27 August 2004).
19. Ibid.
20. Red Ladder, www.redladder.co.uk (accessed 25 August 2004).
21. About Face Theatre, www.aboutfacetheatre.com (accessed 3 March 2005).
22. Kershaw also indicated that community theatre expanded at an even greater rate than feminist, gay or black companies.
23. Fragmentation might also be read as a necessary challenge to political movements that did not take notice of issues of gender, race, and sexuality. Fragmentation enables the possibility of coalition politics, where different groups unite for shared issues, without assuming that everyone is the same, or subject to the same forms and effects of oppression.
24. Nabil Shaban, telephone interview, January 2005.
25. Theatre Workshop, www.theatre-workshop.com (accessed 17 January 2005).
26. Arts Council England, 'A Statistical Survey of Regularly and Fixed Term Funding Organisations, 2001/02'. Some performance activities would fall under the 'combined arts' heading where, of the 136 funded organisations surveyed, nine were 'African, Carribean, Chinese or Asian led' (a definition relating to organisational structures rather than to aesthetic outputs).
27. The work undertaken at Bradford College of Art is discussed in Chapter 2.
28. Catherine Itzin referred to the presentation as one of the classic legendary events in political theatre (Itzin, 1980, p. 20). Roland Muldoon's reflections were more transparent in their judgement, suggesting that

not all such crossings were pleasurable. See Itzin (1980, p. 21) and Kershaw (1992, p. 124).

29. Happenings and Ken Dewey are discussed in Chapter 3. Other influential practitioners to work with the Mime Troupe included the minimalist musician Steve Reich and the actor-director Lee Breuer.

30. Reader programme note.

Notes to Chapter 5: Devising and Communities

1. The complex network and history of the development of this new popular theatre movement in South and Latin America is closely argued in Weiss (1993).

2. Rose Myers, interview, May 2003.

3. J. Cohen-Cruz, 'An Introduction to Community Art and Activism', Community Arts Network www.communityarts.net/readingroom/archive files/2002/02/an_introduction.php (accessed 1 August 2004).

4. For more information on Junebug's practices, particularly its use of oral history in its Story Circles, see <www.gnofn.org/~junebug/thejunebugtheater.html>.

5. Ann Jellicoe's work in Lyme Regis on community play-making lies somewhat outside the scope of this study, with its emphasis on writers working with communities. Her work was modelled in some ways on Cheeseman's style of documentary drama, for example, her first project in 1978, *The Reckoning*, was about the local connections to the Monmouth rebellion of 1685. However, Jellicoe, an experienced playwright whose work had been staged at the Royal Court, used a process that was in some ways more traditional than the experiments at the Victoria Theatre, Stoke-on-Trent, in that she wrote the play herself from research gathered by the community. On the other hand, her work had a more radical connection to the community as the community itself staged and performed the work. The success of community participation in the performance led her to establish the Colway Theatre Trust and to undertake further projects, always with a slow development lasting up to two years, using the many diverse local communities to evolve the work, but always with a core of professional writers and facilitators.

6. Formed in the 1960s, the Craigmillar Festival Society, based on a deprived housing estate in Edinburgh, became an effective political force, winning EU poverty action funding over the heads of the Scottish Office. As well as the annual festival the Society ran a huge number of projects employing local people in landscaping, play area development, play groups, theatre and art works, social work and community development. See Crummy (1992). In October 2004 an exhibition of the 'Arts

the Catalyst' displayed documents, photographs and art work from the history of the project. Devising and making community-written perform-ance was a key part of the evolution of the project. The tradition continues with the community pantomime.

7. This and the following quotation, Rose Myers, interview with the author, May 2003.

8. Incidentally, all these writers began from a position extolling the innate health and positive aspects of 'human nature', which can be 'corrupted' by poor systems or dysfunctional social structures and strictures. As Tony Coult outlined, since the 1960s Gavin Bolton and Dorothy Heathcote had developed this idea to emphasise drama in education as offering a child not a vague creative outlet, but a 'precise emotional and cognitive experience' (Coult, 1980, p. 77).

9. Earlier expressions of a child-centred theatre were developed by Peter Slade at his Rae Street Centre, Birmingham, and by Brian Way at the Theatre Centre, London.

10. Not all programmes were so content orientated. For example, Perspectives Theatre Company's event for infants, *Spaces* (1979), was about physical properties of objects. Using the ideas of Edward de Bono, four actors went into schools with 'inventing kits', collections of shapes of unusual texture, weight etc. and initiated free play as pupils investigated and experimented. Then the class was asked to invent a 'sleep-inducing machine, an animal trap or an explorer's raft, using the shapes as building blocks, endowed with whatever properties they wished', which moved the work from individual to group play. Tony Coult considered that 'although very few conventional theatre techniques were used, there was still a conscious use of dramatic structure, with theatre design and roleplay contributing the greater part of the theatre experience' (Coult, 1980, p. 82).

11. Blah, Blah, Blah, www.blahs.co.uk (accessed January 2005).

12. It is remarkable to think of this experiment in community activism in the same breath as Sir Alan Ayckbourn, one of the most conservative of British establishment playwrights; Peter Cheeseman (1971a, 79).

13. This and the remaining extracts in this section, Rose Myers, interview, May 2003.

14. Other activities included an outpost in the new town Milton Keynes, and acting as a pressure group to inform local government policy, NUBS advisory service on the renovation of local amenities and Inter-Action Game Method and Training.

15. John Turner, *The Albany: A Deptford Ark*, Deptford Albany, www.thealbany.org.uk/aor/aormain/graphics/TheDeptfordArk.pdf (accessed 15 February 2004).

16. See Coult and Kershaw (eds) (1990).

17. See also Fox (1996).

18. Pauline and Denis Peel, two of the company members, had worked at Craigmillar, and Steve Capelin had experience with WEST community theatre, Melbourne.

19. The fact that *Kabaret* was funded not by an Arts Board but by the Human Rights Commission indicates the extent to which this was perceived as social action, as well as aesthetic action.

20. As personnel changed in 1995, Street Arts became Arterial, a visual arts organisation, echoing a move in many community arts companies towards integrating performance arts and contemporary performance practices into their work.

21. Maryat Lee argued: 'Street theater died ... because ... not one of the companies, not *one*, had street people on the stages ... [T]hey were well-intentioned theater folks bringing culture to the streets, or they were activists wanting to stir the people up to action "for their own good". They were, in fact, deadly and shortsighted. ... The naïveté of asking theater people to perform the oral histories belonging to the people is mind boggling' (cited in Richard Owen Geer (1994), pp. 18–23).

22. In recent years, funding criteria have led to an increased move towards specialisation in the target client groups in community work. Particularly well served are youth audiences; particularly poorly served are older communities: Age Exchange (1984) being one of the very few UK companies who work with Reminiscence Theatre. The growth of Boalean influence in this kind of community work is difficult to overemphasise, particularly his characterisation of Freirean pedagogy as Forum Theatre: Cardboard Citizens (1991) specialise in working with the homeless through these means.

Notes to Chapter 6: Contemporary Devising and Physical Performance

1. Lynne Bradley and Simon Woods, interview, May 2003. All quotations from this source will be referred to as (Bradley and Woods).

2. Debra Iris Batton, interview, May 2003. All quotations from this source will be referred to as (Batton).

3. Legs on the Wall, <www.Legsonthewall.com.au> (accessed 1 May 2003).

4. David Clarkson, interview, May 2003. All quotations from this source will be referred to as (Clarkson).

5. For further details see Dixon and Smith (eds) (1995).

6. Lynne Bradley's use of 'jamming' to describe the improvisational, compositional work of this phase echoes the ideological drive of the earlier physical performance groups of the 1960s and 1970s.

7. BTEC National Diploma in Performing Arts.

8. Theatre de Complicite, <www.complicite.org> (accessed 27 June 2004).
9. Ibid.
10. Ibid.
11. Jatinder Verma, email interview, October 2004.
12. Ibid.
13. Lee Simpson came through drama school and comedy improvisation, Phelim McDermott through a Performing Arts degree at Middlesex, where he worked with Jon Wright and Julia Bardsley, and Julian Crouch was a maker who worked with Welfare State International. Simpson and McDermott had been working together on improvised performances in various repertory theatres. As a company, Improbable has, to date, produced eight shows including *70 Hill Lane* (1996), *Lifegame* (1998–2004), *Coma* (1997), *Spirit* (2001) and *The Hanging Man* (2003). In a different formation Julian Crouch and Phelim McDermott collaborated with a producing company, Cultural Industry, to produce the junk-opera *Shockheaded Peter* (1998).
14. McDermott's directing outside Improbable has included *Impossible Tales*, a two hour improvised performance at Nottingham Playhouse.
15. Lee Simpson of Improbable, interview, December 2004. All quotations from this source will be referred to as (Simpson).
16. Improbable, <www.improbable.co.uk> (accessed 1 December 2004).
17. Effective images transfer from one performance to the next: a newspaper man puppet animated by the actors is an opening image in *70 Hill Lane*, while in *Cinderella* (1998/9), newspaper puppets represent a horse, on which Cinderella and the Prince ride away. The luminous sellotape effect of *70 Hill Lane* was adapted on a large scale to become the principle for a huge outdoor spectacular, *Sticky* (2000), where a giant menacing sellotape spider-cum-tower blazes into the sky in a pyrotechnical finale.
18. It will be interesting to see what the company makes of the performance issues surrounding their project *Theatre of Blood*, at the National Theatre, which will use a script of some sort for the first time. The horror film, in which critics meet with gruesome deaths drawn from Shakespeare, will be made through improvisation on a text, not devising.

Notes to Chapter 7: Contemporary Devising and Postmodern Performance

1. Many of these theories developed from and challenged the structuralist insights of Ferdinand de Saussure. There is not space here to list the many publications that appeared during this period but a few examples should adequately suggest the critical landscape: Derrida's *Of Grammatology* was first published in 1967, and translated into English by Spivak in 1976; Cixous's 'The Laugh of the Medusa' was published in 1975;

Foucault's hugely influential study *The History of Sexuality, vol. 1* appeared in 1976, one year after *Discipline and Punish: The Birth of the Prison*; Said's important *Orientalism* was published in 1977, while Lyotard's *The Postmodern Condition* first appeared in 1979.

2. There is not room here to discuss the debates circulating around the terms 'postmodern' and 'postmodernism'. Seminal critical texts remain Jean-François Lyotard's *The Postmodern Condition: A Report on Knowledge* (1979; 1984), Andreas Huyssen's *After the Great Divide* (1986), Frederic Jameson's *Postmodernism, or, The Cultural Logic of Late Capitalism* (1995). Linda Hutcheon's *The Politics of Postmodernism* (1989) is a useful text for the potential political impact of postmodernism in artistic practice; Nick Kaye's *Postmodernism and Performance* (1994) is particularly valuable for students and practitioners of theatre, while Philip Auslander's *Presence and Resistance: Postmodernism and Cultural Politics in Contemporary American Performance* (1992) provides some useful critical discussion around various concepts pertaining to performance, in particular those relating to original and copy, live and mediated.

3. Contemporary devised performance practice is much more a feature of the UK landscape than the USA. Though one of the best known collaborative companies, The Wooster Group, was founded in New York in 1975, and has undoubtedly been influential nationally and internationally, more recent companies such as The Builders Association, Elevator Repair Services, The Civilians, Goat Island and Lucky Pierre remain the exception. This relative scarcity of contemporary devising companies in the USA is all the more marked when placed beside the vibrant scene in the UK, where there are too many companies to mention. In Britain, this realm of performance-making has not only been sustained since the 1970s, but has developed considerably and has undoubtedly benefited from increased subsidy such as the Arts Council's Combined Arts initiative, the New Collaborations Fund (1991–6), which specifically encouraged the development of interdisciplinary practice. The Combined Arts Unit was itself established in 1985, indicating the extent and visibility of cross-disciplinary forms. Elena Holy, director of the New York Fringe Festival, explained the lack of contemporary devising in the USA as a result of inadequate funding opportunities. Without adequate funding provision, it is difficult for people to commit long-term to a group, or even to a devising project (Holy, interview with the author, September 2004). This bears similarities to the experiences of many political companies discussed in Chapter 4.

4. The Special Guests, www.thespecialguests.co.uk (accessed 8 August 2004).

5. Bottoms is here using Gilles Deleuze and Félix Guattari's concept of the rhizome, as introduced in *A Thousand Plateaus: Capitalism and*

Schizophrenia, trans. Brian Massumi (1987). The rhizome is a stem whose shoots grow underground, spreading horizontally.

6. Third Angel, www.thirdangel.co.uk (accessed 27 December 2005).
7. Alexander Kelly, telephone interview, January 2005.
8. Third Angel, www.thirdangel.co.uk (accessed 27 December 2005).
9. Members of the company were students of Drama and English at the University of Exeter. One tutor, Dorinda Hulton, introduced them to the concept of the 'creative actor'.
10. Tim Etchells interview, December 2003. All quotations from this source will be referred to as (Etchells).
11. For an excellent example on the ethics of witnessing, see Nick Kaye's discussion on the responses to The Wooster Group's (contentious) use of blackface in *Route 1 & 9* (Kaye, 1994, p. 140).
12. Paul Clarke, 'Impossible Structures', www.uninvited-guests.net/gh/paul-s_text.htm (accessed 1 August 2004).
13. For a discussion on the problematic status of the 'real' in performance, see Quick (1996).
14. Of course, as Norris highlighted, the diffusion of the online population is highly uneven. 20.4 per cent of the western European population was estimated to be online in 2000, compared with only 0.5 per cent of the population in Africa, 3.1 per cent in South America, and 3.3 per cent in Asia; 42.8 per cent of the North American population were estimated to be online (Norris, 2001, p. 47).
15. Ofcom, 'The Communications Market', 11 August 2004, www.ofcom.org.uk/research/cm/ (accessed 5 February 2005).
16. Blast Theory, *Desert Rain* (1999) programme note. For full descriptions of the performance and its potential effects, see G. Giannachi (2004) and R. Clarke (2001). Blast Theory were prescient in their predictions and perceptions; only a few years later Arnold Schwarzenegger is the elected Governor of California, and a computer video game of the second Gulf War is now available on the market.
17. Third Angel have two directors, who both swap that role and occupy it simultaneously, as the need dictates.
18. Stan's Cafe, www.stanscafe.co.uk/qcollaboration.html (accessed 26 December, 2004).
19. Ibid.
20. It is for this reason that Forced Entertainment dropped the 'Theatre' from their name.
21. The practice of devising within universities and colleges must take some responsibility for this repetition, as frequently professional devising companies are employed to work with students, and the work of certain companies has become a staple part of the curricula. Rachael Walton, co-founder of Third Angel and a Lancaster graduate, remembers being introduced to the work of Forced Entertainment and other companies

where 'the text wasn't the be all and end all' and has suggested the existence of a 'Lancaster theatrical language' (Walton, interview with the author, December 2003). From our surveys of Performance, Theatre and Drama departments, we would suggest that this language is less a 'Lancaster language' than a more widespread 'university contemporary theatre language'.

22. The Special Guests, www.thespecialguests.co.uk/ (accessed 8 August 2004).

23. Whilst acknowledging the deliberately 'open', or 'undecided' nature of many contemporary performances, Harris has importantly extended this responsibility of 'meaning making' to the spectator. See also Harris (1999b).

24. Etchells in fact reviewed Impact Theatre's last show, *The Price of Meat in the Last Days of the Mechanical Age* (1986). In what, armed with the benefit of hindsight and knowledge of Forced Entertainment's own early work, proves to be an instructive and revealing evaluation, Etchells proposed that the piece 'shows us people trying to make order out of chaos, art out of life, fact of fiction. Nothing satisfies.' The company was 'caught between presenting real performance events and dramatic fictions' and instead of 'transcending fiction', Impact 'turns around and attacks it' (Etchells, 1986, p. 10).

Notes to Chapter 8: Conclusions

1. The context in which work is shown is also important. For some audiences, depending on their experiences as spectators, the use of a fragmented dramaturgy, or a multi-layered narrative, might remain bewildering.

2. See Lehmann (1999).

3. David Clarkson, interview, May 2003.

4. Lynne Bradley and Simon Woods, interview, 2003.

5. Given that degree courses are typically three years in duration, 'siblings' is perhaps a more accurate metaphor than 'generation'. There are often only a few years separating companies, which makes cross-fertilisation between them more possible. The 'traffic' of influence might therefore be considered two-way.

6. President George Bush's identification of an 'axis of evil' appears, however, to have reinstated an identifiable 'enemy' of the West, located in the Middle-East. This ideology is not, perhaps, so far removed from the Cold War or 'Yellow Peril' rhetoric.

7. *New York Times*, 8 December 2004; statistics from reports published by the United Nations' Food and Agriculture Organisation and the United Nations' International Labour Organisation.

8. *New York Times*, 13 June 2000; statistics from World Refugee Survey.

Bibliography

Abbot. L. (1996), 'Spiderwoman Theater and the Tapestry of Story', *Canadian Journal of Native Studies*, XVI, 1: 165–80.

Abercrombie, N. and Warde, A. (2000), *Contemporary British Society* (Cambridge: Polity Press).

Adorno, T. (1950), *The Authoritarian Personality* (New York: Harper).

Alfreds, M. and Barker, C. (1981), 'Shared Experience: from Science Fiction to Shakespeare', *Theatre Quarterly*, X, 39: 12–22.

Allain, P. (2002), *The Art of Stillness: The Theatre Practice of Tadashi Suzuki* (London: Methuen).

Alway, J. (1999), *Critical Theory and Political Possibilities: Conceptions of Emancipatory Politics in the Works of Horkheimer, Adorno, Marcuse, and Habermas* (London: Greenwood Press).

Anonymous (1971), 'Paris After the Revolution', *Theatre Quarterly*, 1, 3: 63.

Ansorge, P. (1975), *Disrupting the Spectacle* (London: Pitman).

Apollonio, U. (ed.) (1973), *Futurist Manifestos* (London: Thames and Hudson).

Apple, J. (1991), 'The Life and Times of Lin Hixson: the LA Years', *Drama Review*, 35, 4: 27–45.

Aronson, A. (2000), *American Avant-Garde Theatre* (London: Routledge).

Artaud, A. (1974), *Theatre and its Double*, trans. V. Corti (London: Calder and Boyars).

Ashford, J. (1980), 'The Jazz of Dreams: Performance Art', in S. Craig (ed.), *Dreams and Deconstructions: Alternative Theatre in Britain* (Ambergate: Amber Lane Press), pp. 95–104.

Asquith, R. (1980), 'The Arena of Exploration: Children's Theatre', in S. Craig (ed.), *Dreams and Deconstructions: Alternative Theatre in Britain* (Ambergate: Amber Lane Press), pp. 86–95.

Aston, E. (1999), *Feminist Theatre Practice: A Handbook* (London: Routledge).

Auslander, P. (1992), *Presence and Resistance: Postmodernism and Cultural Politics in Contemporary American Performance* (Ann Arbor: University of Michigan Press).

Babbage, F. (2000), 'The Past in the Present: a Response to Stan's Cafe's Revival of *The Carrier Frequency*', *New Theatre Quarterly*, XVI, 1: 97–9.

Banes, S. (1993), *Greenwich Village, 1963* (Durham: Duke University Press).
—— (2000), 'Institutionalizing Avant-Garde Performance: a Hidden History of University Patronage in the United States', in J. Harding (ed.), *Contours of the Theatrical Avant-Garde* (Ann Arbor: University of Michigan Press), pp. 217–38.
Banes, S. and Baryshnikov, M. (eds) (2003), *Reinventing Dance in the 1960s* (Madison: University of Wisconsin Press).
Barker, C. (1977), *Theatre Games* (London: Methuen).
—— (1979), 'Pip Simmons in Residence', *Theatre Quarterly*, IX, 35: 17–30.
Beck, J. (1965), 'Storming the Barricades', in K. H. Brown, *The Brig* (New York: Hill and Wang) pp. 3–35.
—— (1972), *The Life of the Theatre* (San Francisco: City Lights Books).
Becker, C. (2000), 'Response to Adrian Heathfield', in *Goat Island School Book 2* (Chicago: School of Art Institute of Chicago), pp. 94–9.
Belgrad, D. (1998), *The Culture of Spontaneity* (Chicago: University of Chicago Press).
Berghaus, G. (1995), 'Happenings in Europe: Trends, Events and Leading Figures', in M. Sandford (ed.), *Happenings and Other Acts* (London: Routledge), pp. 310–88.
Berman, E. (1980), 'Foreword', in E. Leyh, *Concrete Sculpture in the Community* (London: Inter-Action Trust).
Bessai, D. (1992), *Playwrights of Collective Creation* (Toronto: Simon and Pierre).
Bicât, T. and Baldwin, C. (eds) (2002), *Devised and Collaborative Theatre: A Practical Guide* (Marlborough: Crowood Press).
Birchall, B. (1978) 'Grant Aid and Political Theatre: Part 2', *Wedge*, 2: 39–43.
Blumenthal, E. (1984), *Joseph Chaikin: Exploring the Boundaries of Theatre* (Cambridge: Cambridge University Press).
Blundell, G. (ed.) (1970), *Plays by Buzo, Hibberd, Romeril* (London: Penguin).
Boal, A. (1979), *Theatre of the Oppressed*, trans. C. and M-O. Leal McBride (London: Pluto Press).
—— (1998), *Legislative Theatre: Using Performance to Make Politics*, trans. A. Jackson (London: Routledge).
Bottoms, S. J. (1998), 'The Tangled Flora of Goat Island: Rhizome, Repetition, Reality', *Theatre Journal*, 50: 421–46.
Bourdieu, P. (1990), *The Logic of Practice* (Stanford: Stanford University Press).
Bradbury, M. and McFarlane, J. (eds), (1976), *Modernism: A Guide to European Literature, 1890–1930* (London: Penguin Books).
Bradby, D. and McCormick, J. (1978), *People's Theatre* (London: Croom Helm).
Bradley, L. and Woods, S. (2003), 'Company History' (Brisbane: Zen Zen Zo).
Brady, S. (2000), 'Welded to the Ladle: Steelbound and Non-radicality in Community-based Theatre', *Drama Review*, 44, 3: 51–74.
Brecht, G. (1996), *Chance-Imagery* (New York: A Great Bear Pamphlet).

Brown, G. (1975), *Plays and Players*, 22, 9: 29–31.

Brown, I., Brannen, R. and Brown, D. (2000), 'The Arts Council Touring Franchise and English Political Theatre after 1986', *New Theatre Quarterly*, XVI, 4: 379–87.

Brunner, C. (1980), 'Roberta Sklar: Towards Creating a Women's Theatre', *Drama Review*, 24, 2: 23–40.

Bullock, A. (1976), 'The Double Image', in M. Bradbury and J. McFarlane (eds), *Modernism: A Guide to European Literature, 1890–1930* (London: Penguin Books), pp. 58–70.

Burt, S. and Barker, C. (1980), 'IOU and the New Vocabulary of Performance Art', *Theatre Quarterly*, X, 37: 70–94.

Butler, C. (1980), *After the Wake: The Contemporary Avant-Garde* (Oxford: Oxford University Press).

Caillois, R. (1961), *Man, Play and Games* (New York: Free Press of Glencoe).

Calder, J. (1967), 'Happenings in the Theatre', in *New Writers IV: Plays and Happenings* (London: Calder and Boyers), pp. 7–10.

Cameron, A. (1996), 'Experimental Theatre in Scotland', in T. Shank (ed.), *Contemporary British Theatre* (Basingstoke: Macmillan), pp. 123–38.

Campbell-Kelly, M. and Aspray, W. (1996), *Computer: A History of the Information Machine* (New York: Basics Books).

Cavallo, D. (1999), *A Fiction of the Past: The Sixties in American History* (New York: Palgrave).

Cave, R. (2003), 'What Price Global Culture? (or Can You Hope to Clone a TapDog?)', in E. Schafer and S. Bradley Smith (eds), *Playing Australia: Australian Theatre and the International Stage* (Amsterdam: Rodopi), pp. 159–79.

Chaikin, J. (1972), *The Presence of the Actor* (New York: Atheneum).

—— (1975), 'Joseph Chaikin: Closing the Open Theatre', interview with Richard Toscan, *Theatre Quarterly*, V, 16: 36–43.

Chamberlain, F. and Yarrow, R. (eds) (2002), *Jacques Lecoq and the British Theatre* (London: Routledge).

Chambers, C. (1980), 'Product into Process: Actor-based workshops', in S. Craig (ed.), *Dreams and Deconstructions: Alternative Theatre in Britain* (Ambergate: Amber Lane Press), pp. 105–15.

Chambers, C. and Steed, M. (2004), 'Acting on the Front Foot', in J. Milling and M. Banham (eds), *Extraordinary Actors* (Exeter: University of Exeter Press), pp. 191–209.

Cheeseman, P. (1971a), 'A Community Theatre in the Round', *Theatre Quarterly*, I, 1: 71–82.

—— (1971b), 'Casebook of the Staffordshire Rebels', *Theatre Quarterly*, I, 1: 86–102.

Christopher, K. (1996), 'Illusiontext', *Performance Research*, 1, 3: 6–10.

Clarke, R. (2001), 'Reigning Territorial Plains – Blast Theory's "Desert Rain"', *Performance Research*, 6, 2: 43–50.

Cockett, R. (1999), 'The New Right and the 1960s: the Dialectics of Liberation', in G. Andrews, R. Cockett, A. Hooper and M. Williams (eds), *New Left, New Right and Beyond: Taking the Sixties Seriously* (Basingstoke: Macmillan Press), pp. 85–105.

Cody, G. (1998), 'Woman, Man, Dog, Tree: Two Decades of Intimate and Monumental Bodies in Pina Bausch's Tanztheater', *Drama Review*, 42, 2: 115–31.

Cohen-Cruz, J. (2000), 'A Hyphenated Field: Community-based Theatre in the USA', *New Theatre Quarterly*, XVI, 4: 364–78.

Copeland, R. (2002), 'Merce Cunningham and the Aesthetic of Collage', *Drama Review*, 46, 1: 11–28.

Coren, M. (1984), *Theatre Royal: 100 Years of Stratford East* (London: Quartet Books).

Coult, T. (1980), 'Agents of the Future: Theatre-in-Education', in S. Craig (ed.), *Dreams and Deconstructions: Alternative Theatre in Britain* (Ambergate: Amber Lane Press), pp. 76–85.

Coult, T. and Kershaw, B. (eds) (1990), *Engineers of the Imagination: The Welfare State Handbook* (London: Methuen, 1983; rev. edn, 1990).

Cousin, G. (1985), 'Shakespeare from Scratch: the Footsbarn Hamlet and King Lear', *New Theatre Quarterly*, I, 1: 105–27.

Craig, S. (1980a), 'The Beginnings of the Fringe: Reflexes of the Future', in S. Craig (ed.), *Dreams and Deconstructions: Alternative Theatre in Britain* (Ambergate: Amber Lane Press), pp. 9–29.

Craig, S. (1980b), 'Unmasking the Lie: Political Theatre', in S. Craig (ed.), *Dreams and Deconstructions: Alternative Theatre in Britain* (Ambergate: Amber Lane Press), pp. 30–48.

Crisell, A. (1997), *An Introductory History of British Broadcasting* (London: Routledge).

Croyden, M. (1974), *Lunatics, Lovers and Poets* (New York: Delta).

Crummy, H. (1992), *Let the People Sing: The Story of Craigmillar* (Newcraighall: H. Crummy).

Dahlgren, P. (2001), 'The Transformation of Democracy', in B. Axford and R. Huggins (eds), *New Media and Politics* (London: Sage), pp. 64–88.

Daly, M. (1979), *Gyn/ecology: The Metaethics of Radical Feminism* (London: Women's Press).

Daniels, R. (1989), *Year of the Heroic Guerrilla: World Revolution and Counter Revolution in 1968* (New York: Basic Books).

Davies, A. (1987), *Other Theatres: The Development of Alternative and Experimental Theatre in Britain* (Basingstoke: Macmillan).

Davis, R. G. (1975a) *The San Francisco Mime Troupe: The First Ten Years* (Palo Alto, CA: Ramperts Press).

—— (1975b), 'Politics, Art, and the San Francisco Mime Troupe', *Theatre Quarterly*, V, 18: 26–7.

—— (1975c), 'The Radical Right in the American Theatre', *Theatre Quarterly*, V, 19: 67–72.

Deleuze, G. and Guattari, F. (1987), *A Thousand Plateaus: Capitalism and Schizophrenia*, trans. B. Massumi (Minneapolis: University of Minnesota Press).

Derrida, J. (1976), *Of Grammatology*, trans. G. C. Spivak (Baltimore, MD: Johns Hopkins University Press; first published 1967).

Devlin, G. (2004), 'The Beginning: 1970s', *ITC Members Matters, Special Birthday Issue*, 2004: 3–4.

Dewey, K. (1963), 'Act of San Francisco at Edinburgh', *Encore*, Nov.–Dec. 1963: 12–16.

—— (1977), 'An Odyssey Out of Theatre', in P. Hulton (ed.), *Theatre Papers*, 1, 11 (Totnes: Dartington College of Arts).

—— (1995), 'X-ings', in M. Sandford (ed.), *Happenings and Other Acts* (London: Routledge), pp. 206–10.

DiCenzo, M. (1996), *The Politics of Alternative Theatre in Britain: The Case of 7:84* (Cambridge: Cambridge University Press).

Dixon, L. (1980) *Performance Magazine*, 8.

—— (1982a), *Performance Magazine*, 17: 25.

—— (1982b), *Performance Magazine*, 15: 23–4.

Dixon, M. and Smith, J. (eds) (1995), *Anne Bogart: Viewpoints* (Lyme, NH: Smith and Kraus).

Dobbin, C. (1984), 'Women's Theatre and the APG', *Meanjin*, 43, 1: 129–38.

'Eclipse (1995): a Traveller's Map' (1999), in R. J. Allen and K. Pearlman (eds), *Performing the Unnameable* (Redfern, NSW: Currency Press), pp. 178–89.

Edgar, D. (1979), 'Ten Years of Political Theatre, 1968–78', *New Theatre Quarterly*, III, 32: 25–33.

Elam, H. J. (1997), *Taking It to the Streets: The Social Protest Theater of Luis Valdez and Amiri Baraka* (Michigan: University of Michigan Press).

Esslin, M. (1976), *Plays and Players*, 24, 2: 32–3.

Etchells, T. (1986), *Performance Magazine*, 40.

—— (1987), *Performance Magazine*, 49.

—— (1988), 'These are a Few of our (half) Favourite Things', *Theatre News and Reviews*, 1988.

—— (1990), 'Elvis Lives', *City Limits*, 1990: 1–8; included in *Forced Entertainment Resource Pack*.

—— (1994), 'Diverse Assembly: Some Trends in Recent Performance', in T. Shank (ed.), *Contemporary British Theatre* (London: Macmillan), pp. 107–22.

—— (1997), 'Addicted to Real Time', *Entropy*, 1997; included in *Forced Entertainment Resource Pack*.

—— (1999a), *Certain Fragments: Contemporary Performance and Forced Entertainment* (London: Routledge).

—— (1999b), 'Tim Etchells', in G. Giannachi and M. Luckhurst (eds), *On Directing: Interviews with Directors* (London: Faber and Faber), pp. 24–9.

—— (2004), 'A Text on 20 Years, with 66 Footnotes', in J. Helmer and F. Malzacher (eds), *Not Even a Game Anymore: The Theatre of Forced Entertainment* (Berlin: Alexander Berlag), pp. 269–90.

Etchells, T. and Forced Entertainment (2003), *Imaginary Evidence* (CD-ROM).

Fabre, G. (1983), *Drumbeats, Masks and Metaphor: Contemporary Afro-American Theatre*, trans. M. Dixon (Cambridge: Harvard University Press).

Feldman, P. (1977–8) 'The Sound and Movement Exercise as Developed by the Open Theatre', in P. Hulton (ed.), *Theatre Papers*, 1, 1 (Totnes: Dartington College of Arts).

Ferguson, R. (ed.) (1988), *Out of Actions: Between Performance and the Object, 1949–1979* (London: Thames and Hudson).

Fink, C., Gassert, P. and Junker, D. (eds) (1998), *1968: The World Transformed* (Cambridge: Cambridge University Press).

Flynn, M. (1984), *The Feeling Circle, Company Collaboration and Ritual Drama: Three Conventions Developed by the Women's Theater, At the Foot of the Mountain* (Ann Arbor: University of Michigan Press).

Forced Entertainment (1998a), *Interactions: Making Performance*, video recording.

—— (1998b), Resource Pack.

Fotheringham R. (ed.) (1992), *Community Theatre in Australia* (Sydney: Currency Press, 1987; rev. edn, 1992).

—— (1998), 'Boundary Riders and Claim Jumpers', in V. Kelly (ed.), *Our Australian Theatre in the 1990s* (Amsterdam: Rodopi), pp. 20–38.

Foucault, M. (1984), *The History of Sexuality: An Introduction* (Harmondsworth: Penguin; first published 1972).

—— (1977), *Language, Counter-memory, Practice*, ed. and trans. D. Bouchard (Ithaca: Cornell University Press, 1977).

Fox, J. (1996), 'Exploring to Fulfil a Genuine Need', *Live* 4 (London: Nick Hern), pp. 33–9.

Freeman, S. (1997), *Putting Your Daughters on the Stage: Lesbian Theatre from the 1970s to the 1990s* (London: Cassell).

Freire, P. (1989), *Pedagogy of the Oppressed* (New York: Continuum).

Freshwater, H. (2001), 'The Ethics of Indeterminacy: Théâtre de Complicité's *Mnemonic*', *New Theatre Quarterly*, XVII, 3: 212–18.

Fricker, K. (2003), 'Tourism, the Festival Marketplace and Robert Lepage's *The Seven Streams of the River Ota*', *Contemporary Theatre Review*, 13, 4: 79–93.

Frisch, N. and Weems, M. (1997), 'Dramaturgy on the Road to Immortality: Inside the Wooster Group', in S. Jonas, G. Proehl and M. Lupu (eds), *Dramaturgy in American Theater: A Source Book* (Orlando: Harcourt Brace), pp. 483–503.

Frost, A. and Yarrow, R. (1990), *Improvisation in Drama* (Basingstoke: Macmillan).

Gale, D. (1985), 'Against Slowness', *Performance Magazine*, 33: 22–6.

Gale, D. and Westlake, H. (1987), 'Doff This Bonnet Before it Becomes the Tea Cosy', *Performance Magazine*, 44/45: 6–8.

Gard, R. and Burley, G. (1959), *Community Theatre: Idea and Achievement* (Westport, CT: Greenwood Press).

Gates, H. (1988), *The Signifying Monkey: A Theory of African American Literary Criticism* (New York: Oxford).

Geer, R. O. (1994), 'Of the People, By the People and For the People: the Field of Community Performance', *High Performance*, 17, 4 (Winter): 18–23.

Giannachi, G. (2004), *Virtual Theatres: An Introduction* (London: Routledge).

Giannachi, G. and Luckhurst, M. (eds) (1999), *On Directing: Interviews with Directors* (London: Faber and Faber).

Giesekam, G. (2000), *Luvvies and Rude Mechanicals: Amateur and Community Theatre in Scotland* (Edinburgh: Scottish Arts Council).

Goat Island (2000), *Goat Island School Book 2* (Chicago: School of Art Institute of Chicago).

—— (2001), *It's an Earthquake in My Heart: A Reading Companion* (Chicago: Goat Island).

Godfrey, P. (1983), 'Performance and the Third Dimension', *Performance Magazine*, 21/21: 24–6.

Goffman, E. (1959), *The Presentation of Self in Everyday Life* (New York: Doubleday).

—— (1963), *Behaviour in Public Spaces* (New York: Free Press of Glencoe).

Goldberg, R. (1988), *Performance Art: From Futurism to the Present* (London: Thames and Hudson).

—— (1998), *Performance: Live Art since the 60s* (London: Thames and Hudson).

Goodman, L. (1993), *Contemporary Feminist Theatres: To Each Her Own* (London: Routledge).

Goodman, P. (1960), *Growing Up Absurd: Problems of Youth in the Organized Society* (New York: Vintage Books).

Goorney, H. (1981), *The Theatre Workshop Story* (London: Eyre Methuen).

Goorney, H. and MacColl, E. (eds) (1986), *Agitprop to Theatre Workshop* (Manchester: Manchester University Press).

Gottlieb, S. (1966), 'The Living Theatre in Exile: Mysteries, Frankenstein', *Tulane Drama Review*, 10, 4.

Goulish, M. (1996), 'Five Microlectures', *Performance Research*, 1, 3: 94–9.

Graver, D. (1995), *The Aesthetics of Disturbance: Anti-Art in Avant-Garde Drama* (Ann Arbor: University of Michigan Press).

Haedicke, S. (2001), 'Theater for the Next Generation: the Living Stage Theatre Company's Program for Teen Mothers', in S. Haedicke and T. Nellhaus (eds), *Performing Democracy: International Perspectives on Urban Community-based Performance* (Ann Arbor: University of Michigan Press), pp. 269–80.

Haedicke, S. and Nellhaus, T. (eds) (2001), *Performing Democracy: International Perspectives on Urban Community-based Performance* (Ann Arbor: University of Michigan Press).

Hall, S. (1983), *Performance Magazine*, 23.

Halprin, A. (1995), *Moving Toward Life: Five Decades of Transformational Dance* (Hanover: Wesleyan University Press).

—— (1977), 'The San Francisco Dancers' Workshop', in A. Feinsten (ed.), *Theatre Papers*, 1, 6 (Totnes: Dartington College of Arts).

—— (1989), 'Planetary Dance', *Drama Review*, 33, 2: 51–66.

Halprin, L. (1969), *RSVP Cycles: Creative Processes in the Human Environment* (New York: G. Braziller).

Hamilton, M. (2003), 'International Fault-Lines: Directions in Contemporary Australian Performance and the New Millennium', in E. Schafer and S. Bradley Smith (eds), *Playing Australia: Australian Theatre and the International Stage* (Amsterdam: Rodopi), pp. 180–94.

Hammond, J. (1973), 'A Potted History of the Fringe', *Theatre Quarterly*, III, 12: 37–46.

Hanna, G. (1991), *Monstrous Regiment: Four Plays and a Collective Celebration* (London: Nick Hern Books).

Harding, J. (ed.) (2000), *Contours of the Theatrical Avant-Garde: Performance and Textuality* (Ann Arbor: University of Michigan Press).

Harris, G. (1999a), 'Repetition, Quoting, Plagiarism and Iterability (*Europe After the Rain* – Again)', *Studies in Theatre Production*, 19: 6–21.

—— (1999b), *Staging Femininities: Performance and Performativity* (Manchester: Manchester University Press).

Harris, J. (1985–6), 'The Combination' in 'Theatre and Communities: a Council of Europe Workshop', *Theatre Papers*, 5, 16 (Totnes: Dartington College of Arts).

Harrop, J. (1973), 'University Theatre USA: Success and Failure', *Theatre Quarterly*, III, 10: 67–78.

Harrop, J. and Huerta, J. (1975), 'The Agitprop Pilgrimage of Luis Valdez and El Teatro Campesino', *Theatre Quarterly*, V, 17: 30–9.

Hassan, I. (1987), *The Postmodern Turn: Essays in Postmodern Theory and Culture* (Columbus: Ohio State University).

Haugo, Ann (2002), 'Weaving a Legacy: an Interview with Muriel Miguel of the Spiderwoman Theater', in R. Uno and L. San Pablo Burns (eds), *The Color of Theater* (London: Continuum), pp. 219–36.

Hawkins, G. (1991), 'Reading Community Arts Policy', in V. Binns (ed.), *Community and the Arts: History, Theory, Practice* (Leichhardt: Pluto Press Australia), pp. 45–53.

Heathfield, A. (2001), 'Coming Undone', in *It's an Earthquake in My Heart: A Reading Companion* (Chicago: Goat Island), pp. 16–20.

—— (ed.) (2004), *Live: Art and Performance* (London: Routledge).

Helmer, J. and Malzacher, F. (eds) (2004), *Not Even a Game Anymore: The Theatre of Forced Entertainment* (Berlin: Alexander Verlag).

Henri, A. (1974), *Environments and Happenings* (London: Thames and Hudson).

Hill, A. (1981a), *Performance Magazine*, 9: 20–1.

—— (1981b), *Performance Magazine*, 10: 23.

Hixson, L. (1995), 'Feminisms: Responses', *P-Form*, 35 (Spring): 22–5.

Hoban, R. (1984), *Performance Magazine*, 32.

Holden, J. (1975), 'Collective Playmaking: the Why and the How', *Theatre Quarterly*, V, 18:28–36.

Holmbert, A. (1997), *The Theatre of Robert Wilson* (Cambridge: Cambridge University Press).

Hornick, N. (1982), *Performance Magazine*, 17:15–16.

Howell, A. and Templeton, F. (1977), *Elements of Performance Art* (London: Ting Theatre of Mistakes; rev. edn).

Hughes, D. (1990), 'Locating Goat Island', *Performance*, 61:10–17.

Huizinga, J. (1955), *Homo Ludens: A Study of the Play Element in Culture* (Boston, MA: Beacon Press).

Hulton, P. (ed.) (1977–86), *Theatre Papers Archive* (DVD recording) (Exeter: Arts Documentation Unit).

Hunt, A. (1971), 'John Ford's Cuban Missile Crises', *Theatre Quarterly*, I, 1:47–55.

—— (1975), 'Political Theatre', *New Edinburgh Review*, 30:5–6.

—— (1978), *Hopes for Great Happenings: Alternatives in Education and Theatre* (London: Eyre Methuen).

Hutcheon, L. (1989), *The Politics of Postmodernism* (London: Routledge).

Hutchins, M. (2004), 'The Middle: 1980s', *ITC Members Matters, Special Birthday Issue* (June): 4–5.

Huyssen, A. (1986), *After the Great Divide: Modernism, Mass Culture, 'Postmodernism'* (Bloomington and Indianapolis: Indiana University Press).

Hyde, P. (1983), *Performance Magazine*, 22:25–6.

Innes, C. (1993), *Avant-Garde Theatre, 1892–1992* (London: Routledge).

Itzin, C. (1979), *British Alternative Theatre Directory* (Eastbourne: John Offord).

—— (1980), *Stages in the Revolution: Political Theatre in Britain since 1968* (London: Eyre Methuen).

Jackson, A. (ed.) (1993), *Learning Through Theatre: New Perspectives on Theatre in Education* (London: Routledge).

Jameson, F. (1995), *Postmodernism, or, The Cultural Logic of Late Capitalism* (Durham, NC: Duke University Press).

Jaremba, T. (1991), 'Lin Hixson: an Interview', *Drama Review*, 35, 4:46–9.

Johnstone, K. (1981), *Impro: Improvisation and the Theatre* (London: Eyre Methuen).

Kanellos, N. (1987), *Mexican American Theater: Legacy and Reality* (Pittsburgh: Latin American Literary Review Press).

Kaprow, A. (1966a), *Assemblage, Environments and Happenings* (New York: Harry N. Abrams).

—— (1966b), *Some Recent Happenings* (New York: A Great Bear Pamphlet).

—— (1995), 'In Response', in M. R. Sandford (ed.), *Happenings and Other Acts* (London: Routledge), pp. 219–20.

Kaye, N. (1994), *Postmodernism and Performance* (London: Macmillan Press).

—— (1996), *Art into Theatre: Performance, Interviews and Documents* (Amsterdam: Harwood Academic).

Kelly, A. (2004), 'Teaching Directing Devising' (unpublished paper).

Kelly, O. (1984), *Community, Art and the State: Storming the Citadels* (London: Comedia).

Keogh, B. (1999), 'All of Me', in R. J. Allen and K. Pearlman (eds), *Performing the Unnameable* (Redfern, NSW: Currency Press).

Kerrigan, S. (2001), *The Performer's Guide to the Collaborative Process* (Portsmouth, NH: Heinemann).

Kershaw, B. (1992), *The Politics of Performance: Radical Theatre as Cultural Intervention* (London: Routledge).

—— (1999a), 'British Theatre and Economics, 1979–1999', *Theatre Journal*, 51: 267–83.

—— (1999b), *The Radical in Performance* (London: Routledge).

Khan, N. (1980), 'The Public-going Theatre: Community and Ethnic Theatre', in S. Craig (ed.), *Dreams and Deconstructions: Alternative Theatre in Britain* (Ambergate: Amber Lane Press), pp. 59–75.

—— (1983), *Drama*, 149: 8–10.

Kiernander, A. (1993), *Ariane Mnouchkine and the Théâtre du Soleil* (Cambridge: Cambridge University Press).

King, B. (2000), 'Landscapes of Fact and Fiction: Asian Theatre Arts in Britain', *New Theatre Quarterly*, XVI, 1: 26–33.

Kirby, M. (1971), *Futurist Performance* (New York: E. P. Dutton).

—— (1995), 'Happenings: an Introduction', in M. Sandford (ed.), *Happenings and Other Acts* (London: Routledge), pp. 1–28.

Kirby, V. N. (1974), 'The Creation and Development of People Show #52', *Tulane Drama Review*, 18, 2: 48–66.

Knapper, S. (2004), 'Complicite's Comintern: Internationalism and *The Noise of Time*', *Contemporary Theatre Review*, 14, 1: 61–73.

Kobialka, M. (ed.) (1993), *A Journey Through Other Spaces: Essays and Manifestos, 1944–1990, Tadeusz Kantor* (Berkeley: University of California Press).

Kostelanetz, R. (1980), *The Theatre of Mixed-Means: An Introduction to Happenings, Kinetic Environments and Other Mixed-Means Presentations* (New York: R. K. Editions).

Kourilsky, F. (1972), 'Vocal Minorities: Agit-Prop in Paris', *Gambit: International Theatre Review*, 6, 22: 46–53.

La Frenais, R. (1985), *Performance Magazine*, 38: 6–11.

Lagden, J. (1971), 'Theatre in the Market Place', *Theatre Quarterly*, I, 1: 83–5.

Laing, R. D. (1965), *The Divided Self: An Existential Study in Sanity and Madness* (Harmondsworth: Penguin).

Laing, R. D. (1967), *The Politics of Experience* (New York: Pantheon Books).

Lambert, J. W. (1977), 'Politics and Theatre', *Drama: The Quarterly Review*, 125: 12–28.

Lamden, G. (2000), *Devising: A Handbook for Drama and Theatre Students* (London: Hodder and Stoughton Educational).

Lane, J. (1979), 'Arts Centres', in C. Itzin (ed.), *The Alternative British Theatre Directory* (Eastbourne: John Offord), pp. 173–4.

Laurie, R. (1984), 'A Thousand Bloomin' Flowers, No Stopping Now', *Meanjin*, 43, 1: 81–5.

Laye, M. (1982), *Performance Magazine*, 18: 18–19.

Leabhart, T. (1989), *Modern and Post-Modern Mime* (Basingstoke: Macmillan).

Leary, T. (1964), *The Psychedelic Experience* (New York: University Books).

Lebel, J-J. (1967), 'Theory and Practice', in *New Writers IV: Plays and Happenings* (London: Calder and Boyers), pp. 13–45.

—— (1969), *Entretiens avec le Living Theatre* (Paris: P. Belfond).

Lehmann, H-T. (1999), *Postdramatisches Theater* (Frankfurt-am-Main: Verlag der Autoren).

Ley, G. (1997), 'Theatre of Migration and the Search for a Multicultural Aesthetic: Twenty Years of Tara Arts', *New Theatre Quarterly*, XIII, 52: 349–71.

Leyh, E. (1980), *Concrete Sculpture in the Community* (London: Inter-Action Trust).

Lippard, L. (1970), *Surrealists on Art* (Englewood Cliffs, NJ: Prentice-Hall).

Littlewood, J. (1995), *Joan's Book* (London: Minerva Press).

Long, M. (1981–2), 'The People Show', in P. Hulton (ed.), *Theatre Papers*, 4, 2 (Totnes: Dartington College of Arts).

Lyotard, J-F. (1984), *The Postmodern Condition: A Report on Knowledge* (Manchester: Manchester University Press).

Lyotard, J-F. and Thébaud, J-L. (1985), *Just Gaming* (Minneapolis: University of Minnesota Press).

Malina, J. (1972), *The Enormous Despair* (New York: Random House).

—— (1984), *The Diaries of Judith Malina: 1947–1957* (New York: Grove Press).

Malina, J. and Beck, J. (1971), *Living Theatre, Paradise Now: Collective Creation of the Living Theatre, written down by Judith Malina and Julian Beck* (New York: Random House).

Malpede, K. (ed.) (1974), *Three Works by the Open Theatre* (New York: Drama Books).

Malzacher, F. (2004), 'There is a Word for People Like You: Audience, the Spectator as Bad Witness and Bad Voyeur', in J. Helmer and F. Malzacher (eds), *Not Even a Game Anymore: The Theatre of Forced Entertainment* (Berlin: Alexander Verlag), pp. 121–35.

Manning, B. (1922), 'Salamanca Theatre', in R. Fotheringham (ed.), *Community Theatre in Australia* (Sydney: Currency Press, 1987; rev. edn, 1992).

Mantegna, G. and Rostagno, A. (1970), *We, The Living Theatre* (New York: Ballatine Books).

Marcuse, H. (1967), 'The Question of Revolution', *New Left Review*, 45.

—— (1968), *One-dimensional Man: The Ideology of Industrial Society* (London: Sphere Books).

—— (1969), *An Essay on Liberation* (London: Penguin).

Marks, E. and de Courtivron, L. (eds) (1981), *New French Feminisms* (Harvester: Brighton).

Marowitz, C. (1961), *The Method as Madness* (London: Herbert Jenkins).
—— (1963), 'Happenings in Edinburgh', *Encore*, Nov.–Dec. 1963: 8–11.
Marranca, B. (2003), 'The Wooster Group: a Dictionary of Ideas', *Performing Arts Journal*, 74: 1–18.
Martin, J. (2004), *The Intercultural Performance Handbook* (London: Routledge).
Marwick, A. (1998), *The Sixties: Cultural Revolution in Britain, France, Italy, and the United States, c.1958–c.1974* (Oxford: Oxford University Press).
Maslow, A. (1970), *Motivation and Personality* (London: Harper and Row; first edition, 1954).
McBurney, S. (1994), *Live 1* (London: Methuen), pp. 13–24.
—— (1999), 'Simon McBurney', in G. Giannachi and M. Luckhurst (eds), *On Directing* (London: Faber and Faber), pp. 67–77.
McGrath, J. (1975a), 'Better a Bad Night in Bootle . . .', *Theatre Quarterly*, V, 19: 39–54.
—— (1975b), 'Boom: an Introduction', *New Edinburgh Review*, 30: 9–10.
—— (1981), *The Cheviot, the Stag, and the Black, Black Oil* (London: Eyre Methuen).
—— (1984), *A Good Night Out: Popular Theatre: Audience, Class and Form* (London: Methuen; first published 1981).
McLeod, D. (1982), *Performance Magazine*, 16: 10–11.
Melzer, A. (1980), *Latest Rage, the Big Drum: Dada and Surrealist Performance* (Ann Arbor: University of Michigan Research Press).
Meyrick, J. (2003), 'Sightlines and Bloodlines: the Influence of British Theatre on Australia in the Post-1945 Era', in E. Schafer and S. Bradley Smith (eds), *Playing Australia: Australian Theatre and the International Stage* (Amsterdam: Rodopi), pp. 43–62.
Miller, E. (1966), *The Edinburgh International Festival, 1947–1996* (Aldershot: Scholar Press).
Milne, G. (2004), *Theatre Australia (Un)limited: Australian Theatre since the 1950s* (Amsterdam: Rodopi).
Muldoon, R. (1976), 'CAST Revival', *Plays and Players*, 24, 3: 40–1.
Murray, S. (2003), *Jacques Lecoq* (London: Routledge).
National Statistics UK 2004 (London: Office for National Statistics).
Newson, L. (1994), *Live 1* (London: Methuen), pp. 43–54.
—— (1999), 'Lloyd Newson', in G. Giannachi and M. Luckhurst (eds), *On Directing* (London: Faber and Faber), pp. 108–14.
Nicholson, H. (2005), *Applied Drama* (Basingstoke: Palgrave).
Nicholson, S. (2005), *The Censorship of British Drama, 1900–1968*, vol. 3 (Exeter: University of Exeter Press).
Norris, P. (2001), *Digital Divide: Civic Engagement, Information Poverty, and the Internet Worldwide* (Cambridge: Cambridge University Press).
Nuttall, J. (1968), *Bomb Culture* (London: Paladin).
—— (1979), *Performance Art: Memoirs*, vol. 1 (London: John Calder).
Oddey, A. (1994), *Devising Theatre: A Practical and Theoretical Handbook* (London: Routledge).

Osinski, Z. (1985), *Grotowski and His Laboratory* (New York: Performing Arts Journal).

Osment, P. (ed.) (1989), *Gay Sweatshop: Four Plays and a Company* (London: Methuen).

O'Toole, J. and Bundy, P. (1993), 'TIE in Australia', in Tony Jackson (ed.), *Learning Through Theatre: New Perspectives on Theatre in Education* (London: Routledge), pp. 133–50.

Pammenter, D. (1993), 'Devising for TIE', in T. Jackson (ed.), *Learning Through Theatre: New Perspectives on Theatre in Education* (London: Routledge), pp. 53–70.

Pasolli, R. (1972), *A Book on the Open Theatre* (New York: Avon).

Patterson, M. (2003), *Strategies of Political Theatre: Post-War British Playwrights* (Cambridge: Cambridge University Press).

Pearson, M. (1997), 'Special Worlds, Secret Maps: a Poetics of Performance', in A. M. Taylor (ed.), *Staging Wales: Welsh Theatre, 1979–1997* (Cardiff: University of Wales Press), pp. 85–99.

—— (2004), 'Anecdotes and Analects', unpublished paper presented at 'We Are Searching … A Forced Entertainment Symposium' (Lancaster University, 16–17 October).

Pilgrim, G. (1982), *Performance Magazine*, 17: 13–14.

Pippen, J. (1997), 'Ranged between Heaven and Hades: Actors' Bodies in Crosscultural Theatre Forms', in D. Batchelor (ed.), *Two-Way Traffic: Aspects of Australian/Asian Interculturalism in Theatre and Dance* (Brisbane: Centre for Innovation in the Arts, QUT Academy of the Arts).

Quick, A. (1996), 'Approaching the Real: Reality Effects and the Play of Fiction', *Performance Research*, 1, 3: 12–22.

—— (2002), unpublished paper, The Wooster Group Symposium, London International Festival of Theatre (14–15 May).

Radic, L. (1991), *State of Play: The Revolution in the Australian Theatre since the 1960s* (London: Penguin).

Ramsay, M. (1991), *The Grand Union (1970–76): An Improvisational Performance Group* (New York: Peter Lang).

Rathbone, N. (2001), *New Theatre Quarterly*, XVII, 1: 90.

Rea, K. (1981), 'Drama Training in Britain, part II', *Theatre Quarterly*, X, 40: 61–73.

Rebellato, D. (1999), *1956 and All That: The Making of Modern British Drama* (London: Routledge).

Redwood, J. (ed.) (1979), *Theatre of the Avant-Garde* (Cambridge: Cambridge University Press).

Rees, R. (1992), *Fringe First: Pioneers of Fringe Theatre on Record* (London: Oberon Books).

Rees-Mogg, W. (1985), *The Political Economy of Art* (London: Arts Council of Great Britain).

Ritchie, R. (ed.) (1987), *The Joint Stock Book: The Making of a Theatre Collective* (London: Methuen).

Robertson, T. (2001), *The Pram Factory: The Australian Performing Group Recollected* (Melbourne: Melbourne University Press).

Rogers, C. (1967), *On Becoming a Person: A Therapist's View of Psychotherapy* (London: Constable; first published 1961).

Rogers, S. (1983), *Performance Magazine*, 22: 5–8.

—— (1985), *Performance Magazine*, 33: 28–9.

—— (1986a), *Performance Magazine*, 40: 12.

—— (1986b), *Performance Magazine*, 43: 16–18.

Roth, M. (1982), 'An Interview with Martha Boesing', *Theaterworks*, 2, 2 (January): 4–5.

Rudlin, J. (1994), *Commedia dell'arte: An Actor's Handbook* (London: Routledge).

Said, E. (1978), *Orientalism* (London: Routledge & Kegan Paul).

Sainer, A. (1997), *The New Radical Theatre Notebook* (New York: Applause).

Sandford, M. (ed.) (1995), *Happenings and Other Acts* (London: Routledge).

Savill, C. (1997), 'Brith Gof', in A. M. Taylor (ed.), *Staging Wales: Welsh Theatre, 1979–1997* (Cardiff: University of Wales Press), pp. 100–10.

Savran, D. (1988), *Breaking the Rules: The Wooster Group* (New York: Theatre Communications Group).

Sayre, H. M. (1992), *The Object of Performance: The American Avant-Garde since 1970* (Chicago: University of Chicago Press).

Schechner, R. (1971), 'Actuals: Primitive Ritual and Performance Theory', *Theatre Quarterly*, I, 2: 49–66.

—— (1973), *Six Axioms for Environmental Theatre* (New York: Hawthorn).

—— (1981), 'The Decline and Fall of the (American) Avant-Garde', *Performing Arts Journal*, 5, 2: 48–63.

—— (1985a), 'Happenings', in M. Sandford (ed.), *Happenings and Other Acts* (London: Routledge), pp. 216–18.

—— (1995b), 'Extensions in Time and Space: An Interview with Allan Kaprow', in M. Sandford (ed.), *Happenings and Other Acts* (London: Routledge), pp. 221–9.

Schumann, P. (1970), 'Bread and Puppets', *Drama Review*, 14, 3: 35.

Schutzman, M. and Cohen-Cruz, J. (eds) (1994), *Playing Boal: Theatre, Therapy, Activism* (London: Routledge).

Seyd, R. (1975), 'The Theatre of Red Ladder', *New Edinburgh Review*, 30: 36–42.

Shank, T. (1977), 'The San Francisco Mime Troupe's Production of *False Promises*', *Theatre Quarterly*, VII, 27: 41–52.

—— (1978), 'Political Theatre in England', *Performing Arts Journal*, 11, 3: 48–61.

—— (1982), *American Alternative Theatre* (New York: St Martins Press).

Shevtsova, M. (2003), 'Performance, Embodiment, Voice: the Theatre/Dance Cross-overs of Dodin, Bausch and Forsythe', *New Theatre Quarterly*, XIX, 1: 3–17.

Short, R. (1976), 'Dada and Surrealism', in M. Bradbury and J. McFarlane (eds), *Modernism: A Guide to European Literature, 1890–1930* (London: Penguin), pp. 292–308.

Smethurst, J. (2005), *The Black Arts Movement: Literary Nationalism in the 1960s and 1970s* (Chapel Hill: University of North Carolina Press).

Sobieski L. (1994), 'Breaking Boundaries: The People Show, Lumiere & Son, and Hesitate and Demonstrate', in T. Shank (ed.), *Contemporary British Theatre* (Basingstoke: Macmillan), pp. 89–106.

Spolin, V. (1963), *Improvisation in the Theater* (Evanston: Northwestern University Press).

Spunner, S. (1981), 'Ways to Shear a Sheep: Community Theatre at the Mill', *Theatre Australia*, April: 13.

Stiles, K. (2000), 'Never Enough is *Something Else*: Feminist Performance Art, Avant-Gardes, and Probity', in J. Harding (ed.), *Contours of the Theatrical Avant-Garde: Performance and Textuality* (Ann Arbor: University of Michigan Press), pp. 239–89.

Sullivan, D. (1998), 'Theater in East Harlem: the Outdoor Audience Gets into the Act', in J. Cohen-Cruz (ed.), *Radical Street Performance: An International Anthology* (London: Routledge), pp. 100–2.

Tait, P. (1988), 'Performing Sexed Bodies in Physical Theatre', in V. Kelly (ed.), *Our Australian Theatre in the 1990s* (Amsterdam: Rodopi), pp. 213–29.

Teer, B. A. (1971), 'The National Black Theatre', *Essence*, March: 50.

Theatre de Complicité (1999), *Mnemonic* (London: Methuen).

Thompson, E. P. (1963), *The Making of the English Working Class* (London: Gollancz).

Tstatsos, I. (1991), 'Talking with Goat Island: an Interview with Joan Dickinson, Karen Christopher, Matthew Goulish, Greg McCain, and Tim McCain', *Drama Review*, 35, 4: 66–74.

Tufnell, M. and Crickmay, C. (1990), *Body Space Image: Notes towards Improvisation and Performance* (London: Virago).

—— (2004), *A Widening Field* (Chailey: Vine House).

Turner, V. (1972), 'Symbols in African Ritual', *Science*, 179 (16 March: 1100–5.

Tytell, J. (1995), *The Living Theatre* (New York: Grove Press).

Van Erven, E. (2001), *Community Theatre: Global Perspectives* (London: Routledge).

Vergine, L. (2000), *Body Art and Performance: The Body as Language* (Milan: Skira Editore).

Verma, J. (2003), 'Asian Arts in the 21st Century', Keynote Address, DNAsia Conference, Watermans Arts Centre (24 March).

—— (1999), 'Jatinder Verma', in G. Giannachi and M. Luckhurst (eds), *On Directing* (London: Faber & Faber), pp. 128–35.

Von Neumann, J. and Morgenstern, O. (1944) *Theory of Games and Economic Behaviour* (Princeton, NJ: Princeton University Press).

Wandor, M. (ed.) (1980), *Strike While the Iron is Hot: Sexual Politics in Theatre: Three Plays from Gay Sweatshop, Red Ladder Theatre, Women's Theatre Group* (Journeyman Press: London).

—— (1986), *Carry On, Understudies: Theatre and Sexual Politics* (London: Routledge and Kegan Paul).

Watt, D. (1991), 'Interrogating "Community": Social Welfare versus Cultural Democracy', in V. Binns (ed.), *Community and the Arts* (Leichhardt: Pluto Press), pp. 55–65.

—— (1992), 'Community Theatre: a Progress Report', *Australasian Drama Studies*, 20: 3–15.

—— (1995), 'The Popular Theatre Troupe and Street Arts: Two Paradigms of Political Activism', in S. Capelin (ed.), *Challenging the Centre: Two Decades of Political Theatre* (Brisbane: Playlab Press), pp. 13–33.

Watt, D. and Pitts, G. (1991), 'Community Theatre as Political Activism: Some Thoughts on Practice in the Australian Context', in V. Binns (ed.), *Community and the Arts* (Leichhardt: Pluto Press), pp. 119–33.

Weiss, J. (1993), *Latin American Popular Theatre* (Albuquerque: University of New Mexico Press).

Wheeler, W. (1999), 'Stars and Moons: Desire and the Limits of Marketisation', in G. Andrews, R. Cockett, A. Hooper and M. Williams (eds), *New Left, New Right and Beyond: Taking the Sixties Seriously* (London: Macmillan), pp. 42–50.

Whitmore, J. (1994), *Directing Postmodern Theatre: Shaping Signification in Performance* (Ann Arbor: University of Michigan Press).

Whitworth, J. (2003), 'Translating Theologies of the Body', *Performance Research*, 8, 2: 21–7.

Williams, D. (1988), *Peter Brook: A Theatrical Case Book* (London: Methuen).

—— (1999), *Collaborative Theatre: The Théâtre du Soleil Sourcebook* (London: Routledge).

Williams, M. (1985), *Black Theatre in the 1960s and 1970s* (London: Greenwood).

Worth, L. and Poynor, H. (2004), *Anna Halprin* (London: Routledge).

Index